STRATEGIC
MANAGEMENT

Second Edition

STRATEGIC MANAGEMENT

THOMAS L. WHEELEN
University of South Florida

J. DAVID HUNGER
George Mason University

ADDISON-WESLEY PUBLISHING COMPANY

READING, MASSACHUSETTS · MENLO PARK, CALIFORNIA · DON MILLS, ONTARIO
WOKINGHAM, ENGLAND · AMSTERDAM · SYDNEY · SINGAPORE · TOKYO
MADRID · BOGOTÁ · SANTIAGO · SAN JUAN

Sponsoring Editor: James Heitker
Production Supervisor: Michael Weinstein
Text Designer and Illustrator: Kenneth J. Wilson
Art Editor: Loretta Bailey
Cover Designer: Richard Hannus
Permissions Editor: Mary Dyer
Manufacturing Supervisor: Hugh Crawford

Library of Congress Cataloging-in-Publication Data
Wheelen, Thomas L.
  Strategic management.

  Includes bibliographies and indexes.
  1. Strategic planning.   I. Hunger, J. David,
1941–   . II. Title.
HD30.28.W429   1987   658.4′012   86–17227
ISBN 0–201–09038–4

Reprinted with corrections June, 1987

DEFGHIJ-HA-8987

To

Betty
Tom, Kathy, Richard   Kari, Suzi, Lori, Merry

PREFACE

This book was written in order to provide the reader with a more comprehensive understanding of the business corporation. By taking a strategic view, it unites the various compartments, majors, and sub-disciplines usually taught within a school of business. Unlike many other areas of study, strategic management directly raises the issue of corporate existence and dares to ask *why*. Other areas deal in depth with procedures and activities designed to answer *how*. Business policy, partly because of its more holistic orientation and partly because strategic management is an emerging area of study, is often a difficult course to teach as well as to take. Consequently, this book is organized around the strategic management model that prefaces each chapter, providing a structure for both chapter content areas and complex case analyses by students.

This text was originally part of a hardcover book titled *Strategic Management and Business Policy*, 2nd ed., published in 1986 by Addison-Wesley. The hardcover book includes the eleven chapters of this text plus thirty-eight comprehensive policy cases. Given the strong demand for the hardcover book in its first year of publication, we decided to publish the text alone in a soft-cover version. This gives policy instructors the opportunity to continue using the textural material with cases or a simulation from another source. The same instructor's manual originally prepared for the hardcover book can be used with this text.

Objectives

This book focuses on the following objectives, which are typically found in most business policy and strategic management courses:

- To develop *conceptual skills* so that a student is able to integrate previously learned aspects of corporations.

- To develop a *framework of analysis* to enable a student to identify central issues and problems in complex, comprehensive cases, to suggest alternative courses of action, and to present well-supported recommendations for future action.

- To develop an understanding of strategic management *concepts, research,* and *theories.*

- To develop an understanding of the *roles* and *responsibilities* of the Board of Directors, Chief Executive Officer, and other key managers in strategic management positions.

- To develop the ability to analyze and evaluate the *performance* of the people responsible for strategic management.

- To bridge the gap between theory and practice by developing an understanding of when and how to apply *concepts* and *techniques* learned earlier in courses focusing on marketing, accounting, finance, management, and production.

- To improve the *research capabilities* necessary to gather and interpret key environmental data.

- To develop a better understanding of the *present and future environments* within which corporations must function.

- To develop and refine *analytical and decision-making skills* to deal with complex conceptual problems.

This book achieves these objectives by presenting and explaining concepts and theories useful in understanding the strategic management process. It provides studies in the field of strategy and policy in order to acquaint the student with the literature of this area and to help develop the student's research capabilities. It also describes the people who manage strategically and suggests a model of strategic management. It recommends a strategic audit as one approach to the systematic analysis of complex organization-wide issues. The book focuses on the business corporation because of its crucial position in the economic system of the free world.

Structure

Part I is an overview of the subject, surveying the basic skills and competencies needed to deal with strategic issues in modern corporations. Chapter 1 presents a descriptive model as well as key terms and concepts that will be used throughout the book. Chapter 2 focuses on the development of the skills necessary to understanding and applying strategic concepts to actual situations.

Part II discusses important concepts that arise from both the external and internal environments of a corporation. It also describes key people in the corporation who are responsible for strategic management. Chapter 3 discusses the role and importance of a corporation's board of directors and top management in the strategic management process. Chapter 4 discusses both the task and societal environments of a corporation and suggests environmental scanning and forecasting as key corporate tasks. Chapter 5 examines the importance of a corporation's structure, culture, and resources to its strategic management.

Part III deals with strategy formulation. It emphasizes long-range planning and the development of alternative courses of action at both the corporate and business levels. Chapter 6 discusses situational analysis. Chapter 7 examines the many possible corporate, business, and functional strategies.

Part IV considers the implementation of strategies and policies, as well as the process of evaluation and control, with continued emphasis on corporate and division-level strategic management. Chapter 8 explains strategy implementation in terms of programs, budgets, and procedures. It tells who are in charge of implementation, what they need to do, and how they should do it. Chapter 9 focuses on evaluation and control. It considers the monitoring of corporate processes and the accomplishment of goals, as well as various methods and criteria used in evaluating performance.

Part V summarizes strategic concerns in areas of increasing importance. Chapter 10 deals with the strategic implications of operating within an international environment, and Chapter 11 describes the strategic management of not-for-profit organizations.

Instructor's Manual

A comprehensive Instructor's Manual has been carefully constructed to accompany *Strategic Management and Business Policy*, 2nd ed., the hardcover version of this text which includes cases. Except for the part dealing with cases, the Manual can be used in conjunction with the soft-cover-text. It is composed of the following four parts.

Part I: *Introduction.* Suggested course outlines, case sequences, and teaching aids.

Part II: *Text Chapters.* A strandardized format is provided for each chapter: (1) chapter abstract, (2) list of key concepts/terms, (3) suggested answers to discussion questions, and (4) multiple choice questions.

Part III: *Case Notes.* A standardized format is provided for each case: (1) case abstract, (2) case issues and subjects, (3) steps covered in the strategic decision-making process (see Fig. 6.1, p. 141), (4) case objectives, (5) suggested classroom approaches, (6) discussion questions, (7) student paper, (8) case author's teaching note, (9) student strategic audit, and (10) a complete list of 30 calculated financial ratios (new to this edition).

Part IV: *Transparency Masters.* Selected figures and tables from the text chapters plus other masters highlighting key strategic management concepts and techniques. *The actual transparencies are also available to those instructors who adopt the book for classroom use* (new to this edition).

Acknowledgments

We are grateful to the many people who reviewed drafts of the first and second editions of this book for their constructive comments and suggestions. Their thought and effort has resulted in a book far superior to our original manuscript.

Sumer Aggarwal, University of Massachusetts, Boston
William Boulton, University of Georgia
Richard Castaldi, San Diego State University
William Crittenden, Northeastern University
Keith Davis, Arizona State University
Richard Deane, Georgia State University
Donald Del Mar, University of Idaho
Roger Evered, Naval Postgraduate School
Jerry Geisler, Eastern Illinois University
Fred Haas, Virginia Commonwealth University
Kathryn Harrigan, Columbia University
William Litzinger, University of Texas at San Antonio
John Logan, University of South Carolina
John Mahon, Boston University
Martin Marsh, California State University at Bakersfield
James Miller, Georgia State University
Thomas Navin, University of Arizona
Henry Odell, University of Virginia
Neil Snyder, University of Virginia
Jeffrey Susbauer, Cleveland State University

James Thurman, George Washington University
Robert Vichas, Old Dominion University
William Warren, College of William and Mary
Carl Zeithaml, Texas A&M University

Our special thanks go to Janis Jackson Hill, Connie Spatz, Cindy Johnson, and Jim Heitker of Addison-Wesley Publishing Company for their encouragement and concern as the book moved from being a series of interrelated ideas to a completed textbook. We are also grateful to Mary Clare McEwing, Michael Weinstein, Shirley Rieger, Jerry Moore, and Barbara Willette for their comments and helpful suggestions. Their hard work is reflected in the quality of production work and in the fact that the book was published on time!

We thank Betty Hunger and Deborah Kluitenberg for cheerful typing of the text revisions and Wayne Spies for his work in indexing. In addition, we express our appreciation to Dr. Robert G. Cox, Dean of the University of South Florida's College of Business, Dr. Charles B. Handy, Dean of Iowa State's College of Business, and to Dr. Coleman Raphael, Dean of George Mason University's School of Business for their provision of the resources so necessary to compile a casebook. We also thank Dr. Jerry Koehler, Dr. Tom Chacko, and Dr. Jack Pearce, chairs of the management departments of U.S.F., I.S.U., and G.M.U., respectively, for their help and encouragement.

Lastly, to the many policy instructors and students who have moaned to us about their problems with the policy course: We have tried to respond to your problems as best we could by providing a comprehensive yet usable text. To you, the people who work hard in the policy trenches, we acknowledge our debt. This book is yours.

Tampa, Florida   T. L. W.
Fairfax, Virginia   J. D. H.

CONTENTS

STRATEGIC
MANAGEMENT

PART ONE

INTRODUCTION TO STRATEGIC MANAGEMENT

- Chapter 1   INTRODUCTION

- Chapter 2   DEVELOPING CONCEPTUAL SKILLS:
  THE CASE METHOD AND THE
  STRATEGIC AUDIT

Chapter 1

INTRODUCTION

STRATEGIC MANAGEMENT MODEL

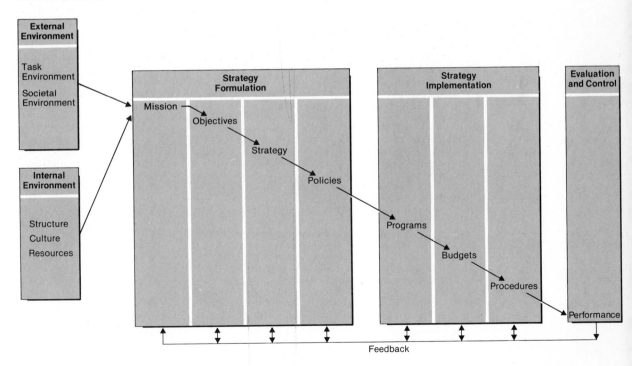

Strategic management and business policy is a fast-developing field of study. It looks at the corporation as a whole and attempts to explain why some firms develop and thrive while others stagnate and go bankrupt. Strategic management typically focuses on analyzing the problems and opportunities faced by people in top management. Unlike many decisions made at lower levels in a corporation, strategic decisions usually deal with the long-run future of the entire organization. The stakes can be very high. For instance, the strategic decision made after World War II by Sears, Roebuck and Company to expand from catalog sales into retail stores and insurance has given Sears many years of successful profits. A similar decision made independently during the 1960s by the top managements of General Motors, Ford, and Chrysler to emphasize the production of large, powerful automobiles over small, fuel-efficient ones resulted in their low profits and even the threat of bankruptcy in the early 1980s.

Other examples of strategic decisions were those made during the early 1980s by the top management of Standard Oil of Ohio (Sohio). Realizing that the $6 billion in annual revenues coming from Sohio's share in the Prudhoe Bay, Alaska, oil field was likely to begin declining by the end of the decade, the firm decided to increase significantly its oil exploration efforts and to diversify into other industries. In 1981, Sohio paid $1.77 billion for Kennecott Corporation, the largest copper producer in the United States. Market demand for copper, however, soon collapsed. In the four years since the acquisition, Kennecott lost more than $350 million. In the meantime, Sohio's top management invested $310 million in a prospective oil field called *Mukluk* in the Beaufort Sea of Alaska. The exploratory well was found in December 1983 to contain water, not oil, and was soon referred to as the most expensive "dry well" in history.

Although a number of Sohio's other acquisitions and exploratory wells have been moderately successful, none appear to have the potential to replace the Prudhoe Bay revenues. Curious about the risky nature of such high-stakes decisions, a reporter from the *Wall Street Journal* asked Alton W. Whitehouse, Jr., the chief executive officer of Sohio, if he would continue to take such strategic gambles. Mr. Whitehouse calmly stated, "If those guys come in with another [enticing prospect like Mukluk] tomorrow, I'll have my neck right back out there."[1]

Alton Whitehouse's comment suggests why top management of large business corporations must manage firms strategically. They cannot make decisions based on long-standing rules, policies, or standard operating procedures. Instead, they must look to the future to plan organization-wide objectives, initiate strategy, and set policies. They must rise above their training and experience in such functional/operational areas as accounting, marketing, production, or finance to grasp the overall picture. They must be willing to ask these key strategic questions:

1. Where is the corporation now?

2. If no changes are made, where will the corporation be in one year, two years, five years, ten years? Are the answers acceptable?

3. If the answers are not acceptable, what specific actions should the corporation undertake? What are the risks and payoffs involved?

1.1 STUDY OF STRATEGIC MANAGEMENT AND BUSINESS POLICY

Most business schools offer a strategic management or business policy course. Although this course typically serves as a capstone or final integrative class in a business administration program, it—also typically—takes on some of the characteristics of a separate discipline.

In the 1950s the Ford Foundation and the Carnegie Corporation sponsored investigations into the business school curriculum.[2] The resulting Gordon and Howell report, sponsored by the Ford Foundation, recommended a broad business education and a course in business policy to "give students an opportunity to pull together what they have learned in the separate business fields and utilize this knowledge in the analysis of complex business problems."[3] The report also suggested the content which should be part of such a course:

> The business policy course can offer the student something he [or she] will find nowhere else in the curriculum: consideration of business problems which are not prejudged as being marketing problems, finance problems, etc.; emphasis on the development of skills in identifying, analyzing, and solving problems in a situation which is as close as the classroom can ever be to the real business world; opportunity to consider problems which draw on a wide range of substantive areas in business; opportunity to consider the external, nonmarket implications of problems at the same time that internal decisions must be made; situations which enable the student to exercise qualities of judgment and of mind which were not explicitly called for in any prior course. Questions of social responsibility and of personal attitudes can be brought in as a regular aspect of this kind of problem-solving practice. Without the responsibility of having to transmit some specific body of knowledge, the business policy course can concentrate on integrating what already has been acquired and on developing further the student's skill in using that knowledge.[4]

By the late 1960s most business schools included such a business policy course in their curriculum. But since that time the typical policy course has evolved to one that emphasizes the total organization and strategic management, with an increased interest in business social responsibilities and ethics as well as nonprofit organizations. This is in line with a recent survey of business school deans that reported a primary objective of undergraduate business education is to develop an understanding of the political, social, and economic environment of business.[5] This increasing concern with the effect of environmental issues on the management of the total organization has led leaders in the field to replace the term *business policy* with the more comprehensive *strategic management*.[6] *Strategic management* is that set of managerial decisions and actions that determines the long-run performance of a corporation. It includes strategy formulation, strategy implementation, and evaluation and control. The study of strategic management therefore emphasizes the monitoring and evaluating of environmental opportunities and constraints in light of a corporation's strengths and weaknesses. In contrast, the study of *business policy,* with its integrative orientation, tends to look inward by focusing on the efficient utilization of a corporation's assets and thus emphasizes the formulation of general guidelines that will better accomplish a firm's mission and objectives. We see, then, that strategic management incorporates the concerns of business policy with a heavier environmental and strategic emphasis.

1.2 RESEARCH ON THE EFFECTIVENESS OF STRATEGIC MANAGEMENT

Many of the concepts and techniques dealing with long-range planning and strategic management have been developed and used successfully by business corporations such as General Electric and the Boston Consulting Group, among others. Nevertheless, not all organizations use these tools or even attempt to manage strategically. Many are able to succeed for a while with unstated objectives and intuitive strategies. American Hospital Supply Corporation was one such example until Karl Bays became chief executive in 1971 and introduced strategic planning to a sales-dominated management. Previously, the company's idea of long-range planning was "Maybe in December we should look at next year's budget," recalled a former AHS executive.[7]

From his extensive work in the area, Bruce Henderson of the Boston Consulting Group concludes that intuitive strategies cannot be continued successfully if (1) the corporation becomes large, (2) the layers of management increase, or (3) the environment changes substantially.[8] Research suggests that the increasing risks of error, costly mistakes, and even economic ruin are causing today's professional managers to take strategic management seriously in order to keep their company competitive in an increasingly volatile environment.[9] Research by Gluck, Kaufman, and Walleck proposes that strategic planning evolves through *four sequential phases* in corporations as top managers attempt to better deal with their changing world:

Phase 1. *Basic financial planning:* seeking better operational control through meeting budgets.

Phase 2. *Forecast-based planning:* seeking more effective planning for growth by trying to predict the future beyond the next year.

Phase 3. *Externally oriented planning:* seeking increased responsiveness to markets and competition by trying to think strategically.

Phase 4. *Strategic management:* seeking to manage all resources to develop competitive advantage and to help create the future.[10]

Concern about external as well as internal factors seems to be increasing in today's large corporations. Recent research studies conducted by Henry indicate that the planning systems of fifty large companies are becoming increasingly sophisticated. For example, there is more effort to formulate, implement, and evaluate strategic plans. There is also a greater emphasis on strategic factors in the evaluation of a manager's performance.[11] Gordon Brunton, president of Britain's International Thomson Organisation, Ltd. emphasized this point when he made the following statement:

> All International Thomson senior managers now understand that unless they demonstrate their ability to think strategically, their future career potential will be limited accordingly.[12]

William Rothschild, staff executive for business development and strategy at General Electric (GE), notes the current trend to push strategic management duties down the organizational hierarchy to operating line managers. He observes that at GE, "over half of our managers are strategic thinkers. Another 20 percent to 25 percent lean that way. The rest don't understand it, and if they're fortunate enough to be in the right business where there is a stable environment, it doesn't matter too much."[13]

Many researchers have conducted studies of corporations to learn if organizations that engage in strategic planning outperform those that do not. One analysis of five companies with sales ranging from $1 billion to $17 billion reports the impact of strategic planning has been to

- help the companies sort their businesses into "winners and losers,"
- focus attention on critical issues and choices, and
- develop a strategic frame of mind among top and upper-level managers.

The study concludes that the results management should expect from strategic planning are improved competitive position and long-term improved profits plus growth in earnings per share.[14]

Research studies attempting to measure objectively this anticipated connection between formal strategic planning and corporate performance have found mixed results.[15] For example, studies by Ansoff, Thune and House, Herold, Burt, Eastlack and McDonald, Wood and La Forge, Karger and Malik, Miller and Friesen, Welch, and Rhyne found that corporations that engaged in strategic planning outperformed those that did not.[16] On the other hand, studies by Rue and Fulmer, Leontiades and Tezel, Kudla, Frederickson and Mitchell, as well as by Lindsay, Boulton, Franklin, and Rue found no such payoff from strategic planning.[17] Rhyne, however, explains these contradictory findings as resulting from the use of different measures for planning and performance plus a typical failure to consider industry effects. When he controlled for industry variation, focused only on the total return to stockholders, and considered strategic planning as different from less-evolved stages of planning (such as budgeting or annual planning), Rhyne found a positive relationship between strategic planning and performance. He concluded that "these results provide assurance that the prescriptions of strategic management theory are indeed valid."[18]

From this evidence we may conclude that a knowledge of strategic management is very important for effective business performance in a changing environment. The use of strategic planning and the selection of alternative courses of action based upon an assessment of important external and internal factors are becoming key parts of a general manager's job.

1.3 HIERARCHY OF STRATEGY

The typical large multidivisional business firm has three levels of strategy: (1) corporate, (2) business, and (3) functional.

Corporate strategy explores the ways a firm can develop a favorable "portfolio strategy" for its many activities.[19] It includes such factors as decisions about the type of businesses a firm should be in, the flow of financial and other resources to and from its divisions, and the way a corporation can increase its return on investment (ROI).

Business strategy, in contrast, usually occurs at the divisional level, with emphasis on improving the competitive position of a corporation's products or services in a specific industry or market segment the division serves. A division may be organized as a *strategic business unit* (SBU) around a group of similar products, such as housewares or electric turbines. Top management usually treats an SBU as an autonomous unit with, generally, the authority to develop its own strategy within corporate objectives and strategy. A division's business strategy probably would stress increasing its profit margin in the production and sales of its products and services. Business strategies also should integrate various functional activities to achieve divisional objectives.

The principal focus of *functional strategy* is on maximizing resource pro-

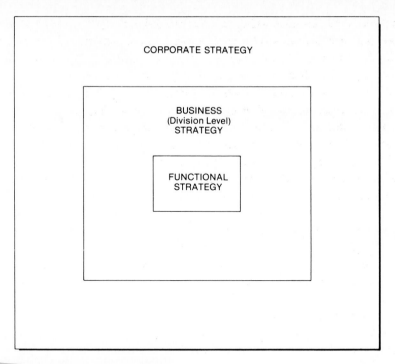

Figure 1.1 Hierarchy of strategy.

ductivity.[20] Given the constraints of corporate and business strategies around them, functional departments develop strategies to pull together their various activities and competencies to improve performance. For example, a typical strategy of a marketing department might center on developing the means to increase the current year's sales over those of the previous year.

The three levels of strategy—corporate, business, and functional—form a *hierarchy of strategy* within a large corporation. They interact closely with each other and must be well integrated if the total corporation is to be successful. As depicted in Fig. 1.1, each level of strategy forms the strategic environment of the next level in the corporation. (The interaction among the three levels is depicted later in the chapter in Fig. 1.5.)

The process of strategic management involves three basic elements: (1) *strategy formulation*, (2) *strategy implementation*, and (3) *evaluation and control*. Figure 1.2 shows how these three elements interact. We will discuss these interactions later in this section.

At the corporate level, the strategic management process includes activities that range from the initial statement of corporate mission to the evalua-

1.4 DESCRIPTIVE MODEL OF STRATEGIC MANAGEMENT

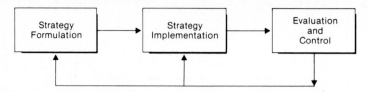

Figure 1.2   **Basic elements of the strategic management process.**

tion of performance. Top management scans both the external environment for opportunities and threats, and the internal environment for strengths and weaknesses. The most important of these to the corporation's future are referred to as strategic factors and are summarized with the acronym S.W.O.T., standing for Strengths, Weaknesses, Opportunities, and Threats. Top management then evaluates the strategic factors to determine corporate mission, which is the first step in the formulation of strategy. A statement of mission leads to a determination of corporate objectives, strategies, and policies. These strategies and policies are implemented through programs, budgets, and procedures. Finally performance is evaluated, and information is fed back into the system to ensure adequate control of organizational activities. Figure 1.3 depicts this process as a continuous one. It is an expansion of the basic model presented in Fig. 1.2.

The model in Fig. 1.3, with minor changes, also reflects the strategic management process at both divisional and functional levels of the corporation. A division's external environment, for example, includes not only task and societal variables, but also the mission, objectives, strategy, and policies of corporate headquarters. Similarly, both corporate and divisional constraints form the external environment of a functional department. The model depicted in Fig. 1.3 therefore is appropriate for any strategic level of a corporation.

External Environment   The *external environment* consists of variables (Opportunities and Threats) that exist outside the organization and are not typically within the short-run control of top management. These variables form the context within which the corporation exists. The external environment has two parts: task environment and social environment. The *task environment* includes those elements or groups that directly affect and are affected by an organization's major operations. Some of these are stockholders, governments, suppliers, local communities, competitors, customers, creditors, labor unions, special interest groups, and trade associations. The *societal environment* includes more general forces—ones that do not directly touch upon the short-run activities of the organization but that can, and often do, influence its long-run

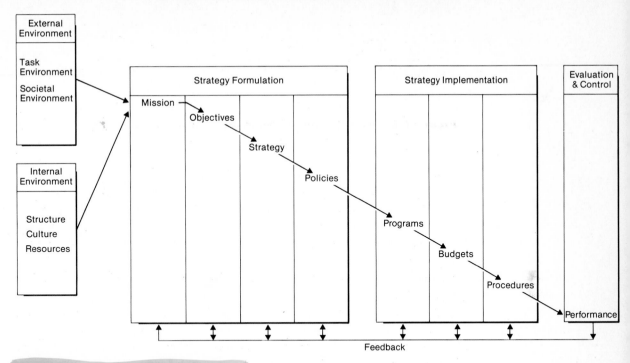

Figure 1.3   Strategic management model.

decisions. Such economic, sociocultural, technological, and political-legal forces are depicted in Fig. 1.4 in relation to a firm's total environment. (These external variables are discussed in more detail in Chapter 4.)

Internal Environment

The *internal environment* of a corporation consists of variables (Strengths and Weaknesses) within the organization itself that are also not usually within the short-run control of top management. These variables form the context in which work is done. They include the corporation's structure, culture, and resources. The *corporate structure* is the way a corporation is organized in terms of communication, authority, and workflow. It is often referred to as the "chain of command" and is graphically described in an organization chart. The *corporation's culture* is that pattern of beliefs, expectations, and values shared by the corporation's members. In a typical firm norms emerge that define the acceptable behavior of people from top management down to the operative employees. *Corporate resources* are those assets that form the raw material for the production of an organization's products or services. These include people and managerial talent as well as financial assets, plant facilities, and functional area skills and abilities.

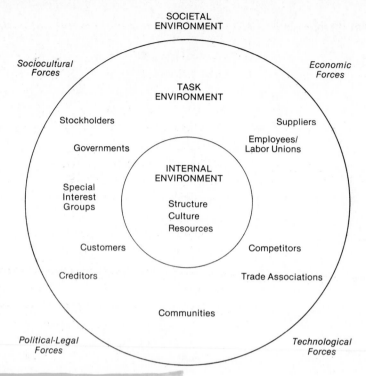

Figure 1.4   **Environmental variables.**

(These internal variables in a firm's environment are discussed in more detail in Chapter 5.)

Strategy Formulation

Strategy formulation is the process of developing long-range plans to deal effectively with environmental opportunities and threats in light of corporate strengths and weaknesses. It includes defining the corporate mission, specifying achievable objectives, developing strategies, and setting policy guidelines.

Mission

The corporate mission is the purpose or reason for the corporation's existence. For example, the mission of a savings and loan association might be to provide mortgage money to people of the community. By fulfilling this mission, the S&L would hope to provide a reasonable rate of return to its depositors. A mission may be *narrow*, like that of the S&L, or it may be *broad*. A broad statement of mission for another S&L might be to offer financial services to anyone who can pay the interest.

The corporate mission, as depicted in Fig. 1.3, determines the parameters of the specific objectives top management chooses to achieve. These objectives are listed as an end result of planned activity. They state *what* is to be accomplished by *when* and should be quantified if possible. (The terms *goals* and *objectives* are used interchangeably.) The achievement of corporate objectives should result in a corporation's fulfilling its mission. An S&L, for example, might set an objective for the year of earning a 15% rate of return on its investment portfolio.

Objectives

The strategy of a corporation forms a comprehensive master plan stating *how* a corporation will achieve its mission and objectives. A strategy of an S&L might be to increase both demand for mortgage loans and the amount of money deposited in its savings accounts. Another strategy might be to expand its financial services so that it is not so dependent on mortgages for income.

Strategy

As broad guidelines for making decisions, policies flow from the strategy. They provide guidance for decision making throughout the organization. In attempting to increase the amount of mortgage loans as well as the amount of deposits available for mortgages, an S&L might set policies of always offering the highest legal interest rate on savings deposits or to offer mortgage borrowers the best deal possible in the area. (Strategy formulation is discussed in more detail in Chapters 6 and 7.)

Policies

Strategy implementation is the process of putting strategies and policies into action through the development of programs, budgets, and procedures. It is typically conducted by middle- and lower-level managers but reviewed by top management. Sometimes referred to as operational planning, it is concerned with day-to-day resource allocation problems.

Strategy Implementation

Division and/or functional managers work to fully develop the programs, budgets, and procedures that will be used to achieve the objectives of the corporate strategy. At the same time, these managers are involved in strategy formulation at the divisional or functional level. If, for example, a corporate program for a steel company is to close down all inefficient plants within two years, a divisional objective might be to close down two specific production facilities. A divisional (business) strategy would then be developed to detail the specifics of the closing.

A program is a statement of activities or steps needed to accomplish a single-use plan. It makes the strategy action-oriented. For instance, to implement its strategy and policies, a savings and loan association might initiate an advertising program in the local area, develop close ties with the local realtors' association, and offer free silverware with every $1,000 savings deposit.

Programs

Budgets   A budget is a statement of a corporation's programs in dollar terms. It lists the detailed cost of each program for planning and control purposes. The S&L might thus draw up separate budgets for each of its three programs: the advertising budget, the public relations budget, and the premium budget.

Procedures   Sometimes referred to as standard operating procedures (SOP), procedures are a system of sequential steps or techniques that describe in detail how to perform a particular task or job. They typically detail the various activities that must be carried out to complete a corporation's program. The S&L, for example, might develop procedures for placing ads in newspapers and on radio. They might list persons to contact, techniques for writing acceptable copy (with samples), and details about payment. They might establish detailed procedures concerning eligibility requirements for silverware premiums. (Strategy implementation is discussed in more detail in Chapter 8.)

Evaluation and Control   *Evaluation and control* is the process of monitoring corporate activities and performance results so that actual performance can be compared with desired performance. Managers at all levels use the resulting information to take corrective action and resolve problems. Although evaluation and control is the final major element of strategic management, it also may serve to stimulate the beginning of the entire process by pinpointing weaknesses in previously implemented strategic plans.

For effective evaluation and control, managers must obtain clear, prompt, and unbiased feedback from the people below them in the corporation's hierarchy. The model in Fig. 1.3 indicates how feedback in the form of performance data and activity reports runs through the entire management process. Managers use this information to compare what is actually happening with what was originally planned in the formulation stage.

For example, the savings and loan would probably ask its internal information systems people to keep track of the number of mortgages being made as well as the level of deposits at the end of each week for each S&L branch office. It may also wish to develop special incentives to reward loan officers who increase their mortgage lending.

Top management of large corporations typically monitors and evaluates results by using periodic reports dealing with key performance indicators, such as return on investment, net profits, earnings per share, and net sales. Corporations are sometimes structured in ways to pinpoint performance problem areas with profit centers, investment centers, expense centers, and revenue centers. (These are discussed in detail in Chapter 9.)

Activities are much harder to monitor and evaluate than are performance results. Because of the many difficulties in deciding which activities to monitor and because of the bias inherent in evaluating job performance, some firms now manage by objectives. Management By Objectives (MBO) has been criticized, however, for ignoring many of the intermediate activities that can lead to the desired results. To counter this criticism, consulting firms have developed management "audits," which assess key organizational activities and provide in-depth feedback to consultants and managers. Management audits complement standard measures of performance and provide a more complete picture of the corporation's activities. (We discuss an example of a comprehensive audit in Chapter 2.)

We illustrate the strategic management model for a large, multidivisional corporation. A fictitious automobile manufacturer called Murphy Motors begins the process by scanning its external environment for any relevant information. It also scans its internal environment to assess the strengths and weaknesses in its divisions and functional areas. Officers of divisions and functional areas are normally requested to provide input in the form of proposals for top management's review. This information provides the data necessary for the formulation and implementation stages of strategic management. As depicted in Illustrative Example 1.1, the firm begins with redefining its mission and ends with developing a feedback system to aid in evaluation and control.

1.5 ILLUSTRATION OF THE MODEL

STRATEGIC MANAGEMENT AT MURPHY MOTORS
(Corporate Level)

Illustrative Example 1.1

STRATEGY FORMULATION

Mission

Broad. Provide transportation vehicles to people throughout the world.
Narrow. Build and sell cars and trucks in noncommunist countries.

Objectives

1. Achieve an ROI of 10% for the period 1988–1993.
2. Become number one in *global* automotive market share by 1990.
3. Increase domestic car and truck market share by 5% by 1991.
4. Reduce unit costs by 6% by 1990.

Strategies

1. Grow by concentrating all resources in the car and truck industry. Focus on developing fuel-efficient cars and trucks to meet EPA requirements and to challenge competition.

(Continued)

2. Vertically integrate and continually modernize manufacturing facilities with state-of-the-art technology to reduce costs and to control raw materials.

3. Engage in joint ventures with foreign auto manufacturers to build and sell cars and trucks in developing countries.

Policies

1. Emphasize research and development to reduce costs and to improve auto efficiency and safety.

2. Emphasize efficiency at all levels. Reward high performers and retire or fire unproductive workers and managers. Increase plant efficiency at all locations.

3. Emphasize the building of safe, fuel-efficient cars and trucks at a quality level equal to the number-one competitor.

4. Emphasize the international marketplace to respond to global competition.

STRATEGY IMPLEMENTATION

Programs

1. Add a new division to build and sell a new low-cost, high-quality "world car" domestically.

2. Engage in negotiations with foreign automakers to set up joint ventures to build and sell the "world car" throughout the world.

3. Purchase a steel company with the capacity to provide sufficient high-quality steel for all divisions' requirements.

4. Reduce manufacturing costs by installing robots at 50% of each division's work stations by 1990.

5. Increase fleet miles per gallon by converting 80% of all autos produced to front-wheel drive by 1990.

Budgets

Prepare budgets showing cost-benefit analysis of each planned program.

Procedures

1. Develop procedures needed to sell enough bonds and common stock to finance the construction of the "world car" division.

2. Develop procedures for negotiation teams to follow when looking for joint venture partners.

3. Develop a series of procedures to follow in order to purchase a steel company.

4. Develop procedures to convert manned to robot work stations.

5. Develop procedures to convert to front-wheel drive.

(Continued)

Illustrative
Example 1.1
(*Continued*)

EVALUATION AND CONTROL

Require monthly status reports on the following:

1. Number of new "world car" dealerships established.
2. Actual versus planned construction time and costs for new "world car" plant.
3. Progress of negotiations with possible joint venture partners.
4. Progress of negotiations with top management of targeted steel company acquisitions.
5. Actual versus standard costs for each division.
6. Actual versus planned sales for each division.
7. Progress toward installing robots.
8. Progress toward front-wheel drive conversion.

Require annual reports on the following:

1. ROI for each division.
2. Domestic and global market shares by product and by division compared to competition in each area.
3. Raw material and manufacturing costs by product line and by division.
4. EPA rating on fleet in terms of miles per gallon.
5. Strategic audit of entire corporation and each division.

A corporation the size of a modern automobile company would tend to be structured on a divisional and a functional basis. Each car line, for example, might form its own division. Each division would have its own production facilities as well as marketing, finance, and human resource departments. As depicted in Fig. 1.5, the corporate level goes through all three stages of the strategic management process. Top management *with input from the divisions* formulates strategies and makes plans for implementation. These implementation plans stimulate the strategy formulation process at the divisional level. Each division formulates objectives, strategies, and policies in order to accomplish the corporate programs. The evaluation and control information from each division feeds upward to the corporate level for its use in evaluation and control.

Just as the implementation stage of corporate strategic planning stimulates the formulation stage of the same process at the divisional level, implementation planning at the divisional level causes each functional department to begin formulating its own strategic plans. For example, a corporate-level program of Murphy Motors might have as its goal the conversion of 80% of the auto fleet to front-wheel drive by 1990. To implement this program, each division must formulate an objective specifying which cars will be con-

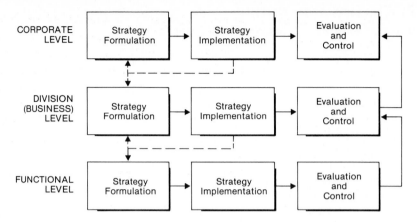

Figure 1.5   **Strategic management process at three corporate levels.**

verted by what time and at what cost and develop a strategy of how it is to be accomplished.

As each division develops its own programs for implementation, separate functional departments within each division begin to formulate their own objectives and strategies. For example, Division A's manufacturing department sets an objective of retooling its assembly line for front-wheel drive cars by 1989. The purchasing department of Division A sets objectives and plans strategies to begin ordering new parts from suppliers. Division A's marketing department initiates plans to change its advertising and promotional activities in order to ready the consumer for front-wheel drive vehicles. Each level develops its own objectives, strategies, and policies to complement the level above.

The specific operation of the hierarchy of strategy may vary from one corporation to another. The one described here of the fictitious Murphy Motors is an example of *top-down* strategic planning in which corporate-level top management initiates the strategy formulation process and calls upon divisions and functional units to formulate their own strategies as a way of implementing corporate-level strategies. Another approach may be *bottom-up* strategic planning in which the strategy formulation process is initiated by strategic proposals from divisional or functional units. This is shown in Fig. 1.5 with dotted arrows leading from functional to divisional level and from divisional to corporate level in the strategy formulation stages. Regardless of whether the initiation for strategy formulation comes from above or below, it is clear that the process involves a lot of negotiation between levels in the hierarchy to ensure that the various strategies fit together and reinforce each other.[21]

This chapter sets the stage for the study of strategic management and business policy. It explains the rationale for including the subject in a business school curriculum. In addition to serving as a capstone to integrate the various functional areas, the course provides a framework for analyzing top management's decision process and the effects of environmental issues on the corporation. Research generally supports the conclusion that corporations that manage strategically perform at higher levels than do those firms that do not. Strategic management is thus an important area of study for anyone interested in organizational productivity.

Our model of strategic management includes formulation and implementation, plus evaluation and control. The mission of a corporation derives from the interaction of internal and external environmental factors, modified by the needs and values of top management. A precise statement of mission guides the setting of objectives and the formulation of strategy and policies. Strategy is implemented through specific programs, budgets, and procedures. Management continually monitors and evaluates performance and activities on the basis of measurable results and audits of key areas. These data feed back into the corporation at all phases of the strategic management process. If results and activities fail to measure up to the plans, managers may then take the appropriate actions.

Although top management and the board of directors have primary responsibility for the strategic management process, many levels of the corporation conduct strategy formulation, implementation, evaluation, and control. Large multidivisional corporations utilize divisional and functional levels that integrate the entire corporation by focusing activities on the accomplishment of the mission.

1.6 SUMMARY AND CONCLUSION

DISCUSSION QUESTIONS

1. What is the difference between business policy and strategic management?
2. How does strategic management typically evolve in a corporation? Why?
3. What is meant by the hierarchy of strategy?
4. Does every business firm have business strategies? Explain.
5. What information is needed to properly formulate strategy? Why?

NOTES

1. G. Brooks, "After Mukluk Fiasco, Sohio Strives To Find, or Perhaps To Buy, Oil," *Wall Street Journal* (April 19, 1984), p. 22.
2. R. A. Gordon and J. E. Howell, *Higher Education for Business* (New York: Columbia University Press, 1959).
   F. C. Pierson et al., *The Education of American Businessmen* (New York: McGraw-Hill, 1959).

3. Gordon and Howell, p. 206.

4. Gordon and Howell, pp. 206–207.

5. J. D. Hunger and T. L. Wheelen, *An Assessment of Undergraduate Business Education in the United States* (Charlottesville, Va.: McIntire School of Commerce Foundation, 1980). Also summarized in "A Performance Appraisal of Undergraduate Business Education," *Human Resource Management* (Spring 1980), pp. 24–31.

6. M. Leontiades, "The Confusing Words of Business Policy," *Academy of Management Review* (January 1982), p. 46.

7. B. Lancaster, "American Hospital's Marketing Program Places Company Atop a Troubled Industry," *Wall Street Journal* (August 24, 1984), p. 19.

8. B. D. Henderson, *Henderson on Corporate Strategy* (Cambridge, Mass.: Abt Books, 1979), p. 33.

9. R. Lamb, *Advances in Strategic Management,* Vol. 2 (Greenwich, Conn.: Jai Press, Inc., 1983), p. x.

10. F. W. Gluck, S. P. Kaufman, and A. S. Walleck, "The Four Phases of Strategic Management," *The Journal of Business Strategy* (Winter 1982), pp. 9–21.

11. H. W. Henry, "Evolution of Strategic Planning in Major Corporations," *Proceedings, American Institute of Decision Sciences* (November 1980), pp. 454–456.
H. W. Henry, "Then and Now: A Look at Strategic Planning Systems," *Journal of Business Strategy* (Winter 1981), pp. 64–69.

12. G. C. Brunton, "Implementing Corporate Strategy: The Story of International Thomson," *Journal of Business Strategy* (Fall 1984), p. 14.

13. P. Pascarella, "Strategy Comes Down to Earth," *Industry Week* (January 9, 1984), p. 51.

14. W. B. Schaffir and T. J. Lobe, "Strategic Planning: The Impact at Five Companies," *Planning Review* (March 1984), pp. 40–41.

15. R. B. Higgins, "Human Resource Management Problems in Strategic Planning: The Challenge of the 1980's," in R. Lamb (ed.) *Advances in Strategic Management,* Vol. 1 (Greenwich, Conn.: Jai Press, Inc., 1983), p. 86.
C. B. Shrader, L. Taylor, and D. R. Dalton, "Strategic Planning and Organizational Performance: A Critical Appraisal," *Journal of Management* (Summer 1984), pp. 149–179.

16. H. I. Ansoff et al., "Does Planning Pay?" *Long Range Planning* (December 1970), pp. 2–7.
S. Thune and R. J. House, "Where Long-Range Planning Pays Off," *Business Horizons* (August 1970), pp. 81–87.
D. M. Herold, "Long-Range Planning and Organizational Performance: A Cross-Validation Study," *Academy of Management Journal* (March 1972), pp. 91–104.
D. Burt, "Planning and Performance in Australian Retailing," *Long Range Planning* (June 1978), pp. 62–66.

J. O. Eastlack and P. R. McDonald, "CEO's Role in Corporate Growth," *Harvard Business Review* (May–June 1970), pp. 150–163.

D. R. Wood and R. L. LaForge, "The Impact of Comprehensive Planning on Financial Performance," *Academy of Management Journal* (September 1979), pp. 516–526.

D. W. Karger and Z. A. Malik, "Long Range Planning and Organizational Performance," *Long Range Planning* (December 1975), pp. 60–64; and Z. A. Malik and D. W. Karger, "Does Long-Range Planning Improve Company Performance?" *Management Review* (September 1975), pp. 27–31.

D. Miller and P. H. Friesen, "Strategy-Making and Environment: The Third Link," *Strategic Management Journal* (July–September 1983), pp. 221–235.

J. B. Welch, "Strategic Planning Could Improve Your Share Price," *Long Range Planning* (April 1984), pp. 144–147.

L. C. Rhyne, "The Impact of Strategic Planning on Financial Performance" (Paper presented at the Forty-Third Annual Meeting of the Academy of Management, Dallas, Texas, August 1983).

17. M. Leontiades and A. Tezel, "Planning Perceptions and Planning Results," *Strategic Management Journal* (January–March 1980), pp. 65–75.

W. Rue and R. M. Fulmer, "Is Long-Range Planning Profitable?" *Proceedings, Academy of Management* (August 1973), pp. 66–73.

R. J. Kudla, "The Effects of Strategic Planning on Common Stock Returns," *Academy of Management Journal* (March 1980), pp. 5–20.

J. W. Fredrickson and T. R. Mitchell, "Strategic Decision Processes: Comprehensiveness and Performance" (Paper presented at the Forty-Second Annual Meeting of the Academy of Management, New York, August 1982).

W. M. Lindsay, W. R. Boulton, S. Franklin, and L. W. Rue, "Strategic Management Effectiveness: A Longitudinal Study" (Paper presented at the Forty-First Annual Meeting of the Academy of Management, San Diego, California, 1981).

18. L. C. Rhyne, p. 9.

19. P. Lorange, *Corporate Planning: An Executive Viewpoint* (Englewood Cliffs, N.J.: Prentice-Hall, 1980), p. 18.

20. C. W. Hofer and D. Schendel, *Strategy Formulation: Analytical Concepts* (St. Paul, Minn.: West Publishing Co., 1978), p. 29.

21. M. E. Naylor, "Regaining Your Competitive Edge," *Long Range Planning* (February 1985), pp. 33–34.

Chapter 2

DEVELOPING CONCEPTUAL SKILLS: THE CASE METHOD AND THE STRATEGIC AUDIT

STRATEGIC MANAGEMENT MODEL

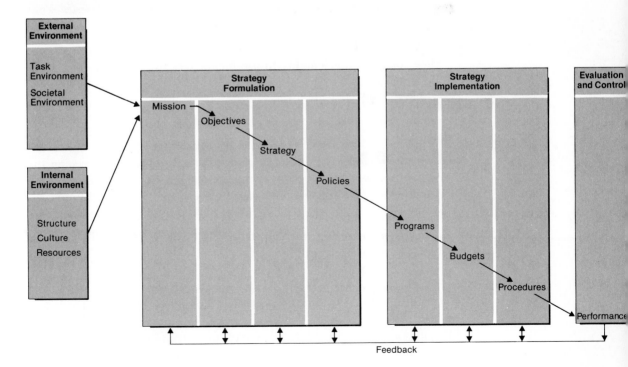

An analysis of a corporation's strategic management calls for a top-down view of the organization. In our analysis we view the corporation as an entity composed of interrelated units and systems, such as accounting, marketing, and finance. We examine the interrelationships of these areas in light of the opportunities and threats in the corporation's environment. We carry out our analysis through the use of complex cases or management simulations. These techniques will give you the opportunity to move from a narrow, specialized view to a broader, less precise analysis of the overall corporate picture. Consequently, the emphasis in case analysis is on developing and refining conceptual skills, which are different from the skills you developed in your technical and function-oriented courses. As you will see, conceptual skills are vital to performing successfully in the business world.

2.1 IMPORTANCE OF CONCEPTUAL SKILLS IN BUSINESS

Many have attempted to specify the characteristics necessary for a person to successfully advance from an entry-level position to one in top management. Few of these studies have been successful.[1] But Robert L. Katz has suggested one interesting approach. He focused on the skills successful managers exhibit in performing their jobs, an approach that negates the need to identify specific personality traits.[2] These skills imply abilities that can be developed and are manifested in performance.

Katz suggests that effective administration rests on three basic skills: technical, human, and conceptual. He defines them as follows:[3]

- *Technical skills* pertain to *what* is done and to working with *things*. They comprise one's ability to use technology to perform an organizational task.

- *Human skills* pertain to *how* something is done and to working with *people*. They comprise one's ability to work with people to achieve goals.

- *Conceptual skills* pertain to *why* something is done and to seeing the corporation as a *whole*. They comprise one's ability to understand the complexities of the corporation as it affects and is affected by its environment.

Katz further suggests that the optimal mix of these three skills varies at the different corporate levels:

At lower levels, the major need is for technical and human skills. At higher levels, the administrator's effectiveness depends largely on human and conceptual skills. At the top, conceptual skill becomes the most important of all for successful administration.[4]

Results of a survey of 300 presidents of *Fortune's* list of the top fifty banking, industrial, insurance, public utility, retailing, and transportation firms support Katz's conclusion regarding the different skill mixes needed at

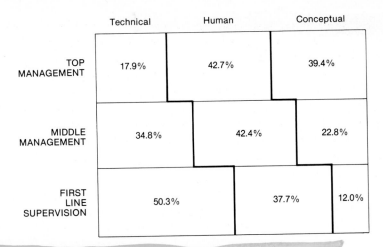

Figure 2.1   **Optimal skill mix of a manager by hierarchical level.**
SOURCE: T. L. Wheelen, G. K. Rakes, and J. D. Hunger, "Skills of an Executive," a paper presented to the Academy of Management, Kansas City, Mo., August 1976.

the different organizational levels.[5] As shown in Fig. 2.1, the need for technical skills decreases and the need for conceptual skills increases as a person moves from first line supervision to top management.

In addition, when executives were asked, "Are there certain skills necessary to move from one organizational level to another?" fifty-five percent reported conceptual skills to be the most crucial in moving from middle to top management.[6] Similar results have been reported concerning accountants in CPA firms.[7] Most theorists therefore agree that conceptual work carried out by organization leaders is the heart of strategy-making.[8]

The strategic management and business policy course attempts to develop conceptual skills through the use of comprehensive cases or complex simulations. Of course, you also need technical skills in order to analyze various aspects of each case. And you will use human skills in team presentations, study groups, or team projects. But in this course you will primarily develop and refine your conceptual skills by focusing on strategic issues. Concentrating on strategic management processes forces you to develop a better understanding of the political, social, and economic environment of business and to appreciate the interactions of the functional specialties required for corporate success.

Consulting firms, management scholars, boards of directors, and practicing managers are increasingly suggesting the use of audits of corporate activities.[9] An audit provides a checklist of questions by area or issue to enable a

2.2 AUDITS

systematic analysis of various corporate activities. It is extremely useful as a diagnostic tool to pinpoint problem areas and to highlight strengths and weaknesses.

Management Audit

The National Association of Regulatory Utility Commissioners analyzed thirty-one management audits that had been completed or were in progress. The report concluded that the regulatory agencies using management audits were pleased with the results and intended to continue using them. In general, these audits recommended changes in the operating practices of management and suggested areas where substantial reductions in operating costs could be made. The audits gave the boards of directors and management the opportunity to establish new priorities in their objectives and planning, and provided specific recommendations that had impact on the "bottom line."[10]

Typically, the term *management audit* is used to describe a checklist of questions for an in-depth analysis of a particular area of importance to the corporation. Recent examples are the inflation audit, sales force management audit, the social audit, the stakeholder audit, and the forecasting audit, among others.[11] Rarely, however, does it include a consideration of more than one issue or functional area. The *strategic audit* is, in comparison, a *type of management audit* which takes a corporate-wide perspective to provide a comprehensive assessment of a corporation's strategic situation. Most business analysts predict the use of management audits of all kinds to increase. As corporate boards of directors become more aware of their expanding duties and responsibilities, they should call for more corporate-wide management audits to be conducted.

Strategic Audit

As contrasted with the typically more specialized management audit, the strategic audit considers external as well as internal factors and includes alternative selection, implementation, and evaluation and control. It therefore covers the key aspects of the strategic management process and places them within a decision-making framework. This framework is composed of the following eight interrelated steps:

1. Evaluation of a corporation's current performance results in terms of (a) return on investment, profitability, etc., and (b) the current mission, objectives, strategies, and policies.

2. Examination and evaluation of a corporation's strategic managers—its board of directors and top management.

3. A scanning of the external environment to locate strategic factors that pose opportunities and threats.

4. A scanning of the internal corporate environment to determine strategic strengths and weaknesses.

5. Analysis of the strategic factors (a) to pinpoint problem areas and (b) to review and revise the corporate mission and objectives as necessary.

6. Generation, evaluation, and selection of the best alternative strategy in light of the analysis conducted in step 5.

7. Implementation of selected strategies via programs, budgets, and procedures.

8. Evaluation of the implemented strategies via feedback systems, and the control of activities to ensure minimum deviation from plans.

This strategic decision-making process is depicted in Fig. 2.2 and basically reflects the approach to strategic management being used successfully by corporations such as Warner-Lambert and Dayton Hudson.[12] Although some research suggests that this type of "normative" approach may not work so well for firms in very unstable environments,[13] a recent survey of 956 corporate long-range planners reveals actual business practice to agree

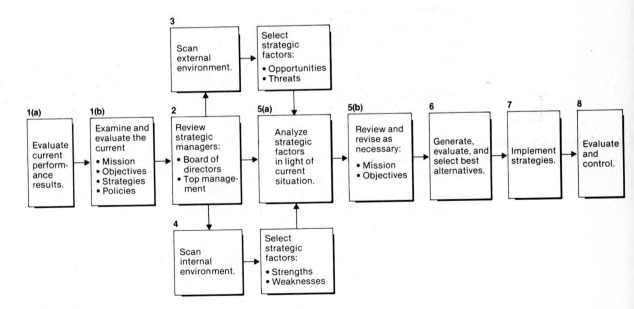

NOTE: Steps 1 through 6 are **strategy formulation.**
Step 7 is **strategy implementation.**
Step 8 is **evaluation and control.**

Figure 2.2   **Strategic decision-making process.**

generally with the model presented in Fig. 2.2.[14] This strategic decision-making process is made operational through the strategic audit.

The audit presents an integrated view of strategic management in action. It not only describes how objectives, strategies, and policies are formulated as long-range decisions, but also how they are implemented, evaluated, and controlled by programs, budgets, and procedures. The strategic audit, therefore, enables a person to better understand the *ways* in which various functional areas are interrelated and interdependent, as well as the *manner* in which they contribute to the achievement of the corporate mission. Consequently, the strategic audit is very useful to those people, such as boards of directors, whose job is to evaluate the overall performance of a corporation and its management.

Appendix 2.A at the end of this chapter is an example of a strategic audit proposed for use in analyzing complex business policy cases and for strategic decision making. The questions in the audit parallel the steps depicted in Fig. 2.2, the strategic decision-making process. It is *not* an all-inclusive list, but it presents many of the critical questions needed to strategically analyze any business corporation. You should consider the audit as a guide for analysis. Some questions or even some areas may be inappropriate for a particular case; in other areas, the questions may be insufficient for a complete analysis. However, each question in a particular area of the strategic audit can be broken down into an additional series of subquestions. It is up to you to develop these subquestions when they are needed.

A strategic audit fulfills three major *functions* in a case-oriented strategy and policy course:

1. It serves to highlight and review important concepts from previously studied subject areas.

2. It provides a systematic framework for the analysis of complex cases. (It is especially useful if you are unfamiliar with the case method.)

3. It generally improves the quality of case analysis and reduces the amount of time you might spend in learning how to analyze a case.

Students also find the audit helpful in organizing a case for written or oral presentation and in seeing that all areas have been considered. The strategic audit thus enables both students and teachers to maximize the amount of time spent both in analyzing why a certain area is creating problems for a corporation and in considering solutions to the problems.

2.3 CASE METHOD   The analysis/discussion of case problems has been the most popular method of teaching strategy and policy for many years.[15] Cases present actual business situations and enable you to examine both successful and unsuccessful corporations. For example, you may be asked to critically analyze a situation where a manager had to make a decision of long-run corporate importance. This approach gives you a feel for what it is like to work in a large corporation and to be faced with making a business decision.

Case Analysis and Presentation

There is no one best way to analyze or present a case report. Each instructor has personal preferences in terms of format and approach. Nevertheless, we present one suggested approach for both written and oral reports in Appendix 2.B at the end of the chapter. This approach provides a systematic method for successfully attacking a case.

The presentation of case analysis can be organized on the basis of a number of frameworks. One obvious framework to follow is the strategic audit as detailed in Appendix 2.A. Another is the McKinsey 7-S Framework composed of the seven organization variables of *structure, strategy, staff, management style, systems and procedures, skills,* and *shared values.*[16] Regardless of the framework chosen, be especially careful to include a complete analysis of key environmental variables—especially of trends in the industry and of the competition.

The focus in case discussion is on critical analysis and logical development of thought. A solution is satisfactory if it resolves important problems and is likely to be implemented successfully. What the corporation may actually have done to deal with the case problems has no real bearing on the analysis because its management may have analyzed its problems incorrectly and implemented a series of flawed solutions.

Researching the Case

You should undertake outside research to provide the environmental setting of the case. Check each case to find out when the case situation occurred and then screen the business periodicals for that time period. This background will give you an appreciation for the situation as it was experienced by the people in the case. A company's annual report from that year can be very helpful. An understanding of the economy during that period will help you avoid making a serious error in your analysis—for example, suggesting a sale of stock when the stock market is at an all-time low or taking on more debt when the prime interest rate is over 15%. Information on the industry will provide insights on its competitive activities. Some resources available for research into the economy and a corporation's industry are suggested in Appendix 2.C at the end of the chapter.

If you are unfamiliar with these business resources we urge you to read *How to Use the Business Library: With Sources of Business Information,* 5th ed., by H. W. Johnson, A. J. Faria, and E. L. Maier (Cincinnati: South-Western Publishing Co., 1984).

Table 2.1 **Financial Ratios**

Ratio	Formula	How Expressed
1. Liquidity Ratios		
Current ratio	$\dfrac{\text{Current assets}}{\text{Current liabilities}}$	Decimal
Quick (acid test) ratio	$\dfrac{\text{Current assets} - \text{Inventory}}{\text{Current liabilities}}$	Decimal
Inventory to net working capital	$\dfrac{\text{Inventory}}{\text{Current assets} - \text{Current liabilities}}$	Decimal
Cash ratio	$\dfrac{\text{Cash} + \text{cash equivalents}}{\text{Current liabilities}}$	Decimal
2. Profitability Ratios		
Net profit margin	$\dfrac{\text{Net profit after taxes}}{\text{Net sales}}$	Percentage
Gross profit margin	$\dfrac{\text{Sales} - \text{Cost of goods sold}}{\text{Net sales}}$	Percentage
Return on investment (ROI)	$\dfrac{\text{Net profit after taxes}}{\text{Total assets}}$	Percentage
Return on equity (ROE)	$\dfrac{\text{Net profit after taxes}}{\text{Stockholders equity}}$	Percentage
Earnings Per Share (EPS)	$\dfrac{\text{Net profit after taxes} - \text{Preferred stock dividends}}{\text{Average number of common shares}}$	Dollar per share
Productivity of Assets	$\dfrac{\text{Gross income} - \text{Taxes}}{\text{Stockholders equity}}$	Percentage
3. Activity Ratios		
Inventory turnover	$\dfrac{\text{Net sales}}{\text{Inventory}}$	Decimal
Days of inventory	$\dfrac{\text{Inventory}}{\text{Cost of goods sold} \div 365}$	Days
Net working capital turnover	$\dfrac{\text{Net sales}}{\text{Net working capital}}$	Decimal
Asset turnover	$\dfrac{\text{Sales}}{\text{Total assets}}$	Decimal
Fixed asset turnover	$\dfrac{\text{Sales}}{\text{Fixed assets}}$	Decimal
Average collection period	$\dfrac{\text{Accounts receivable}}{\text{Sales for year} \div 365}$	Days
Accounts receivable turnover	$\dfrac{\text{Annual credit sales}}{\text{Accounts receivable}}$	Decimal
Accounts payable period	$\dfrac{\text{Accounts Payable}}{\text{Purchases for year} \div 365}$	Days

Table 2.1 **Financial Ratios (Cont.)**

Ratio	Formula	How Expressed
Cash turnover	$\dfrac{\text{Cash}}{\text{Net sales for year} \div 365}$	Days
4. *Leverage Ratios*		
Debt to asset ratio	$\dfrac{\text{Total debt}}{\text{Total assets}}$	Percentage
Debt to equity ratio	$\dfrac{\text{Total debt}}{\text{Stockholders equity}}$	Percentage
Long-term debt to equity ratio	$\dfrac{\text{Long-term debt}}{\text{Stockholders equity}}$	Percentage
Times interest earned	$\dfrac{\text{Profit before taxes} + \text{Interest charges}}{\text{Interest charges}}$	Decimal
Coverage of fixed charges	$\dfrac{\text{Profit before taxes} + \text{Interest charges} + \text{Lease charges}}{\text{Interest charges} + \text{Lease obligations}}$	Decimal
Current liabilities to equity	$\dfrac{\text{Current liabilities}}{\text{Stockholders equity}}$	Percentage
5. *Other ratios*		
Price earning ratio	$\dfrac{\text{Market price per share}}{\text{Earnings per share}}$	Decimal
Dividend payout ratio	$\dfrac{\text{Annual dividends per share}}{\text{Annual earnings per share}}$	Percentage
Dividend yield on common stock	$\dfrac{\text{Annual dividends per share}}{\text{Current market price per share}}$	Percentage
Cash flow per share	$\dfrac{\text{After-tax profits} + \text{Depreciation}}{\text{Number of common shares outstanding}}$	Decimal

NOTE: In using ratios for analysis, calculate ratios for the corporation and compare them to the average ratios for the particular industry. Refer to Standard and Poor's and Robert Morris Associates for average industry data. For an in-depth discussion of ratios and their use, refer to J. F. Weston and E. F. Brigham, *Essentials of Managerial Finance,* 7th ed. (Hinsdale, Ill.: Dryden Press, 1985), pp. 59–93.

Financial Analysis: A Place To Begin

A review of key financial ratios may help you assess the company's overall situation and pinpoint some problem areas. Table 2.1 lists some of the most important financial ratios. Included are (1) *liquidity ratios,* which measure the corporation's ability to meet its financial obligations, (2) *profitability ratios,* which measure the degree of corporate success in achieving desired profit levels, (3) *activity ratios,* which measure the effectiveness of the corporation's use of resources, and (4) *leverage ratios,* which measure the contributions of owners' financing compared with creditors' financing.

In your analysis do *not* simply make an exhibit including all the ratios, but select and discuss only those ratios that have an impact on the company's problems. For instance, external resources, accounts receivable, and inventory may provide a source of funds. If receivables and inventories are double the industry average, reducing them may provide needed cash. In this situation, the case report should include not only sources of funds, but also the number of dollars freed for use.

A typical financial analysis of a firm would include a study of the operating statements for five or ten years, including a trend analysis of sales, profits, earnings per share, debt/equity ratio, return on investment, etc., plus a ratio study comparing the firm under study with industry standards. To begin, scrutinize historical income statements and balance sheets. These two basic statements provide most of the data needed for analysis. Compare the statements over time if a series of statements is available. Calculate changes that occur in individual categories from year to year, as well as the total change over the years. Determine the percentage change along with the absolute amount and the amount *adjusted for inflation*. Examination of this information may reveal developing trends. Compare trends in one category with trends in related categories. For example, an increase in sales of 15% over three years may appear to be satisfactory until you note an increase of 20% in the cost of goods sold during the same period. The outcome of this comparison may suggest that further investigation into the manufacturing process is necessary.

Another approach to analyzing financial statements is to convert them into *common-size* statements. Convert every category from dollar terms to percentages. In the case of the balance sheet, give the total assets or liabilities a value of 100%, and calculate all other categories as percentages of the total assets or liabilities. For the income statement, net sales represent 100%: calculate the percentage of each category so that the categories sum to the net sales percentage (100%). When you convert statements to this form, it is relatively easy to note the percentage each category represents of the total. Comparisons over the years may point out areas for additional analysis. To get a proper picture, however, make comparisons with industry data, if available, to see if fluctuations are merely reflecting industry-wide trends. If a firm's trends are generally in line with those of the rest of the industry, there is less likelihood of problems than if the firm's trends are worse than industry averages.

If the corporation being studied appears to be in poor financial condition, calculate its "Z-value." Developed by Edward Altman, the formula combines five ratios by weighting them according to their importance to a corporation's financial strength (see Illustrative Example 2.1). The formula predicts the likelihood of the company going bankrupt. Firms in serious trouble have Z values below 1.81.

THE ALTMAN BANKRUPTCY FORMULA

Illustrative
Example
2.1

Edward I. Altman developed a formula to predict a company's likelihood of going bankrupt. His system of multiple discriminate analysis is used by stockholders to determine if the corporation is a good investment. The formula was developed from a study of 33 manufacturing companies with assets averaging $6.4 million that had filed Chapter X bankruptcies. These were paired with 33 similar but profitable firms with assets between $1 million and $25 million. The formula is:

$$Z = 1.2x_1 + 1.4x_2 + 3.3x_3 + 0.6x_4 + 1.0x_5$$

where

x_1 = Working capital divided by total assets.
x_2 = Retained earnings divided by total assets.
x_3 = Earnings before interest and taxes divided by total assets.
x_4 = Market value of equity divided by book value of total debt.
x_5 = Sales divided by total assets.
Z = Overall index of corporate fiscal health.

The range of the Z-value for most corporations is -4 to $+8$. According to Altman, financially strong corporations have Z values above 2.99. Corporations in serious trouble have Z values below 1.81. Those in the middle are question marks that could go either way. The closer a firm gets to bankruptcy, the more accurate the Z-value is as a predictor.

SOURCE: M. Ball, "Z Factor: Rescue by the Numbers," *INC.* (December 1980), p. 48. Reprinted with the permission of *INC.* Magazine, December 1980. Copyright © 1980 by INC. Publishing Company, Boston.

Adjusting for Inflation

Many of the cases in business policy/strategy textbooks take place during a period of rapid inflation. When analyzing these cases, you should calculate sales and profits in constant dollars in order to perceive the "true" performance of the corporation in comparison with that of the industry, or of the economy in general. Remember that chief executive officers wish to keep their jobs and that some will tend to bias the figures in their favor. Sales stated in current dollars may look like substantial growth, but when they're converted to constant dollars, they may show a steady decline. In 1980, Peter Drucker, a renowned author and consultant, stated, ". . . corporate profits of the last ten years would be all wiped out if they were adjusted for inflation."[17]

As of 1980, the Financial Accounting Standards Board (FASB) required the largest U.S. corporations to report the last five years' sales, dividends and market price in constant dollar terms. It also required corporations to

Table 2.2   **Scott Paper Company's Annual Report Adjusted for Inflation: An Excerpt**

(Constant dollar and current cost expressed in average 1983 dollars)	1983	1982	1981	1980	1979
Average consumer price index	**298.4**	289.1	272.4	246.8	217.4
(In millions, except on a per share basis)					
Sales					
As reported	**$2,465.1**	$2,293.4	$2,309.4	$2,083.2	$1,908.1
In constant dollars	**2,465.1**	2,367.2	2,529.8	2,518.8	2,619.0
Net income (loss)					
As reported	**$123.7**	$74.5	$133.3	$133.0	$136.5
In constant dollars	**(4.5)**	(40.5)	31.7	55.6	103.5
At current cost	**8.6**	(29.7)	37.4	54.7	103.7
Earnings (loss) per common share					
As reported	**$2.58**	$1.61	$3.22	$3.41	$3.50
In constant dollars	**(.24)**	(1.09)	.75	1.42	2.65
At current cost	**.05**	(.84)	.90	1.40	2.66
Dividends per common share					
As reported	**$1.00**	$1.00	$1.00	$1.00	$ .90
In constant dollars	**1.00**	1.03	1.09	1.21	1.24
Net assets at year end					
As reported	**$1,481.2**	$1,335.7	$1,287.6	$1,114.0	$1,019.8
In constant dollars	**2,515.8**	2,497.7	2,528.3	2,406.4	2,334.8
At current cost	**2,753.9**	2,741.7	2,792.3	2,681.8	2,659.0
Current cost decrease in inventory and property, plant and equipment relative to general price level	**$15.4**	$30.8	$23.7	$30.8	$42.7
Unrealized gain from decline in purchasing power of net amounts owed	**$30.7**	$31.5	$67.6	$90.0	$100.3
Market price per common share at year end					
As reported	**$31.63**	$20.50	$16.38	$21.38	$18.75
In constant dollars	**31.09**	20.92	17.36	24.69	24.34

SOURCE: Scott Paper Company, *1983 Annual Report*, p. 45.

report what they have paid for goods and services at current cost in addition to the usual historical cost.[18] In 1984, the FASB decided to continue only the current cost requirement. Table 2.2 shows a page from the 1983 annual report of the Scott Paper Company, which provided constant dollar figures so that investors could make comparisons quickly. Note that, as originally stated, Scott Paper sales increased 29 percent from 1979 to 1983. When recalculated in constant dollars, however, sales actually declined. Note also

Table 2.3   **Consumer Price Index for All Items (1967 = 100.0)**

Year	CPI	Year	CPI
1972	125.3	1979	217.4
1973	133.1	1980	246.8
1974	147.7	1981	272.4
1975	161.2	1982	289.1
1976	170.5	1983	298.4
1977	181.5	1984	311.1
1978	195.4	1985	322.2

SOURCE: U.S. Department of Commerce, *1984 Statistical Abstract of the United States,* 10th edition, Chart no. 797, p. 478.

Table 2.4   **Changes in Prime Interest Rates***

Year	Low	High	Year	Low	High
1972	5	6	1979	11½	15¾
1973	6	10	1980	11	21½
1974	8¾	12	1981	15¾	20½
1975	7	10½	1982	11½	17
1976	6¼	7¼	1983	10½	11½
1977	6½	7¾	1984	10¾	12¾
1978	6	11¾	1985	9½	10¾

SOURCE: D. S. Benton, "Banking and Financial Information," Table 1.1, p. 2 in *Thorndike Encyclopedia of Banking and Financial Tables,* Revised Edition, *1986 Yearbook* (Boston, Mass.: Warren, Gorham & Lamont, 1986).

* The rate of interest that banks charge on the lowest-risk loans they make.

that when 1983 net income is calculated using constant dollars, a profit of $123.7 million becomes a $4.5 million net loss!

As an additional method of dealing with the distortions caused by inflation, firms such as DuPont and General Electric use inflation-adjusted figures throughout their operations. To adjust for inflation, most firms use the Consumer Price Index (CPI). Table 2.3 presents the index for all items. Table 2.4 provides information on prime interest rates.

2.4 SUMMARY AND CONCLUSION

The strategic management/business policy course is concerned with developing the conceptual skills that successful top management needs. The emphasis is therefore on improving your analytical and problem-solving abilities. The case method develops those skills and gives you an appreciation of environmental issues and the interdependencies among the functional units of a large corporation. The strategic audit is one recommended technique for systematizing the analysis of fairly long and complex policy cases. It also provides a basic checklist for investigating any large corporation. Nevertheless, the strategic audit is only one of many techniques with which you can analyze and diagnose case problems. We expect consultants, managers, and boards of directors to increasingly employ the audit as an analytical technique.

DISCUSSION QUESTIONS

1. Should people be selected for top management positions primarily on the basis of their having a particular combination of skills? Explain.

2. What are the strengths and weaknesses of the strategic audit as a technique for assessing corporate performance?

3. What value does the case method hold for the study of strategic management/business policy?

4. Why should one begin a case analysis with a financial analysis? When are other approaches appropriate?

5. Reconcile the strategic decision-making process depicted in Fig. 2.2 with the strategic management model depicted in Fig. 1.3.

NOTES

1. B. M. Bass, *Stogdill's Handbook of Leadership* (New York: Free Press, 1981), p. 73.

2. R. L. Katz, "Skills of an Effective Administrator," *Harvard Business Review* (January–February 1955), p. 33.

3. Katz, pp. 33–42. These definitions were adapted from the material in this article.

4. Katz, p. 42.

5. T. L. Wheelen, G. K. Rakes, and J. D. Hunger, "Skills of an Executive" (Paper presented at the Thirty-Sixth Annual Meeting of the Academy of Management, Kansas City, Mo., August 1976).

6. Wheelen, Rakes, and Hunger, p. 7.

7. W. G. Shenkir, T. L. Wheelen, and R. H. Strawser, "The Making of an Accountant," *CPA Journal* (March 1973), p. 219.

8. E. E. Chaffee, "Three Models of Strategy," *Academy of Management Review* (January 1985), pp. 89–90.

9. R. B. Buchele, "How to Evaluate a Firm," *California Management Review* (Fall 1962), pp. 5–16.
   W. T. Greenwood, *Business Policy: A Management Audit Approach* (New York: Macmillan, 1967).
   A. Elkins, *Management: Structures, Functions, and Practices* (Reading, Mass.: Addison-Wesley, 1980), pp. 441–454.
   B. H. Marcus and E. M. Tauber, *Marketing Analysis and Decision Making* (Boston: Little, Brown & Co., 1979), p. 25.
   J. A. F. Stoner, *Management,* 2nd ed. (Englewood Cliffs, N.J.: Prentice-Hall, 1982), p. 526.

J. Martindell, *The Appraisal of Management* (New York: Harper & Row, 1962).

R. Bauer, L. T. Cauthorn, and R. P. Warner, "Management Audit Process Guide," (Boston: Intercollegiate Case Clearing House, no. 9-375-336, 1975).

J. D. Hunger and T. L. Wheelen, "The Strategic Audit: An Integrative Approach To Teaching Business Policy" (Paper presented at the Forty-Third Annual Meeting of the Academy of Management, Dallas, Texas, August 1983).

M. Lauenstein, "The Strategy Audit," *Journal of Business Strategy* (Winter 1984), pp. 87–91.

10. T. Barry, "What a Management Audit Can Do for You," *Management Review* (June 1977), p. 43.

11. A. Michel, "The Inflation Audit," *California Management Review* (Winter 1981), pp. 68–74.

A. J. Dubinsky and R. W. Hansen, "The Sales Force Management Audit," *California Management Review* (Winter 1981), pp. 86–95.

A. B. Carroll and G. W. Beiler, "Landmarks in the Evolution of the Social Audit," *Academy of Management Journal* (September 1975), pp. 589–599.

R. E. Freeman, *Strategic Management: A Stakeholder Approach* (Boston: Pitman Publishing, 1984), p. 111.

J. S. Armstrong, "The Forecasting Audit," in S. Makridakis and S. C. Wheelwright (eds.), *The Handbook of Forecasting* (New York: Wiley and Sons, 1982), pp. 535–552.

A. L. Wilkins, "The Culture Audit," *Organization Dynamics* (Autumn 1983), pp. 24–38.

12. E. E. Tallett, "Repositioning Warner-Lambert as a High-Tech Health Care Company," *Planning Review* (May 1984), pp. 12–16, 41.

K. A. Macke, "Managing Change: How Dayton Hudson Meets the Challenge," *Journal of Business Strategy* (Summer 1983), pp. 78–81.

13. J. W. Fredrickson, "The Comprehensiveness of Strategic Decision Processes: Extension, Observation, Future Directions," *Academy of Management Journal* (September 1984), pp. 445–466.

14. P. M. Ginter and A. C. Rucks, "Relative Emphasis Placed on the Steps of the Normative Model of Strategic Planning by Practitioners," *Proceedings, Southern Management Association* (November 1983), pp. 19–21.

15. C. Boyd, D. Kopp, and L. Shufelt, "Evaluative Criteria in Business Policy Case Analysis: An Exploratory Study," *Proceedings, Midwest Academy of Management* (April 1984), pp. 287–292.

16. T. J. Peters and R. W. Waterman, Jr., *In Search of Excellence* (New York: Harper & Row, 1982), pp. 9–12.

17. D. Pauly, "Tomorrow's Rules for World Business," *Newsweek,* April 28, 1980, p. 71.

18. "Financial Statements Restated for General Price-Level Changes," *Financial Accounting Standards,* APB Statement no. 3 (Stamford, Conn.: Financial Accounting Standards Board, July 1, 1979).

STRATEGIC AUDIT OF A CORPORATION

Appendix 2.A

I. Current Situation

    A. How is the corporation performing in terms of return on investment, overall market share, profitability trends, earnings per share, etc.?

    B. What are the corporation's current mission, objectives, strategies, and policies?

        1. Are they clearly stated or are they merely implied from performance?

        2. *Mission:* What business(es) is the corporation in? Why?

        3. *Objectives:* What are the corporate, business, and functional objectives? Are they consistent with each other, with the mission, and with the internal and external environments?

        4. *Strategies:* What strategy or mix of strategies is the corporation following? Are they consistent with each other, with the mission and objectives, and with the internal and external environments?

        5. *Policies:* What are they? Are they consistent with each other, with the mission, objectives, and strategies, and with the internal and external environments?

II. Strategic Managers

    A. Board of Directors

        1. Who are they? Are they internal or external?

        2. Do they own significant shares of stock?

        3. Is the stock privately held or publicly traded?

        4. What do they contribute to the corporation in terms of knowledge, skills, background, and connections?

        5. How long have they served on the board?

        6. What is their level of involvement in strategic management? Do they merely rubber stamp top management's proposals or do they actively participate and suggest future directions?

    B. Top Management

        1. What person or group constitutes top management?

        2. What are top management's chief characteristics in terms of knowledge, skills, background, and style?

3. Has top management been responsible for the corporation's performance over the past few years?

4. Has it established a systematic approach to the formulation, implementation, and evaluation and control of strategic management?

5. What is its level of involvement in the strategic management process?

6. How well does top management interact with lower-level management?

7. How well does top management interact with the board of directors?

8. Is top management sufficiently skilled to cope with likely future challenges?

III. External Environment: Opportunities and Threats (S.W.<u>O</u>.T.)

   A. Societal Environment

     1. What general environmental factors (that is, sociocultural, economic, political-legal, and technological factors) are affecting the corporation?

     2. Which of these are the most important at the present time? In the next few years?

   B. Task Environment

     1. What key factors in the immediate environment (that is, customers, competitors, suppliers, creditors, labor unions, governments, trade associations, interest groups, local community, and stockholders) are affecting the corporation?

     2. Which of these are most important at the present time? In the next few years?

IV. Internal Environment: Strengths and Weaknesses (<u>S</u>.<u>W</u>.O.T.)

   A. Corporate Structure

     1. How is the corporation presently structured?

       a) Is decision-making authority centralized around one group or decentralized to many groups or units?

       b) Is it organized on the basis of functions, projects, geography, or some combination of these?

     2. Is the structure clearly understood by everyone in the corporation?

     3. Is the present structure consistent with current corporate objectives, strategies, policies, and programs?

     4. In what ways does this structure compare with those of similar corporations?

(*Continued*)

    B. Corporate Culture

        1. Is there a well-defined or emerging culture composed of shared beliefs, expectations, and values?

        2. Is the culture consistent with the current objectives, strategies, policies, and programs?

        3. What is the culture's position on important issues facing the corporation (that is, on productivity, quality of performance, adaptability to changing conditions)?

    C. Corporate Resources

        1. Marketing

           a) What are the corporation's current marketing objectives, strategies, policies, and programs?

             i) Are they clearly stated or merely implied from performance and/or budgets?

             ii) Are they consistent with the corporation's mission, objectives, strategies, policies, and with internal and external environments?

           b) How well is the corporation performing in terms of analysis of market position and marketing mix (that is, of product, price, place, and promotion)?

             i) What trends emerge from this analysis?

             ii) What impact have these trends had on past performance and how will they probably affect future performance?

             iii) Does this analysis support the corporation's past and pending strategic decisions?

           c) How well does this corporation's marketing performance compare with those of similar corporations?

           d) Are marketing managers using accepted marketing concepts and techniques to evaluate and improve product performance? (Consider product life cycle, market segmentation, market research, and product portfolios.)

           e) What is the role of the marketing manager in the strategic management process?

        2. Finance

           a) What are the corporation's current financial objectives, strategies, policies, and programs?

             i) Are they clearly stated or merely implied from performance and/or budgets?

             ii) Are they consistent with the corporation's mission, objectives, strategies, policies, and with internal and external environments?

b) How well is the corporation performing in terms of financial analysis? (Consider liquidity ratios, profitability ratios, activity ratios, leverage ratios, capitalization structure, and constant dollars.)

   i) What trends emerge from this analysis?

   ii) What impact have these trends had on past performance and how will they probably affect future performance?

   iii) Does this analysis support the corporation's past and pending strategic decisions?

c) How well does this corporation's financial performance compare with that of similar corporations?

d) Are financial managers using accepted financial concepts and techniques to evaluate and improve current corporate and divisional performance? (Consider financial leverage, capital budgeting, and ratio analysis.)

e) What is the role of the financial manager in the strategic management process?

3. Research and Development (R&D)

a) What are the corporation's current R&D objectives, strategies, policies, and programs?

   i) Are they clearly stated or implied from performance and/or budgets?

   ii) Are they consistent with the corporation's mission, objectives, strategies, policies, and with internal and external environments?

   iii) What is the role of technology in corporate performance?

   iv) Is the mix of basic, applied, and engineering research appropriate given the corporate mission and strategies?

b) What return is the corporation receiving from its investment in R&D?

c) Is the corporation technologically competent?

d) How well does the corporation's investment in R&D compare with the investments of similar corporations?

e) What is the role of the R&D manager in the strategic management process?

4. Manufacturing/Service

a) What are the corporation's current manufacturing/service objectives, strategies, policies, and programs?

(*Continued*)

i) Are they clearly stated or merely implied from performance and/or budgets?

ii) Are they consistent with the corporation's mission, objectives, strategies, policies, and with internal and external environments?

b) What is the type and extent of production capabilities of the corporation?

i) If product-oriented, consider plant facilities, type of manufacturing system (continuous mass production or intermittent job shop), age and type of equipment, degree and role of automation and/or robots, plant capacities and utilization, productivity ratings, availability and type of transportation.

ii) If service-oriented, consider service facilities (e.g., hospital, theater, or school buildings), type of operations systems (continuous service over time to same clientele or intermittent service over time to varied clientele), age and type of supporting equipment, degree and role of automation and/or use of mass communication devices (e.g., diagnostic machinery, videotape machines), facility capacities and utilization rates, efficiency ratings of professional/service personnel, availability and type of transportation to bring service staff and clientele together.

c) Are manufacturing or service facilities vulnerable to natural disasters, local or national strikes, reduction or limitation of resources from suppliers, substantial cost increases of materials, or nationalization by governments?

d) Is operating leverage being used successfully with an appropriate mix of people and machines in manufacturing firms or of support staff to professionals in service firms?

e) How well is the corporation performing compared to the competition? Consider costs per unit of labor, material, and overhead; downtime; inventory control management and/or scheduling of service staff; production ratings; facility utilization percentages; and number of clients successfully treated by category (if service firm), or percentage of orders shipped on time (if product firm).

i) What trends emerge from this analysis?

ii) What impact have these trends had on past performance and how will they probably affect future performance?

iii) Does this analysis support the corporation's past and pending strategic decisions?

f) Are manufacturing/service managers using appropriate concepts and techniques to evaluate and improve current performance? Consider cost systems, quality control and reliability systems, inventory control management, personnel scheduling, learning curves, safety programs, engineering programs to improve efficiency of manufacturing or of service.

g) What is the role of the manager of manufacturing or services in the strategic management process?

5. Human Resources Management (HRM)

a) What are the corporation's current HRM objectives, strategies, policies, and programs?

i) Are they clearly stated or merely implied from performance and/or budgets?

ii) Are they consistent with the corporation's mission, objectives, strategies, policies, and with internal and external environments?

b) How well is the corporation's HRM performing in terms of improving the fit between the individual employee and the job? Consider turnover, grievances, strikes, layoffs, quality of work life.

i) What trends emerge from this analysis?

ii) What impact have these trends had on past performance and how will they probably affect future performance?

iii) Does this analysis support the corporation's past and pending strategic decisions?

c) How does this corporation's HRM performance compare with that of similar corporations?

d) Are HRM managers using appropriate concepts and techniques to evaluate and improve corporate performance? Consider job analysis program, performance appraisal system, up-to-date job descriptions, training and development programs, attitude surveys, job design programs, quality of relationship with unions.

e) What is the role of the HRM manager in the strategic management process?

6. Information Systems (MIS)

a) What are the corporation's current MIS objectives, strategies, policies, and programs?

(Continued)

i) Are they clearly stated or merely implied from performance and/or budgets?

ii) Are they consistent with the corporation's mission, objectives, strategies, policies, and with internal and external environments?

b) How well is the corporation's MIS performing in terms of providing a useful database, automating routine clerical operations, assisting managers in making routine decisions, and providing information necessary for strategic decisions?

i) What trends emerge from this analysis?

ii) What impact have these trends had on past performance and how will they probably affect future performance?

iii) Does this analysis support the corporation's past and pending strategic decisions?

c) How does this corporation's MIS performance and stage of development compare with that of similar corporations?

d) Are MIS managers using appropriate concepts and techniques to evaluate and improve corporate performance? Do they know how to build and manage a complex database, conduct system analyses, and implement interactive decision support systems?

e) What is the role of the MIS manager in the strategic management process?

V. Analysis of Strategic Factors

A. What are the key internal and external factors (S.W.O.T.) that strongly affect the corporation's present and future performance?

1. What are the short-term problems facing this corporation?

2. What are the long-term problems facing this corporation?

B. Are the current mission and objectives appropriate in light of the key strategic factors and problems?

1. Should the mission and objectives be changed? If so, how?

2. If changed, what will the effect be on the firm?

VI. Strategic Alternatives

A. Can the current or revised objectives be met by simply implementing more carefully those strategies presently in use (for example, fine tuning the strategies)?

B. What are the feasible alternative strategies available to this corporation?

1. Do you recommend stability, growth, retrenchment, or a combination of these strategies?

2. What are the pros and cons of each?

C. What is the *best* alternative (that is, *your* recommended strategy)?

1. Does it adequately resolve the long- and short-term problems?

2. Does it take into consideration the key strategic factors?

3. What policies should be developed or revised to guide effective implementation?

VII. Implementation

A. What kinds of programs (for example, restructuring the corporation) should be developed to implement the recommended strategy?

1. Who should develop these programs?

2. Who should be in charge of these programs?

B. Are the programs financially feasible? Can *pro forma* budgets be developed and agreed upon? Are priorities and timetables appropriate to individual programs?

C. Will new standard operating procedures need to be developed?

VIII. Evaluation and Control

A. Is the current information system capable of providing sufficient feedback on implementation activities and performance?

1. Can performance results be pinpointed by area, unit, project, or function?

2. Is the information timely?

B. Are adequate control measures in place to ensure conformance with the recommended strategic plan?

1. Are appropriate standards and measures being used?

2. Are reward systems capable of recognizing and rewarding good performance?

SUGGESTED TECHNIQUES FOR CASE ANALYSIS AND PRESENTATION

Appendix 2.B

A. Case Analysis

1. Read the case rapidly to get an overview of the nature of the corporation and its environment. Note the date the case was written so that you can put it into proper context.

(Continued)

2. Read the case a second time, giving it a detailed analysis according to the strategic audit (see Appendix 2.A) when appropriate. The audit will provide a conceptual framework to examine the corporation's objectives, mission, policies, strategies, problems, symptoms of problems, and issues. You should end up with a list of the salient issues and problems in the case. Perform a financial analysis.

3. Undertake outside research, when appropriate, to uncover economic and industrial information. Appendix 2.C suggests possible sources for outside research. These data should provide the environmental setting for the corporation. Conduct an in-depth analysis of the industry. Analyze the important competitors. Consider the bargaining power of suppliers as well as buyers which may affect the firm's situation. Consider also the possible threats of future competitors in the industry as well as the likelihood of new or different products or services which may substitute for the company's present ones.

4. Marshal facts and evidence to support selected issues and problems. Develop a framework or outline to organize the analysis. Your method of organization could be one of the following:

   a) The case as organized around the strategic audit.

   b) The case as organized around the key individual(s) in the case.

   c) The case as organized around the corporation's functional areas: production, management, finance, marketing, and R&D.

   d) The case as organized around the decision-making process.

   e) The case as organized around the seven variables (McKinsey 7-S Framework) of structure, strategy, staff, management style, systems and procedures, skills, and shared values.

5. Clearly identify and state the central problem(s) as supported by the information in the case. Use the S.W.O.T. format to sum up the key strategic factors facing the corporation: Strengths and Weaknesses of the company; Opportunities and Threats in the environment.

6. Develop a logical series of alternatives that evolve from the analysis to resolve the problem(s) or issue(s) in the case.

7. Evaluate each of the alternatives in light of the company's environment (both external and internal), mission, objectives, strategies, and policies. For each alternative, consider both the possible obstacles to its implementation and its financial implications.

8. Make recommendations on the basis of the fact that action must be taken. (Don't say, "I don't have enough information." The individuals in the case may have had the same or even less information than is in the case.)

a) Base your recommendations on a total analysis of the case.

b) Provide the evidence gathered in step A4 to justify suggested changes.

c) List the recommendations in order of priority—those to be done immediately and those to be done in the future.

d) Show how your recommendation(s) will solve each of the problems mentioned in step A5.

e) Explain how each recommendation will be implemented. How will the plan(s) deal with anticipated resistance?

f) Suggest feedback and control systems to ensure that the recommendations are carried out as planned and to give advance warning of needed adjustments

B. Written Presentation

1. Use the outline from step A4 to write the first draft of the case analysis.

a) Don't rehash the case material; rather supply the salient evidence and data to support your recommendations.

b) Develop exhibits on financial ratios and other data for inclusion in your report. The exhibits should provide meaningful information. Mention key elements of an exhibit in the text of the written analysis. If you include a ratio analysis as an exhibit, explain the meaning of the ratios in the text and cite only the critical ones in your analysis.

2. Review your case analysis after it is written for content and grammar. Remember to compare the outline (step A4) with the final product. Make sure you've presented sufficient data or evidence to support your problem analysis and recommendations. If the final product requires rewriting, do so. Keep in mind that the written report is going to be judged not only on *what* is said but also on the *manner* in which it is said.

3. If your written or oral presentation requires *pro forma* statements, you may wish to develop a scenario for each quarter and/or year in your forecast. A well-constructed scenario will help improve the accuracy of your forecast. Chapters 4 and 8 suggest methods to develop scenarios.

C. Oral Presentation by Teams

1. Each team member should develop his or her own outline from step A4.

2. The team should consolidate member outlines into one comprehensive team outline.

3. Divide the work of the case analysis among the team members for further modification and for presentation.

(Continued)

4. Modify the team outline, if necessary, and have one or two rehearsals of the presentation. If there is a time constraint, apply it to the practice presentation. If exhibits are used, make sure to allow sufficient time to explain them. Critique one another's presentations and make the necessary modifications to the analysis.

5. During the class presentation, if a presenter misses a key fact, either slip a note to him or her, or deal with it in the summary speech.

6. Answer the specific questions raised by the instructor or classmates. If one person acts as a moderator for the questions and refers the questions to the appropriate team member, the presentation runs more smoothly than it will if everyone (or no one!) tries to deal with each question.

RESOURCES FOR CASE RESEARCH

Appendix 2.C

A. Company Information
   1. Annual Reports
   2. *Moody's Manuals on Investment* (a listing of companies within certain industries that contains a brief history of each company and a five-year financial statement)
   3. Securities and Exchange Commission Annual Report Form 10-K
   4. *Standard and Poor's Register of Corporations, Directors, and Executives*
   5. *Value Line Investment Survey*
B. Economic Information
   1. Regional statistics and local forecasts from large banks
   2. *Business Cycle Development* (Department of Commerce)
   3. Chase Econometric Associates' publications
   4. Census Bureau publications on population, transportation, and housing
   5. *Current Business Reports* (Department of Commerce)
   6. *Economic Indicators* (Joint Economic Committee)
   7. *Economic Report of the President to Congress*
   8. *Long-Term Economic Growth* (Department of Commerce)
   9. *Monthly Labor Review* (Department of Labor)
   10. *Monthly Bulletin of Statistics* (United Nations)

11. "Survey of Buying Power," *Sales Management*

12. Standard and Poor's Statistical Service

13. *Statistical Abstract of the United States* (Department of Commerce)

14. *Statistical Yearbook* (United Nations)

15. *Survey of Current Business* (Department of Commerce)

16. *U.S. Industrial Outlook* (Department of Defense)

17. *World Trade Annual* (United Nations)

18. *Overseas Business Reports* (published by country by U.S. Department of Commerce)

C. Industry Information

1. Analysis of companies and industries by investment brokerage firms

2. *Annual Report of American Industry* (a compilation of statistics by industry and company published by *Fortune*)

3. *Business Week* (provides weekly economic and business information and quarterly profit and sales rankings of corporations)

4. *Fortune Magazine* (publishes listings of financial information on corporations within certain industries)

5. *Industry Survey* (published quarterly by Standard and Poor Corporation)

D. Directory and Index Information

1. *Business Information: How to Find and Use It*

2. *Business Periodical Index*

3. *Directory of National Trade Associations*

4. *Encyclopedia of Associations*

5. *Funk and Scott Index of Corporations and Industries*

6. *Thomas's Register of American Manufacturers*

7. *Wall Street Journal Index*

E. Ratio Analysis Information

1. *Almanac of Business and Industrial Ratios* (Prentice-Hall)

2. *Annual Statement Studies* (Robert Morris Associates)

3. *Dun's Review* (Dun and Bradstreet: published annually in September–December issues)

F. General Sources

1. *Commodity Yearbook*

2. *U.S. Census of Business*

(Continued)

     3. *U.S. Census of Manufacturers*

     4. *World Almanac and Book of Facts*

G. Business Periodicals

     1. *Business Week*

     2. *Forbes*

     3. *Wall Street Journal*

     4. *Fortune*

     5. Industry-specific periodicals (e.g., *Oil and Gas Journal*)

H. Academic/Practitioner Journals

     1. *Harvard Business Review*

     2. *Journal of Business Strategy*

     3. *Long-Range Planning*

     4. *Strategic Management Journal*

     5. *Planning Review*

     6. *Academy of Management Review*

PART TWO

SCANNING THE ENVIRONMENT

Chapter 3

STRATEGIC MANAGERS

STRATEGIC MANAGEMENT MODEL

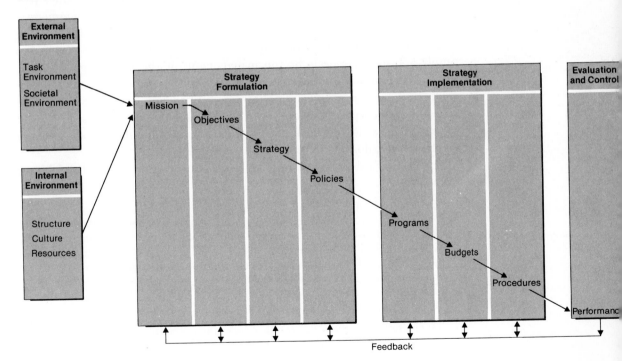

Strategic managers are the people in a corporation who are involved in the strategic management process. They are the people who scan the internal and external environments, formulate and implement objectives, strategies and policies, and evaluate and control the results. The people with direct responsibility for this process are the board of directors and top management. The chief executive officer (CEO), the chief operations officer (COO) or president, the executive vice-president, and the vice-presidents in charge of operating divisions and functional areas typically form the top management group. Traditionally, boards of directors have engaged in strategic management only to the extent that they passively approved proposals from top management and hired and fired their CEOs. Their role, however, is changing dramatically. The strategic management process, therefore, is also changing.

3.1 CORPORATE BOARD OF DIRECTORS

Directors conduct a far different meeting from those in the past. Pressures—from regulatory agencies, shareholders, lenders, and the public—have practically forced greater awareness of directors' responsibilities. The board as a rubber stamp or a bastion of the "old-boy" selection system has largely been replaced by more active, more professional boards.[1]

Even in the recent past, boards of directors have functioned rather passively. Members were selected because of their prestige in the community, regardless of their knowledge of the specific functioning of the corporation they were to oversee. Traditionally, members of the board were requested to simply approve proposals by top management or the firm's legal counsel, and the more important board activities generally were conducted by an executive committee composed of insiders.[2] Even now, the boards in some family-owned corporations are more figureheads than overseers; they exist on paper because the laws of incorporation require their presence, but rarely, if ever, do they question management's plans.

Lee Iacocca describes how such a situation existed at the Ford Motor Company.

> The Ford Motor Company had gone public in 1956, but Henry never really accepted the change. As he saw it, he was like his grandfather, the rightful owner—Henry Ford, Prop. (Proprietor)—and the company was his to do [with] as he pleased. When it came to the board, he, more than most CEO's, believed in the mushroom treatment—throw manure on them and keep them in the dark. That attitude, of course, was fostered by the fact that Henry and his family, with only 12% of the stock, held on to 40% of the voting rights.[3]

Over the past decade, stockholders and various interest groups have seriously questioned the role of the board of directors. As a result, the general public has become more aware and more critical of many boards' apparent lack of responsibility for corporate activities. Who is responsible for radioactive leaks in nuclear power plants? For the manufacture and sale of unsafe toys? For not properly safeguarding employees from hazards in the workplace? For bribery attempts by corporate officers? Can boards, especially those of multinational corporations, realistically monitor the decisions and actions of corporate employees in countries halfway around the world? What are the legal liabilities of a board for the actions taken by the corporation?

At this time, there are no national standards defining the accountability or responsibility of a board of directors. The law offers little guidance on this question. Specific requirements of directors vary, depending on the state in which the corporate charter is issued. According to Conference Board reports authored by Bacon and Brown, "State corporation laws give boards of directors rather sweeping powers couched in general language that does not specify to whom they are accountable nor clarify what it is they are accountable for.[4] There is, nevertheless, a developing consensus concerning the major responsibilities of a board.

Responsibilities of the Board

The board of directors of a corporation is appointed or elected by the stockholders for the following purposes:

- To oversee the management of the corporation's assets;
- To establish or approve the corporation's mission, objectives, strategy, and policies;
- To review management's actions in light of the financial performance of the corporation; and
- To hire and fire the principal operating officers of the corporation.

In a legal sense, the board is required to direct the affairs of the corporation but not to manage them. It is charged by law to act with "due care." As Bacon and Brown put it, "Directors must act with that degree of diligence, care and skill which ordinarily prudent men would exercise under similar circumstances in like positions."[5] If a director or the board as a whole fails to act with due care and, as a result, the corporation is in some way harmed, the careless director or directors may be held personally liable for the harm done.

For example, after the Federal Deposit Insurance Corporation (FDIC) put together a $4.5 billion package to rescue the failing Continental Illinois Bank of Chicago in 1984, it dismissed nine of the bank's sixteen directors.

Two other directors resigned. Even though each director had sworn the Joint Oath of the National Bank Directors to "diligently and honestly administer the affairs" of the bank, the FDIC contended that the directors should have monitored more carefully what was happening at Continental Illinois.[6]

The increasing popularity of personal liability insurance for board members suggests that a number of people on boards of directors are becoming very concerned that they might be held personally responsible not only for their own actions but also for the actions of the corporation as a whole. This is reinforced by the requirement of the Securities and Exchange Commission (SEC) that a majority of directors must sign the Annual Report Form 10-K. A recent survey found that of 606 major U.S. corporations, 51% go beyond the SEC requirement by requiring that *all* directors sign the 10-K.[7]

In addition to these duties, directors must make certain that the corporation is managed in accordance with the laws of the state in which it is incorporated. They must also ensure management's adherence to laws and regulations, such as those dealing with the issuance of securities, insider trading, and other conflict-of-interest situations. They must also be aware of the needs and demands of constituent groups so that they can achieve a judicious balance among the interests of these diverse groups while ensuring the continued functioning of the corporation.

Role of the Board in Strategic Management

In terms of strategic management, a board of directors has three basic tasks.[8]

- *To initiate and determine.* A board can delineate a corporation's mission and specify strategic options to its management.

- *To evaluate and influence.* A board can examine management proposals, decisions, and actions; agree or disagree with them; give advice and offer suggestions; outline alternatives.

- *To monitor.* By acting through its committees, a board can keep abreast of developments both inside and outside the corporation. It can thus bring to management's attention developments it may have overlooked.

Even though any board will be composed of people with varying degrees of commitment to the corporation, we can make some generalizations about a board of directors as a whole in its attempt to fulfill these three basic tasks. We can characterize a board as being at a specific point on a continuum on the basis of its degree of involvement in corporate strategic affairs. As types, boards may range from phantom boards with no real involvement to catalyst boards with a very high degree of involvement. Highly involved boards tend

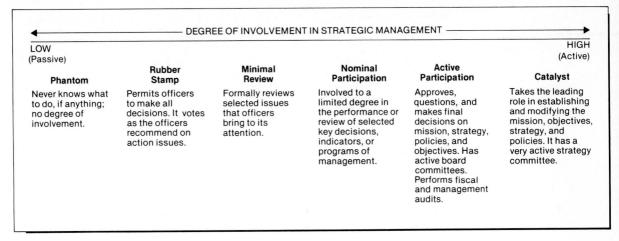

Figure 3.1   Board of directors continuum.

to be very active. They take their tasks of initiating, evaluating and influencing, and monitoring very seriously by providing advice when necessary and keeping management alert. As depicted in Fig. 3.1, they may be deeply involved in the strategic management process. At Texas Instruments, for example, the board attends a four-day strategic planning conference each year to discuss business opportunities of the next decade. Several members of the board also attend, during the following two days, management meetings attended by 500 managers from throughout the company. Kenneth Andrews, an authority on the role of the board of directors in strategic management, indicates the result:

> By the time the board comes to approve the company's plans, via ten days' annual work of the corporate objectives committee, it is presumably informed enough to play an important role in the company's planning processes.[9]

As a board becomes less involved in the affairs of the corporation, it is found further to the left on the continuum. These are passive boards that typically *never* initiate or determine strategy unless a crisis occurs. Most large, publicly owned corporations probably have boards that operate at some point between nominal and active participation. Few have catalyst boards, except for those with major problems (that is, pending bankruptcies, mergers, or acquisitions).

A recent survey of the nation's 2,235 largest commercial banks by Egon Zehnder International, a management consulting firm, supports this characterization of boards of directors.[10] The chief executive officers were asked:

"What phrase best characterizes the role of your Board of Directors in the *strategic* success of your bank?" They responded as follows:

- Critical contributor to our strategic success (catalyst)   5%
- Very active contributor (active participation)   22%
- Somewhat active contributor (nominal participation)   45%
- Passive (minimal review)   21%
- Largely ceremonial (phantom/rubber stamp)   8%

Surprisingly, only *one* CEO from the very biggest banks viewed his board as a critical contributor to his bank's strategic success.

Many CEOs and board members do not want the board to be involved in strategy matters at more than a superficial level. Andrews suggests why:

> Many chief executive officers, rejecting the practicality of conscious strategy, preside over unstated, incremental, or intuitive strategies that have never been articulated or analyzed—and therefore could not be deliberated by the board. Others do not believe their outside directors know enough or have time enough to do more than assent to strategic recommendations. Still others may keep discussions of strategy within management to prevent board transgression onto management turf and consequent reduction of executives' power to shape by themselves the future of their companies.[11]

Nevertheless, a recent survey of more than 1,000 outside directors reveals that one of the most pressing concerns of these directors is strategic management. "In the past," said one director, "strategic planning has been exclusively a management function. But now it has been intertwined with the role and functions of the board."[12] As a result, board members are now coming to think of themselves as being participants in the corporation's strategic management.[13]

Board Membership: Inside versus Outside Directors

The boards of most publicly owned corporations are comprised of both inside and outside directors. Inside directors are typically officers or executives employed by the corporation. The outside director may be an executive of another firm but is not an employee of the board's corporation. A survey sponsored by the Financial Executives Institute found that an average of 72% of the board members of nearly 800 responding *publicly* held corporations were nonmanagement (outside) directors. In comparison, only 55% of the board members of approximately 200 *privately* held corporations were outside directors.[14]

Although the 1984 Hay Survey of Directors reported outside directors to be compensated for their work at an average rate of $21,661 in industrial companies and \$17,210 in financial companies,[15] the median pay in the largest companies is probably closer to the \$20,000 to \$30,000 range.[16] Few inside directors are paid for assuming this extra duty.

The American Law Institute, an association of 1,800 leading lawyers, judges, and law professors proposes in its "Principles of Corporate Governance and Structure: Restatement and Recommendations" that all corporations be required to have outside directors form a majority of the membership of their boards of directors.[17] The Securities and Exchange Commission (SEC) now requires corporations whose stock is listed on the New York Exchange to have at least two outside directors. The ALI and the SEC apparently take the view that outside directors are less biased and more likely to evaluate objectively management's performance than are inside directors. Vance, an authority on boards of directors, contends, however, that outside directors are less effective than are insiders because of their "questionable interest, availability, or competency."[18] Recent research by Pearce found that a director's orientation toward the external environment was more associated with corporate performance than was the ratio of outsiders to insiders.[19] Nevertheless, the general trend seems to be one of an increasing percentage of outsiders on the boards of U.S. corporations.

Surveys of manufacturing companies disclose that a majority (51%) of the outside directors are presidents, managing partners, or chairmen of the boards of other corporations. Outside directors come from a variety of organizations, some even from the ministry, but a majority of them come from the manufacturing, banking, law, and investment industries. With the current concern for productivity, there appears to be a movement toward having more executives on boards with strong operating experience and away from investment bankers and attorneys. A majority (58%) of the inside directors include the president, chairman of the board, and vice-presidents; the rest are key officers or former employees. Lower-level operating employees, including managers, form only 1% of the total employee board membership of the companies surveyed.[20]

Codetermination

The dearth of nonmanagement employee directors on the boards of U.S. corporations may be changing. Codetermination, the inclusion of a corporation's workers on its board, began only recently in the United States. The addition of Douglas Fraser, President of the United Auto Workers, to the board of Chrysler Corporation in 1980 was a controversial move designed to placate the union while Chrysler was attempting to avoid bankruptcy. Critics of this plan raise the issue of conflict of interest. Can a member of the board who is privy to confidential managerial information function as a union leader whose primary duty is to fight for the best benefits for his members?

With the replacement of Douglas Fraser in 1984 by Owen Bieber, the newly elected president of the UAW, a seat for labor in the Chrysler boardroom appeared to become permanent. Eastern Airlines and Western Air Lines have also added representatives from employee associations to their boards. As in the case of Chrysler, both corporations had appointed employee directors as part of an agreement with their union to accept major pay concessions. Research in fourteen other U.S. firms with workers on the board found that "worker board representation is no guarantee that workers will have an effective role in the governance of the organization."[21] The need to work for the corporation as a whole as well as to represent the workers creates role conflict and stress among the worker directors—thus cutting into their effectiveness.

While the movement to place employees on the boards of directors of American companies is only just beginning, the European experience reveals an increasing acceptance of worker participation on corporate boards. The Federal Republic of Germany pioneered the practice with its Co-Determination Acts of 1951 and 1976 and Works Constitution Act of 1952. Worker representatives in the coal, iron, and steel industries were given equal status with management on policy-making boards. Management in other industries, however, retained, a two-thirds majority on policy-making boards.

Other countries, such as Sweden, Denmark, Norway, and Austria have passed similar codetermination legislation. Belgium, Luxembourg, France, Italy, Ireland, and the Netherlands use worker councils to work closely with management, but are seriously considering moving closer toward the German model. The British government in the 1960s established the codetermination concept in nationalized industries but found it to be a failure. It did not cause better labor–management relations.[22] Recent research on German codetermination found that legislation requiring firms to put employee representatives on their boards "lowered dividend payments, led to a more conservative investment policy, and reduced firm values."[23]

Interlocking Directorates

Boards that are primarily composed of outside directors will not necessarily be more objective than those primarily composed of insiders. CEOs may nominate for board membership chief executives from other firms for the purpose of exchanging important information and guaranteeing the stability of key marketplace relationships. One or more individuals serving on the boards of directors of two or more corporations create an *interlocking directorate*. Although the Clayton Act and the Banking Act of 1933 prohibit interlocking directorates by companies competing in the same industry,[24] interlocking continues to occur in almost all corporations, especially large ones.[25] Research has shown that the larger the firm, the greater the number of different corporations represented on its board of directors. Corporations also have members of their management teams on the boards of other corporations. General Motors, for example, has 284 connections (11 through ownership, 67 through direct interlocking, and 206 through indirect interlocking).[26] Interlocking occurs because large firms have a large impact on other corporations; and these other corporations, in turn, have some control over the firm's inputs and marketplace. Interlocking directorates are also a useful method to gain both inside information about an uncertain environment and objective expertise about a firm's strategy. As a result, capital-intensive firms tend to be involved in extensive interlocking.[27] Family-owned corporations, however, are less likely to have interlocking directorates than are corporations with highly dispersed stock ownership, probably because family-owned corporations do not like to dilute their corporate control by adding outsiders to boardroom discussions.[28]

Nomination and Election of Board Members

Traditionally, the CEO of the corporation decided whom to invite to board membership and merely asked the stockholders for approval. This practice continues to occur in approximately 40% of all corporations. The chief criteria used by most CEOs in nominating board members are that the persons be compatible with the CEO and that they bring some prestige to the board.[29]

There are some dangers, however, in allowing the CEO free reign in nominating directors. The CEO may select board members who, in the CEO's opinion, will not disturb the company's policies and functioning. More importantly, directors selected by the CEO often feel that they should go along with any proposals made by the CEO. Thus, board members find themselves accountable to the very management they are charged to oversee. Because of the likelihood of these occurrences, there is an increasing tendency for a special board committee to nominate new outside board members.

A survey by Korn and Ferry reveals that the percentage of corporations using nominating committees to select new directors rose from less than 20% in the 1970s to approximately 60% in the 1980s.[30]

Term of Office

A recent survey by The Hay Group reports that 65% of industrial corporations and 69% of banks elect all directors annually for a one-year term of office. In contrast, 60% of insurance companies elect directors for a three-year term.[31] Virtually every corporation whose directors serve terms of more than one year divide the board into classes and stagger elections so that only a portion of the board stands for election each year. Arguments in favor of this practice are that it provides continuity by reducing the chance of an abrupt turnover in its membership and that it reduces the likelihood of people unfriendly to management being elected through cumulative voting.

Among the many companies recently attempting to switch from one-year terms to longer-term staggered elections to reduce the likelihood of a take-over are Beatrice Foods, Union Oil, Sterling Drug, and Quaker Oats.

Cumulative Voting

The practice of cumulative voting allows a stockholder to concentrate his or her votes in an election of directors. Cumulative voting is required by law in 18 states and is mandatory on request or permitted as a corporate option in 32 other states or territories. Under cumulative voting, the number of votes allowed is determined from multiplying the number of voting shares held by the number of directors to be elected. Thus, a person owning 1,000 shares in an election of 12 directors would have 12,000 votes. These votes may then be distributed in any manner—for instance, divided evenly (or unevenly) between two directors or concentrated on one. This is contrasted with straight voting in which the stockholder votes simply yes or no for each director to be elected.[32]

Only a minority of companies surveyed provide for cumulative voting in their bylaws or certificate of incorporation.[33] Although few stockholders use this privilege, it is a powerful way for them to influence a board of directors. For example, a minority of stockholders could concentrate their voting power and elect one or more directors of their choice. In contrast, straight voting allows the holders of the majority of outstanding shares to prevent the election of any director not to their liking.

Those in favor of cumulative voting argue that it is the only system under which a candidate not on the management slate can hope to be elected to the board. Otherwise, under straight voting, an entrenched management could insulate itself from criticism and use the board as a rubber stamp. Critics of cumulative voting argue that it allows the board to deteriorate into interest groups more concerned with protecting their own special concerns than in working for the good of the corporation. This could become a serious problem if the corporation is in danger of being bought or controlled by another firm. For instance, by purchasing some shares, another firm (such as a potential acquirer) could, through cumulative voting, elect enough board members to directly influence or even incapacitate the board. Nevertheless, the practice of cumulative voting has been recommended as a way to achieve minority representation on the boards of directors of major corporations.

Organization of the Board

The size of the board is determined by the corporation's charter and its bylaws in compliance with state laws. Although some states require a minimum number of board members, most corporations have quite a bit of discretion in determining board size. Surveys of U.S. business corporations reveal that the average *privately* held company has eight board members who meet four times a year as compared to the average *publicly* held corporation with thirteen directors who meet seven times a year. In addition, there appears to be a direct relationship between company size as measured by sales volume and the number of people on the board.[34]

A fairly common practice in U.S. corporations is to have the chairman of the board also serve as the chief executive officer. The CEO concentrates on strategy, planning, external relations, and responsibility to the board. The chairman's responsibility is to ensure that the board and its committees perform their functions as stated in their charter. Further, the chairman schedules board meetings and presides over the annual stockholders' meeting. In over 75% of the Fortune 500 corporations, the CEO also serves as chairman of the board.[35]

Chairman

The most effective boards of large corporations accomplish much of their work through committees.[36] Although the committees do not have legal duties, unless detailed in the bylaws, most committees are granted full power to act with the authority of the board between board meetings. Typical standing committees are the executive committee, audit committee, compensation committee, finance committee, and nominating committee. The executive committee is formed from local directors who can meet between board meetings to attend to matters that must be settled quickly. This committee acts as an extension of the board and, consequently, may have almost unrestricted authority in certain areas. A recent survey reports that in 68% of industrial and 72% of financial corporations, the executive committee includes at least a majority of outside directors.[37] Other less common committees are the strategy, corporate responsibility, investments (pension funds), and conflict-of-interest committees.[38]

Committees

A study by Northwestern University and McKinsey & Company, Inc. sees several following trends for future responsibilities and organizations of boards.[39] Although the study concludes that it is not likely there will be significant changes in the typical board structure, it does predict a reduction in board size and a greater use of committees. The board of the future will tend to direct its own affairs with less reliance on the CEO. It will have fewer inside members and will be under less CEO influence in the selection of its members. There will be greater emphasis on systematically monitoring and appraising top management's performance, with more involvement by the board in the management succession process. Boards will also have more influence in determining executive compensation, and there will probably be more open communication between the board and management as the boards become more active. Boards will most likely form audit committees for the purpose of ensuring a formalized evaluation of overall corporate per-

Trends for the Future

formance. Their membership will become more representative of minorities and women. In addition, there will be a continuing pressure on board members in terms of their liabilities, plus greater expectations by the public for higher standards of public responsibility.

3.2 TOP MANAGEMENT

The top management function is usually conducted by the CEO of the corporation in coordination with the COO or president, executive vice-president, and vice-presidents of divisions and functional areas. As we mentioned earlier in this chapter, some corporations combine the office of CEO with that of chairman of the board of directors. Although this plan has the advantage of freeing the president or COO of the firm from many strategic responsibilities so that he or she may focus primarily on operational matters, it has been criticized because it gives the combined CEO/chairman too much power and serves to undercut the independence of the board.[40]

Responsibilities of Top Management

Top management, and especially the CEO, is responsible to the board of directors for the overall management of the corporation. It is tasked with getting things accomplished through and with others in order to meet corporate objectives. Top management's job is thus multidimensional and oriented toward the welfare of the total organization. Specific top management tasks vary from firm to firm and are developed from an analysis of the mission, objectives, strategies, and key activities of the corporation. But all top managers are people who see the business as a whole, who can balance the present needs of the business against the needs of the future, and who can make final and effective decisions.[41] The chief executive officer, in particular, must successfully handle three responsibilities crucial to the effective strategic management of the corporation: (1) fulfill key roles; (2) provide corporate leadership; and (3) manage the strategic planning process.

Fulfill Key Roles

From five weeks of in-depth observation of five chief executives, Henry Mintzberg concluded that the job of a top manager contains ten interrelated *roles*. The importance of each role and the amount of time demanded by each probably varies from one job to another. These roles are as follows:

Figurehead	Acts as legal and symbolic head; performs obligatory social, ceremonial, or legal duties (hosts retirement dinners, luncheons for employees, and plant dedications; attends civic affairs; signs contracts on behalf of firm).
Leader	Motivates, develops, and guides subordinates; oversees staffing, training, and associated activities (intro-

duces Management By Objectives [MBO], develops a challenging work climate, provides a sense of direction, acts as a role model).

Liaison

Maintains a network of contacts and information sources outside top management in order to obtain information and assistance (meets with key people from the task environment, meets formally and informally with corporate division managers and with CEOs of other firms).

Monitor

Seeks and obtains information in order to understand the corporation and its environments; acts as nerve center for the corporation (reviews status reports from vice-presidents, reviews key indicators of corporate performance, scans *Wall Street Journal* and key trade journals, joins select clubs and societies).

Disseminator

Transmits information to the rest of the top management team and other key people in the corporation (chairs staff meetings, transmits policy letters, communicates five-year plans).

Spokesman

Transmits information to key groups and people in the task environment (prepares annual report to stockholders, talks to the Chamber of Commerce, states corporate policy to the media, participates in advertising campaigns, speaks before congressional committees).

Entrepreneur

Searches the corporation and its environment for projects to improve products, processes, procedures, and structures; then supervises the design and implementation of these projects (introduces cost reduction programs, makes plant trips to divisions, changes forecasting system, brings in subcontract work to level the work load, reorganizes the corporation).

Disturbance Handler

Takes corrective action in times of disturbance or crisis (personally talks with key creditors, interest groups, congressional committees, union leaders; establishes investigative committees; revises objectives, strategies, and policies).

Resource Allocator

Allocates corporate resources by making and/or approving decisions (reviews budgets, revises program scheduling, initiates strategic planning, plans personnel load, sets objectives).

Negotiator   Represents the corporation in negotiating important agreements; may speak directly with key representatives of groups in the task environment or work through a negotiator; negotiates disagreements within the corporation by working with conflicting division heads (works with labor negotiator; resolves jurisdictional disputes between divisions; negotiates with key creditors, suppliers, and customers).[42]

Provide Corporate Leadership

People who work in corporations look to top management for leadership. Their doing so, says Drucker, reflects a need for standard setting and example setting.[43] According to Mintzberg, this is a key role of any manager.

Corporate leadership is important because it sets the tone for the entire corporation. Since most middle managers look to their boss for guidance and direction, they will tend to emulate the characteristics and style of successful top managers. People in an organization want to have a vision of what they are working toward—a sense of mission. Only top management is in the position to specify and communicate this sense of mission to the general work force. Top management's enthusiasm (or lack of it) about the corporation tends to be contagious.

For instance, a positive attitude characterizing many well-known industrial leaders—such as Alfred Sloan at General Motors, Ed Watson at IBM, Robert Wood at Sears, Ray Kroc at McDonald's, and Lee Iacocca at Chrysler—have energized their respective corporations. In their book *In Search of Excellence,* Peters and Waterman report that "associated with almost every excellent company was a strong leader (or two) who seemed to have a lot to do with making his company excellent in the first place."[44] A two-year study by McKinsey & Co. found the CEOs of midsized high-growth companies to be "almost inevitably consummate salesmen who radiate enormous contagious self-confidence" . . . and "take pains to communicate their strong sense of mission to all who come in contact with them."[45]

Chief executive officers with a clear sense of mission are often perceived as dynamic and charismatic leaders. They are able to command respect and to influence strategy formulation and implementation because they tend to have three key characteristics.

1. The CEO *presents a role* for others to identify with and to follow. The leader sets an example in terms of behavior and dress. The CEO's attitudes and values concerning the corporation's purpose and activities are clear-cut and constantly communicated in words and deeds.

2. The CEO *articulates a transcendent goal* for the corporation. The CEO's vision of the corporation goes beyond the petty complaints and grievances of the average work day. This vision puts activities and conflicts in a new perspective, giving renewed meaning to everyone's work activities and enabling them to see beyond the details of their own jobs to the functioning of the total corporation.

3. The CEO *communicates high performance standards* but also *shows confidence* in the followers' abilities to meet these standards. No leader ever improved performance by setting easily attainable goals that provide no challenge. The CEO must be willing to follow through by coaching people.[46]

Top management must initiate and manage the strategic planning process. It must take a very long-range view in order to specify the corporate mission, delineate corporate objectives, and formulate appropriate strategies and policies. As depicted in Fig. 3.2, the ideal time horizon varies according to one's level in the corporate hierarchy. The president of a corporation, for example, should allocate the largest proportion of planning time to looking two to

Manage Strategic Planning

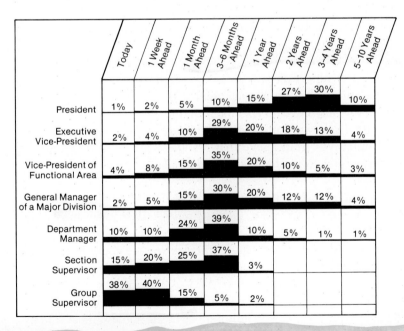

	Today	1 Week Ahead	1 Month Ahead	3–6 Months Ahead	1 Year Ahead	2 Years Ahead	3–4 Years Ahead	5–10 Years Ahead
President	1%	2%	5%	10%	15%	27%	30%	10%
Executive Vice-President	2%	4%	10%	29%	20%	18%	13%	4%
Vice-President of Functional Area	4%	8%	15%	35%	20%	10%	5%	3%
General Manager of a Major Division	2%	5%	15%	30%	20%	12%	12%	4%
Department Manager	10%	10%	24%	39%	10%	5%	1%	1%
Section Supervisor	15%	20%	25%	37%	3%			
Group Supervisor	38%	40%	15%	5%	2%			

Figure 3.2 **"Ideal" allocations of time for planning in the "average" company.**
SOURCE: Reprinted with permission of The Free Press, a division of Macmillan, Inc. from *Top Management Planning* by G. A. Steiner. Copyright © 1969 by the Trustees of Columbia University in the City of New York.

four *years* ahead. A department manager, however, should put the heaviest proportion of planning time on looking only three to six *months* ahead.

To accomplish its tasks, top management must use information provided by three key corporate groups: a long-range planning staff, division or SBU managers, and managers of functional departments.

A *long-range planning staff* typically consists of six people, headed by a senior vice-president or director of corporate planning.[47] It continuously monitors both internal and external environments in order to generate data for strategic decisions by top management. It also suggests to top management possible changes in the corporate mission, objectives, strategies, and policies. Although only one in five companies with sales under $100 million have a separate, formal planning department, nearly all corporations with sales of at least $2 billion have such departments.[48]

Divisional or SBU managers, with the assistance of the long-range planning staff and with input from their product managers, perform the strategic planning function for each division. These SBU managers typically initiate proposals for top management's consideration and/or respond to requests for such proposals by corporate headquarters. They may also be tasked to carry out strategies and policies decided upon at the corporate level for organization-wide implementation. These division managers typically work with the heads of various functional units within the division to develop the appropriate functional strategies to implement planned business-level strategies.

Managers of functional departments (marketing, engineering, R&D managers, etc.) report directly either to divisional managers in a multidivision corporation or to top management if the corporation has no divisions. Although they may develop specific functional strategies, they generally do so within the framework of divisional or corporate strategies. They also respond to initiatives from above that ask them for input or require them to develop strategies to implement divisional plans.

Characteristics of Top Management Tasks

Top management tasks have two characteristics that differentiate them from other managerial tasks.[49] First, *very few of them are continuous*. Rarely does a manager work on these tasks all day. The responsibilities, however, are always present, even though the tasks themselves are sporadic. And when the tasks do arise, they are of crucial significance, such as the selection of a person to head a new division.

Mintzberg reports that the activities of most executives are characterized by brevity, variety, and fragmentation: "Half of the observed activities were completed in less than nine minutes and only one-tenth took more than an hour. In effect, the managers were seldom able or willing to spend much time on any one issue in any one session."[50]

It is likely that serious objective-setting and strategy formulation will not occur in corporations if most top managers are as activity-oriented as those in the Mintzberg study. John De Lorean suggests as much in his comments about "The Fourteenth Floor" (the executive offices) of General Motors.

> I was trying to bring a set of new eyes to the job of group executive, as one only can do in the first few months in a new position. But I had no time to perform the real function of my position. Instead, I was being tied down and totally consumed by this constant parade of paperwork and meetings.[51]

The second characteristic of top management tasks is that *they require a wide range of capabilities and temperaments.* Some tasks require the capacity to analyze and carefully weigh alternative courses of action. Some require an awareness of and an interest in people; whereas others call for the ability to pursue abstract ideas, concepts, and calculations.

One result of these two task characteristics is that top managers are often drawn back into the functional work of the corporation. Since the activities of top management are not continuous, people in top management often have unplanned free time. They tend therefore to get caught up in the day-to-day work in manufacturing, marketing, accounting, engineering, or in other operations of the corporation. They may find themselves constantly solving crises that could probably have been better handled by lower-level managers. These managers are also usually fond of protesting, "How can I be expected to drain the swamp when I'm up to my eyeballs in alligators!?"

A second result of the task characteristics is that top managers tend to perceive only those aspects and responsibilities of the top management function that are compatible with their abilities, experience, and temperaments. And, if the board of directors fails to state explicitly what it considers to be the key responsibilities and activities of top management, the top managers are free to define the job themselves. As a result, important tasks may be overlooked until a crisis occurs.

Top Management Team

Many executives believe that top management work is a job for a team rather than for one person. The large amount and variety of the work may be too great for one person to handle capably. Furthermore, when one person is in charge, he or she becomes extremely involved in the organization and tends to take personally any criticism of corporate activities. Consequently, that person is less willing to change personal management practices as situations change. According to Drucker, ". . . one-man top management is a major reason why businesses fail to grow."[52]

Analysts argue, therefore, that a large complex corporation needs a clearly structured top management team. This team may be organized as an office of the president in which a number of people serve as equals, each with an assigned area of primary responsibility. Corporations such as DuPont, Standard Oil of New Jersey, Royal Dutch Shell, and Unilever have taken this approach.[53] Or the team may include one person who carries the title of CEO and several colleagues, each of whom has clearly assigned authority and responsibility for a segment of the top management task. Another common structure is a three- or four-person team, each person having clearly assigned top management responsibilities even though one person is officially in charge. General Motors and Xerox Corporation use this structure. GM's team includes a chairman, a vice-chairman, a chairman of the executive committee, and a president. General Electric has taken a similar approach, although it refers to its four-man top management group as the Corporate Executive Office.

The use of top management teams has increased dramatically from only 37 in 1970 to 113 in 1980.[54] An advantage of the team approach to top management is the sharing of roles, responsibilities, and tasks, a sharing that depends on the strengths and weaknesses of the people involved. It makes more sense for large corporations to put together a top management team to achieve synergy, rather than try to find the perfect person to be CEO. Certainly succession problems are minimized by the team approach; decisions can be made even though the CEO has resigned, is incapacitated or otherwise absent.

3.3 STRATEGIC MANAGEMENT STYLES

Just as boards of directors vary widely on a continuum of involvement in the strategic management process, so do top management teams. For example, a top management team with low involvement in strategic management will tend to be functionally oriented and will focus its energies on day-to-day operational problems; this type of team is likely either to be disorganized or to have a dominant CEO who continues to identify with his or her old division. In contrast, a top management team with high involvement will be active in long-range planning. It will try to get division managers involved in planning so that it will have more time to scan the environment for challenges and opportunities.

Both the board of directors and top management can be placed on a matrix to reflect four basic styles of corporate strategic management. These styles are depicted in Fig. 3.3.

Chaos Management

When both the board of directors and top management have little involvement in the strategic management process, their style is referred to as chaos management. The board waits for top management to bring it proposals. Top management is operationally oriented and continues to carry out strate-

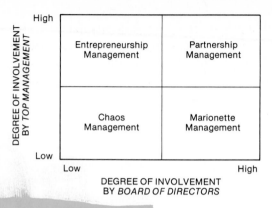

Figure 3.3   Strategic management styles.

gies, policies, and programs specified by the founding entrepreneur who died years ago. The basic strategic philosophy seems to be, "If it was good enough for old J. B., it's good enough for us." There is no strategic management being done here.

A corporation with an uninvolved board of directors but with a highly involved top management has entrepreneurship management. The board is willing to be used as a rubber stamp for top management. The CEO, operating alone or with a team, dominates the corporation and its strategic decisions. An example is the Calhoun First National Bank of Calhoun, Georgia, whose CEO is Bert Lance. Returning to the bank after serving in the cabinet of President Jimmy Carter, Lance tried to regain control of the corporation as its president. He wanted, among other things, the bank to initiate new loan policies and to hire his 26-year-old son as an officer. After the board turned him down, Lance began a proxy fight for control of the bank. The resulting new board not only approved all the changes desired by Lance, it fired both the previous chairman of the board and the president without severance pay. Lance, of course, returned to his job as president of the bank and gained total control of all strategic management.[55]

Entrepreneurship Management

Probably the rarest form of strategic management styles, marionette management occurs when the board of directors is deeply involved in strategic decision making, whereas top management is primarily concerned with operations. Such a style evolves when a board is composed of key stockholders who refuse to delegate strategic decision making to the president. The president is forced into a COO role and can do only what the board allows him to do. This style also occurs when a board fires a CEO but is slow to find a replacement. The COO or executive vice-president stays on as "acting" presi-

Marionette Management

dent or CEO until the selection process is complete. In the meantime, strategic management is firmly in the hands of the board of directors. In one specific bank (which will remain unnamed), the board of directors is so involved in managing that it requires the president to ask its permission before offices are painted. The board actually votes on the color!

Partnership Management

Probably the most effective style of strategic management, partnership management is epitomized by a highly involved board and top management. The board and the top management team work closely to establish mission, objectives, strategies, and policies. Board members are active in committee work and utilize strategic audits to provide feedback to top management on its actions in implementing agreed-upon strategies and policies. This appears to be the style emerging in a number of successful corporations such as Texas Instruments, Dayton Hudson Corporation, and General Electric Company.[56]

3.4 SUMMARY AND CONCLUSION

The strategy makers of a modern corporation are the board of directors and top management. Both must be actively involved in the strategic management process if the corporation is to have long-term success in accomplishing its mission.

An effective board is the keystone of the modern corporation. Without it, management would tend to focus on short-run problems and solutions or go off on tangents at odds with the basic mission. The personal needs and goals of executives would tend to overrule the interests of the corporation. Even the strongest critics of boards of directors are more interested in improving and upgrading boards than in eliminating them.[57] An active board is critical in determining an organization's mission, objectives, strategy, and policies.

Top management, in contrast, is responsible for the overall functioning of the corporation. People in top management must view the corporation as a whole rather than as a series of functional departments or decentralized divisions. They must constantly visualize and plan for the future, setting objectives, strategies, and policies that will allow the corporation to successfully meet that future. They must set standards and provide a vision not only of what the corporation is but also of what it is trying to become. They must develop working relationships with the board of directors, key staff personnel, and managers from divisions and functional areas.

The interaction between the board of directors and the top management of a corporation usually results in an overall strategic management style. The long-run success of a corporation is best ensured through a partnership style in which both the board and top management are genuinely involved in strategic issues.

1. Does a corporation really need a board of directors? Why or why not?

2. What aspects of a corporation's environment should be represented on a board of directors?

3. Should cumulative voting for the election of board members be *required* by law in all political jurisdictions?

4. Do you agree that a chief executive officer (CEO) should fulfill Mintzberg's ten roles in order to be effective?

5. Is partnership management always the best style of strategic management?

DISCUSSION QUESTIONS

1. W. L. Shanklin and J. K. Ryans, Jr., "Should the Board Consider This Agenda Item?" *MSU Business Topics* (Winter 1981), p. 35.

2. W. R. Boulton, "The Evolving Board: A Look at the Board's Changing Roles and Information Needs," *Academy of Management Review* (October 1978), p. 828.

3. L. Iacocca, *Iacocca: An Autobiography* (Toronto: Bantam Books, 1984), p. 104.

4. J. Bacon and J. K. Brown, *Corporate Directorship Practices: Role, Selection and Legal Status of the Board* (New York: The Conference Board, Report no. 646, 1975), p. 7.

5. Bacon and Brown, p. 75.

6. G. Smith, "Who Was Watching the Store?" *Forbes* (July 30, 1984), pp. 37–38.
"Rolling Heads," *Time* (December 17, 1984), p. 69.

7. L. B. Korn and R. M. Ferry, *Board of Directors Ninth Annual Study* (New York: Korn/Ferry International, February 1982), p. 8.

8. Bacon and Brown, p. 15.

9. K. R. Andrews, "Corporate Strategy as a Vital Function of the Board," *Harvard Business Review* (November–December 1981), p. 175.

10. *Third Annual Banking Survey of Chief Executive Officers* (Atlanta, Chicago, New York: Egon Zehnder International, Inc., 1984), p. 9.

11. K. R. Andrews, "Directors' Responsibility for Corporate Strategy," *Harvard Business Review* (November–December 1980), p. 30.

12. T. R. Horton, "The Case for Planning Committees," *Directors & Boards* (Summer 1984), p. 26.

13. A. Tashakori and W. Boulton, "A Look to the Board's Role in Planning," *Journal of Business Strategy* (Winter 1983), pp. 64–70.

14. E. Mruk and J. Giardina, *Organization and Compensation of Boards of Directors* (New York: Financial Executives Institute, Arthur Young & Co., 1981), pp. 11 and 39.

NOTES

15. L. Barker, "Director Compensation 1984," *Directors & Boards* (Spring 1984), p. 35.

16. S. C. Vance, *Corporate Leadership: Boards, Directors, and Strategy* (New York: McGraw-Hill Book Company, 1983), p. 64.

17. K. R. Andrews, "The American Law Institute's Proposals for Regulating Corporate Governance," *Harvard Business Review* (November–December 1982), p. 34.

18. S. C. Vance, p. 274.

19. J. A. Pearce, "The Relationship of Internal versus External Orientations to Financial Measures of Strategic Performance," *Strategic Management Journal* (December 1983), pp. 297–306.

20. E. S. Buffa, "Making American Manufacturing Competitive," *California Management Review* (Spring 1984), p. 39.
J. Bacon, *Corporate Directorship Practices: Membership and Committees of the Board* (New York: The Conference Board, Report no. 588, 1973), pp. 28–29.

21. T. H. Hammer and R. N. Stern, "Worker Representation on Company Boards of Directors," *Proceedings, Academy of Management,* 1983, p. 368.

22. R. J. Kuhne, *Co-Determination in Business* (New York: Praeger Publishers, 1980), pp. 41–71.

23. L. H. Clark, Jr., "What Economists Say about Business—and Baboons," *Wall Street Journal* (June 7, 1983), p. 33. Article summarizes a research paper by G. Benelli, C. Loderer, and T. Lys presented to the Interlaken Seminar on Analysis and Ideology, Interlaken, Switzerland, 1983.

24. E. F. Donaldson and J. K. Pfahl, *Corporate Finance,* 3rd ed. (New York: Ronald Press, 1969), p. 742.
F. D. Schoorman, M. H. Bazerman, and R. S. Atkin, "Interlocking Directorates: A Strategy for Reducing Environmental Uncertainty," *Academy of Management Review* (April 1981), p. 244.

25. M. H. Bazerman and F. D. Schoorman, "A Limited Rationality Model of Interlocking Directorates," *Academy of Management Review* (April 1983), pp. 206–217.
M. Ornstein, "Interlocking Directorates in Canada: Intercorporate or Class Alliance?" *Administrative Science Quarterly* (June 1984), pp. 210–231.

26. R. S. Burt, "Cooptive Corporate Actor Networks: A Reconsideration of Interlocking Directorates Involving American Manufacturing," *Administrative Science Quarterly* (December 1980), p. 566.

27. Burt, p. 559.

28. For a more in-depth discussion of this topic, refer to J. M. Pennings, *Interlocking Directorates* (San Francisco: Jossey-Bass, 1980), and M. S. Mizruchi, *The American Corporate Network 1904–1974* (Beverly Hills, Calif.: Sage Publications, 1982).

29. R. F. Lewis, "Choosing and Using Outside Directors," *Harvard Business Review* (July–August 1974), p. 71.

30. Korn and Ferry, p. 5.

31. Barker, p. 40.

32. Bacon, pp. 7–8.

33. Bacon, p. 6.

34. Korn and Ferry, p. 3; and Mruk and Giardina, p. 39.

35. H. S. Geneen, "Why Directors Can't Protect the Stockholders," *Fortune* (September 17, 1984), p. 29.

36. W. Wommack, "The Board's Most Important Function," *Harvard Business Review* (September–October 1979), p. 48.

37. Barker, p. 39.

38. For further information on board committees, refer to Bacon and Brown, pp. 99–140. For detailed information on the audit committee, see L. Braiotta, *The Audit Director's Guide* (New York: John Wiley & Sons, 1981).

39. R. P. Neuschel, Conference Summary (p. 60), "The Changing Role of the Corporate Board," proceedings of a conference held in Chicago on April 13, 1977, and sponsored jointly by Northwestern University's Graduate School of Management and McKinsey & Company, Inc. Privately published by the sponsors.

40. Bacon and Brown, p. 25.
    Andrews, 1980, p. 36.
    W. R. Boulton, "Effective Board Development: Five Areas of Concern," *Journal of Business Strategy* (Spring 1983), pp. 94–100.
    H. S. Geneen, "Why Directors Can't Protect the Stockholders," *Fortune* (September 17, 1984), p. 29.

41. P. F. Drucker, *Management: Tasks, Responsibilities, Practices* (New York: Harper & Row, 1974), p. 613.

42. Adapted from H. Mintzberg, *The Nature of Managerial Work* (New York: Harper & Row, 1973), pp. 54–94.

43. Drucker, pp. 611–612.

44. T. J. Peters and R. H. Waterman, *In Search of Excellence* (New York: Harper & Row, 1982), p. 26.

45. A. Levitt, Jr., and J. Albertine, "The Successful Entrepreneur: A Personality Profile," *Wall Street Journal* (August 29, 1983), p. 12.

46. Adapted from R. J. House, "A 1976 Theory of Charismatic Leadership," *Leadership: The Cutting Edge,* eds. J. G. Hunt and L. L. Larson (Carbondale, Ill.: SIU Press, 1977), pp. 189–207. Bernard M. Bass refers to this model as *transformational leadership* in his article "Leadership: Good, Better, Best" in *Organizational Dynamics* (Winter 1985), pp. 26–40.

47. S. Matlins and G. Knisely, "Update: Profile of the Corporate Planners," *Journal of Business Strategy* (Spring 1981), pp. 75 and 77.

48. C. D. Burnett, D. P. Yeskey, and D. Richardson, "New Roles for Corporate

Planners in the 1980's," *Journal of Business Strategy* (Spring 1984), p. 67.

49. Drucker, pp. 615–617.

50. Mintzberg, p. 33.

51. J. P. Wright, *On a Clear Day You Can See General Motors* (Grosse Pointe, Mich.: Wright Enterprises, 1979), p. 28.

52. Drucker, p. 618.

53. Drucker, p. 619.

54. S. C. Vance, p. 203.

55. D. Russakoff, "Bert Lance on the Rebound," *Washington Post* (May 17, 1981), pp. A6–A7.

56. K. Andrews, "Corporate Strategy as a Vital Function of the Board," *Harvard Business Review* (November–December 1981), p. 175.
    K. N. Dayton, "Corporate Governance: The Other Side of the Coin," *Harvard Business Review* (January–February 1984), p. 35.

57. R. P. Neuschel, Introductory Remarks (p. 11), "The Changing Role of the Corporate Board," proceedings of a conference held in Chicago on April 13, 1977 and sponsored jointly by Northwestern University's Graduate School of Management and McKinsey & Company, Inc. Privately published by the sponsors.

Chapter 4

THE EXTERNAL ENVIRONMENT

STRATEGIC MANAGEMENT MODEL

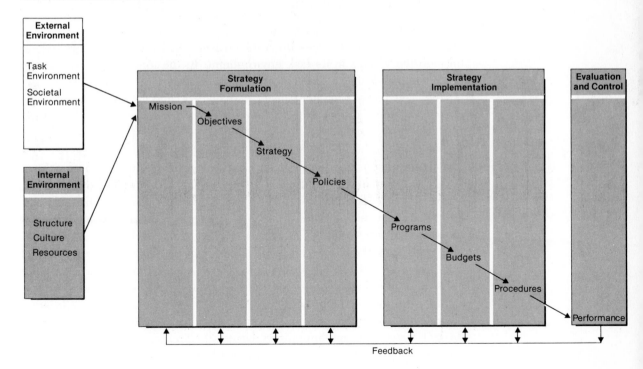

Business corporations do not exist in a vacuum. They arise out of society's need for a particular product or service and can continue to exist in freedom only so long as they acknowledge their role in the larger society. As a result, corporations must constantly be aware of the key variables in their environment. These variables may be within a firm's task environment or in its larger societal environment (see Fig. 4.1). The *task environment* includes those elements or groups that directly affect the corporation and, in turn, are affected by it. These are governments, local communities, suppliers, competitors, customers, creditors, employees/labor unions, special interest groups, and trade associations. The *societal environment* includes the more general forces that do not directly touch on the short-run activities of the organization but that can, and often do, influence its long-run decisions. These, also shown in Fig. 4.1, are as follows:

- *Economic forces* that regulate exchange of materials, money, energy, and information.

- *Sociocultural forces* that regulate values, mores, and customs.

- *Technological forces* that generate problem solving inventions.

- *Political-legal forces* that allocate power and provide constraining and protecting laws and regulations.

All of these variables and forces constantly interact with each other. In the short run, societal forces affect the decisions and actions of a corporation through the groups in its task environment. In the long run, however, the corporation also affects these groups through its activities. For example, the possible collapse of Chrysler Corporation in 1980 had wide-ranging and serious effects upon almost every group and force in its task and societal environment.

4.1 BUSINESS AND SOCIETY: A DELICATE RELATIONSHIP

For centuries, business corporations have lived in an uneasy truce with society. Exchange and commercial activities, along with laws governing them, are as old as recorded history. The Code of Hammurabi, established about 2000 B.C., provided guidelines for merchants and peddlers.[1] The Old Testament is filled with examples of commercial activity and the laws and regulations governing them. Greek philosophers, in general, regarded commercial activities as necessary but distasteful. The Romans, like the Greeks, were necessarily tolerant of commercial activity, but gave those so engaged a low status.[2] During the early years of the Middle Ages, the Roman Christian Church held business and commercial activity in disdain and governed it through strict rules and limitations. Usury, the lending of money at interest, for instance, was decreed a mortal sin for Christians, who were forbidden the

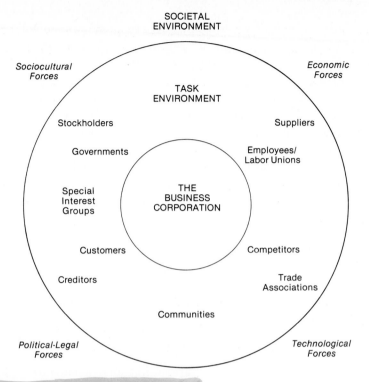

Figure 4.1 Key environmental variables.

practice, although Jews were permitted to engage in it. Trade itself was of dubious purity, and the gathering of wealth was considered an action directly opposed to the charitable teachings of Jesus Christ. This view of trade and commerce and the associated accumulation of capital as necessary evils was commonly accepted in the Western world until the Protestant Reformation. The Eastern world, in contrast, was much more tolerant and accepting of business activities.

With the end of the Middle Ages, values began to change in the West, and business activities were viewed more positively. Max Weber, noted economist and sociologist, postulated that changes in the religious ethic resulting from the Reformation and the Protestant movement provided an economic climate highly favorable for the development of capitalism.[3] A new spirit of individualism developed out of the Renaissance and was encouraged by humanism and Protestantism. Society placed a high value on frugality, thrift, and hard work—key elements of what is commonly referred to as the *Protestant ethic.*

Development of the Capitalistic Ethic

Free trade was not, however, commonly accepted until much later. After the Reformation, kings and queens replaced the Church as earthly rulers. They established their right to regulate business activity through the concept of *mercantilism*. According to this concept, the individual was subordinate to the state, and all economic and business activity was dedicated to support the power of the state. Under mercantilism, Europeans set up organizations, such as the East India Company, to trade with the natives of distant lands and to return with goods valuable to crown and country.

In 1776, however, economist Adam Smith advanced a theory justifying and underlying capitalism in his book *An Inquiry into the Nature and Causes of the Wealth of Nations*. Smith argued that economic freedom would enable individuals through self-interest to fulfill themselves and thereby benefit the total society. He used the term *laissez-faire* to suggest that government should leave business alone. The "invisible hand" of the marketplace would, through pure competition, ensure maximum benefit to society.

The doctrine of *laissez-faire*, as postulated by Smith and refined by others, called for society to give business corporations increasing autonomy so that they could accomplish their work—the production and sale of goods and services. In the rapidly changing world of the eighteenth and nineteenth centuries such work was considered worthwhile and valuable to society. For example, James Watt's development of a usable steam engine permitted muscle power to be replaced by an external power source and resulted in enormous increases in the production and distribution of scarce goods. Because of these benefits, governments relaxed many of their restrictions on commerce and trade, and allowed capital to accumulate and business to flourish.

Society Supports Free Enterprise

With changes in sociocultural values fed by the benefits of new technology and *laissez-faire* economics, governments in the West began to support independent businesses. During much of the early part of the nineteenth century in the United States, government favored the development of commerce and industry. The Supreme Court, for example, ruled that the private corporation was a legal entity, and Congress passed tariff laws protecting business interests. In addition, the government provided vast sums of money and land for the rapidly expanding railroads.[4] As pointed out by McGuire,

> . . . the Federal government attempted to encourage business activities with a minimum of regulation and intervention. . . . Government's task in these years, it was thought by many politicians and businessmen, was to aid business enterprise in accord with the best principles of mercantilism and still leave business free to grow and develop without restraint, as set

forth in the doctrine of *laissez-faire*. The tradition thus grew that businessmen in the United States could do what so few people were able to do—have their cake and eat it too.[5]

Beginnings of Regulation

In the late 1800s and early 1900s, the public began to find some business practices antisocial. This dissatisfaction was expressed increasingly. Karl Marx, who wrote *The Communist Manifesto* with Friedrich Engels in 1848 and *Das Kapital* in 1867, put into words much of this dissatisfaction. He, as well as many others, rejected the capitalistic ethic because of its many unsavory side-effects, such as child labor, unsafe working conditions, and subsistence wages. The development of monopolistic corporations and cartels caused various groups within the United States to demand some form of regulation. Although most U.S. citizens rejected the Marxist view, they challenged the *laissez-faire* concept by suggesting that Adam Smith's economic system was based on a pure, competitive model that was ineffective in a system of entrenched monopolies and oligopolies. As a result, the federal government reclaimed some of the freedom and autonomy it had granted business by enacting such legislation as the Interstate Commerce Act (1887), the Sherman Antitrust Act (1890), the Pure Food and Drug Act (1906), the Clayton Act (1914), and the Federal Trade Commission Act (1914). More restrictive laws were to follow.

A Question of Autonomy

The Great Depression of the 1930s, Keynesian economics, and the increasing popularity of socialism as a political force resulted in business losing even more of its autonomy to government. Governments all over the world assumed responsibility for their economies. In 1946, the U.S. Congress passed the Fair Employment Act, which states that the federal government has prime responsibility for the maintenance of full employment and full utilization of economic resources.[6] Through the decades of the 50s, 60s, and 70s, *laissez-faire*, if not dead, was certainly forgotten as people put their faith in a democratically elected central government rather than the self-interest of capitalists.

Consecutive years of profits earned by American big business during these prosperous decades suggested to a number of people that business was not truly paying its way in society. Increasingly, problems with product safety and environmental pollution were seen as the negative consequences of a selfish concern only with profits by business people. Some of these feelings were expressed in 1962 by President Kennedy after the U.S. steel industry ignored his request to refrain from raising prices during a time of inflation.

Some time ago I asked each American to consider what he would do for his country, and I asked steel companies. In the last 24 hours we had their answer. . . . My father always told me that all businessmen were sons of bitches, but I never believed it until now.[7]

Business people were increasingly constrained in their decision making by laws regarding air and water pollution, product safety, and employment practices, among others. In the United States, the number of federal agencies involved in regulating business activity increased from 49 in 1960 to 83 in 1970. Firms in the steel industry alone faced 5,600 regulations from 27 federal agencies.[8] All around the world businesses were threatened by governments with more regulation or even outright nationalization. Business autonomy was seriously threatened.

National Policy—Modern Mercantilism?

With the coming of the 1980s, the relationship between business and government changed. The labor productivity growth rate which had steadily increased in the United States for nearly two hundred years slowed and became negative during the period from 1978 to 1980.[9] Focusing upon high-volume standardized production, major Western firms found to their chagrin that companies in the developing nations had copied their technology. With lower production costs due to lower wages, among other factors, these companies in the third world were able to seriously erode the market share and profits of the business corporations in the industrialized countries of the West. Faced with serious problems of unemployment and balance of trade problems, governments of the United States, Great Britain, and other Western nations acted to reduce some of the constraints they had previously placed on business activity.

A number of people argued that not only should business be given more autonomy, but also that the national government in the United States be an active supporter of business development. Stating that other nations with supportive industrial policies—such as Japan, Korea, and Singapore—had more competitive business corporations than did many Western nations, proposals for a sort of modern mercantilism were developed. Reich, in his influential book *The Next American Frontier*, contended that the federal government should develop a better system to help move U.S. industry more quickly out of high-volume standardized production into more flexible, quality-oriented systems of production using skilled labor.[10] National governments throughout the world were coming to think of business activity as the key to economic well-being. Questions of social responsibility were temporarily forgotten as people worried more about unemployment than pollution. Nevertheless, by the mid-1980s, problems of toxic waste, hazardous chemical plants, and unsafe products again became important topics for discussion as people once more became concerned about the distasteful side-effects of economic activity.

The concept that business must be socially responsible sounds appealing until one asks, "Responsible to whom?" As was shown in Fig. 4.1, the task environment includes a large number of groups with interest in a corporation's activities. These groups are referred to as *stakeholders* because they affect or are affected by the achievement of the firm's objectives.[11] Should a corporation be responsible only to some of these groups, or does business have a responsibility to society at large?

The corporation must pay close attention to its task environment because its stakeholders are very responsive to the general trends in the societal environment and will typically translate these trends into direct pressure to affect corporate activities. Even if top management assumes the traditional *laissez-faire* stance that the major concern of its corporation is to make profits, it will find (often to its chagrin) that it must also be concerned with the effect of its profit making on stakeholders within its task environment. Each stakeholder uses its own criteria to determine how well a corporation is performing, and each is constantly judging top management's actions by their effect on itself. Therefore top management must be aware not only of the key stakeholders in the corporation's task environment but also of the criteria each group uses to judge the corporation's performance. The following is a list of some of these stakeholders and their probable criteria.

Stakeholders	Criteria
Stockholders	Price appreciation of securities. Dividends (How much and how often?).
Unions	Comparable wages. Stability of employment. Opportunity for advancement.
Governments	Support of government programs. Adherence to laws and regulations.
Suppliers	Rapidity of payment. Consistency of purchases.
Creditors	Adherence to contract terms. Dependability.
Customers/Distributors	Value given for the price paid. Availability of product or service.
Trade associations	Participation in association programs (*time*). Participation in association programs (*money*).

Competitors	Rate of growth (encroachment on their markets). Product or service innovation (source of new ideas to use).
Communities	Contribution to community development through taxes, participation in charitable activities, etc. Employment of local people. Minimum of negative side-effects (e.g., pollution).
Special interest groups	Employment of minority groups. Contributions to urban improvement programs. Provision of free services to the disadvantaged.

Priority of Concerns

In any one decision regarding corporate strategy, the interests of one stakeholder can conflict with another. For example, a business firm's decision to build a plant in an inner-city location may have a positive effect on community relations but a negative effect on stockholder dividends. Which group's interests have priority?

In a survey sponsored by the American Management Association, 6,000 managers and executives were asked to rate on a seven-point scale the importance of a number of corporate stakeholders.[12] As shown in Table 4.1, executives felt customers to be the most important concern. Employees were also rated highly. Interestingly, the general public was felt to be of similar

Table 4.1   Importance to Executives of Various Stakeholders

Stakeholder	*Rank*
Customers	6.40
Employees	6.01
Owners	5.30
General public	4.52
Stockholders	4.51
Elected public officials	3.79
Government bureaucrats	2.90

SOURCE: Adapted from B. Z. Posner and W. H. Schmidt, "Values and the American Manager: An Update." Copyright © 1984 by the Regents of the University of California. Adapted by permission of the Regents from *California Management Review,* vol. xxvi, no. 3, p. 206.

NOTE: The ranking is calculated on a scale of 7 (most important) to 1 (least important).

importance to stockholders. Owners (presumably those who own large blocks of stock), however, were rated as more important than either the public or more typical stockholders. Government representatives were rated as least important of all the groups considered.

Pressures on the Business Corporation

Given the wide range of interests and concerns present in any corporation's task environment, one or more groups, at any one time, probably will be dissatisfied with a corporation's activities. For example, consider General Motors' decision to build a new plant in a run-down area of Detroit (sometimes referred to as "Poletown"). In 1980, when corporate profits were turning to losses, General Motors advised the city of Detroit that in 1983 it would close its Cadillac and Fisher Body plants, both of which were located within city boundaries. Realizing its responsibility to Detroit, GM suggested that if the city could find a rectangular area of 450 to 500 acres with access to highways and long-haul railroad lines, it would build a new plant within the city. The city government in cooperation with the town of Hamtramck decided on the vacant Dodge "main plant" (abandoned previously by Chrysler Corporation), along with the adjacent area. As Detroit and Hamtramck began to appropriate the homes, factories, and churches in the area, protests developed. Lawsuits were filed. General Motors was in a situation of being damned if it left Detroit and damned if it stayed.[13]

Another controversial issue is the presence of over 300 United States business corporations in South Africa. Given the apartheid policy of strict racial segregation and discrimination against non-whites of the South African government, many critics of apartheid have been urging U.S. firms to withdraw their business. With American corporations controlling nearly 70% of South Africa's computer industry and half of its petroleum business, anti-apartheid spokespeople argue that the presence of such important firms as IBM, Exxon, G.E., GM, Kodak, Johnson and Johnson, Hewlett-Packard, Ford, among others, gave tacit approval and financial support to a "racist" government. Calls for the *disinvestment* of American business in South Africa were criticized, however, by other black South Africans with a different point of view. Mangosutu Gatsha Buthelezi, hereditary prime minister of the Zulu nation, commented: "No one has proved to us that the suffering which will ensue within the black community as a result of disinvestment will actually force the regime to effect the fundamental changes all of us are clamoring for."[14] Torn between two conflicting demands, around 150 U.S. business corporations have chosen a compromise position. They remained in South Africa, but signed and followed the *Sullivan Code*, a set of equal opportunity and fair treatment principles drawn up by Leon H. Sullivan, minister of Philadelphia's Zion Baptist Church and a director of General Motors. Nevertheless, by mid-1985 approximately forty U.S. universities had removed more than $300 million in investments from firms dealing with South Africa as had more than eighteen cities and five states.[15]

The previous examples indicate how easily a business corporation can run into problems—even when top management is trying to achieve the best outcome for all involved. There are other examples, however, of business firms engaging in very questionable, unethical, or even illegal actions. These examples reveal the dark side of corporate decision making and support those who favor more governmental regulation and less business autonomy. There is no doubt that top management of some business firms has sometimes made decisions emphasizing short-term profitability or personal gain over long-term relations with governments, local communities, suppliers, and even customers and employees. For example, here are some of the questionable practices that have been exposed in recent years:

- Possible negligent construction and management practices at nuclear power and chemical plants (for example, nuclear plants at Three Mile Island and Diablo Canyon and Union Carbide's chemical plant in Bhopal, India).[16]

- Improper disposal of toxic wastes (for instance, at Love Canal).[17]

- Production and sale of defective products (for example, A. H. Robbins' Dalkon Shield birth control device).[18]

- Declaring bankruptcy to cancel a labor contract and cut wages (for instance, Wilson Foods).[19]

- Insufficient safeguarding of employees from exposure to dangerous chemicals and materials in the workplace (for instance, the asbestos problem at Johns-Manville).[20]

- Continuous instances of fraud, bribery, and price fixing at corporations of all sizes and locations (for example, National Semiconductor's defrauding the Defense Department by failing to test electronic components properly and General Electric's illegal claims for more than $800,000 in cost overruns on Minuteman missile contracts).[21]

Ethics: A Question of Values   Such questionable practices by business corporations run counter to the values of society as a whole and are justly criticized and prosecuted. Why are actions taken that so obviously harm important stakeholders in the corporation's task environment? Are business corporations and the people who run them amoral, or are they simply ignorant of the many consequences of their actions?

One reason for such behavior is that there is no worldwide standard of con-   ***Cultural Differences***
duct for businesspeople. Cultural norms and values vary between countries
and even between different geographic regions and ethnic groups within a
country. One example is the use of payoffs and bribes to influence a potential
customer to buy from a particular supplier. Although this practice is considered illegal in the United States, it is deeply entrenched in many countries.
In Mexico, for instance, the payoff, referred to as *la mordida* (the bite), is
considered a fringe benefit or *propina* (a tip).[22]

Another possible reason for a corporation's questionable practices lies in dif-   ***Personal Differences***
ferences in values between top management and key stakeholders in the task
environment. Some businesspeople may believe profit maximization is the
key goal of their firm, whereas concerned interest groups may have other
goals, such as the hiring of minorities and women or the safety of their
neighborhoods.

Economist Milton Friedman, in urging a return to a *laissez-faire* style
worldwide economy, argues against the concept of social responsibility. If a
businessperson acts "responsibly" by cutting the price of the firm's product
to prevent inflation, or by making expenditures to reduce pollution, or by
hiring the hard-core unemployed, that person, according to Friedman, is
spending the stockholder's money for a general social interest. Even if the
businessperson has stockholder permission or encouragement to do so, he or
she is still acting from motives other than economic and may, in the long run,
cause harm to the very society the firm is trying to help. By taking on the
burden of these social costs, the business becomes less efficient; and either
prices go up to pay for the increased costs, or investment in new activities
and research is postponed. These results negatively affect—perhaps fa-
tally—the long-term efficiency of a business. Friedman thus referred to the
social responsibility of business as a "fundamentally subversive doctrine"
and stated that "there is one and only one social responsibility of business—
to use its resources and engage in activities designed to increase its profits so
long as it stays within the rules of the game, which is to say, engages in open
and free competition without deception or fraud."[23]

Friedman's stand on free enterprise has been both criticized and praised.
Businesspeople tend to agree with Friedman because his views are compatible not only with their own self-interests but also with their hierarchy of
values. Research by Guth and Tagiuri points out that high-level U.S. executives hold most highly a combination of economic, theoretical, and political
values. Religious, aesthetic, and social values have less importance in their
lives. The following comparison of the value systems of business executives
and ministers shows large differences (the values are arranged in order from
most important to least important).[24]

Executives	Ministers
Economic	Religious
Theoretical	Social
Political	Aesthetic
Religious	Political
Aesthetic	Theoretical
Social	Economic

Imagine the controversy that would result if a group composed of ministers and executives had to decide the following strategy issues: Should business firms close on Sunday? Should the corporation hire handicapped workers and accept the increased training costs associated with their employment? In discussing these issues, the executive would probably be very concerned with the effects on the "bottom line" (profits), whereas the minister would probably be concerned with the effects on society and salvation (a very different bottom line).

This conclusion is supported by a study of 6,000 executives and managers who were asked to rate a representative sample of typical organizational goals as depicted in Table 4.2. The results clearly show community service and public service ranked at the bottom of the list under organizational effectiveness and profit maximization.[25] This study generally agrees with previous studies which revealed a desire by businesspeople to limit their social responsibilities to those areas where they can clearly see benefits to the corporation in terms of reduced costs and less governmental regulation.[26]

This very narrow view of businesses' responsibilities to society typically will cause conflicts between the business corporation and certain members of

Table 4.2   Importance to Executives of Various Organizational Goals

Organizational Goal	Degree of Importance
Organizational effectiveness	6.26
High productivity	6.16
High morale	6.01
Organizational efficiency	5.93
Profit maximization	5.44
Organizational growth	5.20
Organizational value to community	4.82
Service to the public	4.68

SOURCE: Adapted from B. Z. Posner and W. H. Schmidt, "Values and the American Manager: An Update." Copyright © 1984 by the Regents of the Univesity of California. Adapted by permission of the Regents from *California Management Review*, vol. xxvi, no. 3, p. 205.

NOTE: The ranking is calculated on a scale of 7 ("very important to me") to 1 (" of little or no importance to me").

its task environment. Carroll, in his research on social responsibility, suggests that in addition to the obvious economic and legal responsibilities, businesses have ethical and discretionary ones.[27] The *economic* responsibilities of a business corporation are to produce goods and services of value to society. Its *legal* responsibilities are defined by governments in the laws that corporations are expected to obey. Its *ethical* responsibilities are to follow the generally held beliefs about how one should act in a society. *Discretionary* responsibilities, in contrast, are the purely voluntary obligations a corporation assumes. Examples are philanthropic contributions, training the hard-core unemployed, and providing day-care centers. Carroll suggests that to the extent that business corporations fail to acknowledge discretionary or ethical responsibilities, society, through government, will act, making them legal responsibilities. This may be done by governments, moreover, without regard to a corporation's economic responsibilities. As a result, the corporation may have greater difficulty in earning a profit than it would have had in assuming voluntarily some ethical and discretionary responsibilities. For example, it has been suggested by some people in the American automobile industry that the large number of safety and pollution regulations passed in the 1960s and 1970s were partially responsible for the poor health of the industry in the early 1980s.[28]

Nevertheless, studies in the area have *failed* to find any significant relationship between a business corporation's social responsibility and its financial performance. Examples can be cited of both highly profitable and marginally profitable companies with both poor and excellent social records.[29] One interesting example is Control Data Corporation. Under the leadership of socially concerned William C. Norris as founder, chairman, and CEO, Control Data has organized assembly plants in ghettos and prisons and spent millions of dollars on computer systems for education and training in schools and industry. Unfortunately, corporate earnings have fallen and Norris has been criticized for allowing his "pet businesses" to drain investment away from the company's profitable ventures.[30]

Even with the finding that social responsibility has no relationship to profits, one conclusion seems clear. The *iron law of responsibility* applies: If business corporations are unable or unwilling to police themselves by considering their responsibilities to all stakeholders in their task environment, then society—usually in the form of government—will police their doing so, and once again governments will reduce business's autonomy via increased rules and regulations.

Because they are a part of a larger society that constantly affects them in many ways, corporations must be aware of changes and potential changes within the key variables in their task and societal environments. In 1973, for

4.3 ENVIRONMENTAL SCANNING

example, the Arab oil embargo caught many firms completely by surprise, with the result that goods dependent on oil as a raw material or energy source could not be produced. The resulting shortages and price adjustments caused chaos throughout the world's economy. The top management of many business corporations then realized just how dependent they were on seemingly unpredictable external events. It was at this time, in the early 1970s, that many corporations established for the first time formal strategic planning systems. By 1984, between 92 and 95% of the world's largest corporations were using planning departments to monitor the environment and to prepare forecasts.[31]

Before strategy makers can begin formulating specific strategies, they must scan the external environment to identify possible *opportunities* and *threats*. Environmental scanning is the monitoring, evaluating, and disseminating of information from the external environment to key people within the corporation.[32] It is a tool used by a corporation to avoid strategic surprise and to ensure its long-run health.[33] Both the societal and task environments must be monitored to detect strategic factors that are likely to have a strong impact on corporate success or failure.

Monitoring Strategic Factors

Usually environmental scanning begins with the identification of strategic factors in the societal and task environments. *Strategic factors* are those variables that top management believes have great potential for affecting its corporation's activities. They are the patterns of events that will influence the corporation in the future. These factors are typically ones that have strongly affected a corporation in the past or are presently doing so. But, unfortunately, few firms attempt to anticipate them.[34] Furthermore, the values of the top managers are likely to bias both their perceptions of what is or is not important to monitor in the external environment and their interpretations of what they perceive.

For example, a recent research study of presidents of savings and loan associations revealed that a president's perception of the environment strongly affected strategic planning. Those presidents who believed the present uncertain environment to be only temporary used no long-term planning staff or planning committees. They simply chose to wait for the "good old days" to return. In contrast, those presidents who believed the days of the stable, regulated environment to be long gone spent 30 to 50% of their time considering long-range strategic issues and using planning staffs extensively.[35]

Societal Environment

The number of possible strategic factors in the societal environment is enormous. As noted in Table 4.3, large corporations categorize the societal en-

Table 4.3 **Some Important Factors in the Societal Environment**

Sociocultural	Economic	Technological	Political-Legal
Life-style changes	GNP trends	Total federal spending for R&D	Antitrust regulations
Career expectations	Interest rates	Total industry spending for R&D	Environmental protection laws
Consumer activism	Money supply	Focus of technological efforts	Tax laws
Rate of family formation	Inflation rates	Patent protection	Special incentives
Growth rate of population	Unemployment levels	New products	Foreign trade regulations
Age distribution of population	Wage/Price controls	New developments in technology transfer from lab to marketplace	Attitudes toward foreign companies
Regional shifts in population	Devaluation/revaluation	Productivity improvements through automation	Laws on hiring and promotion
Life expectancies	Energy availability and cost		Stability of government
Birth rates	Disposable and discretionary income		

vironment into four areas and focus their scanning in each area on trends with corporate-wide relevance. The economic area is usually the most significant, followed by the technological, political–legal, and sociocultural in decreasing order of importance.[36] Obviously, trends in any one area may be very important to the firms in one industry but of lesser importance to firms in other industries. For example, the demographic bulge in the U.S. population caused by the "baby boom" in the 1950s strongly affects the brewing industry, among others. As this demographic group becomes older during the decade of the 80s, the percentage of the population in the 18–25 years of age category—prime beer drinking age—decreases. Thus sales and profits of breweries decrease and corporations like Anheuser-Busch find that they must diversify if they are to stay profitable. In contrast, as the number of people in the 25–34 years of age category becomes larger, demand increases considerably for day-care facilities like Kinder-Care Learning Centers. As this group of "Yuppies" (young urban professionals) have children, businesses are forced to alter their product and service offerings. For example, Jerry Jones, senior vice-president of Colorado's Keystone Resort, says that the baby boomers who once flocked to the ski slopes are now young parents who ski less often and spend fewer dollars when they do. To survive, even fashionable resorts are now using discount rates and promotions to lure families.[37]

John Naisbitt, in his influential book, *Megatrends,* states that America's present societal environment is turbulent because we are moving from one era to another. From a content analysis of newspapers, he proposes that

American society is being restructured by *ten broad influences* or "mega-trends" that are defining the new society.

1. We are moving from an industrial to an information society.

2. We are moving from forced technology to matching each new technology with a compensatory human response ("Hi tech–hi touch").

3. We are moving from a national to a world economy.

4. We are moving from short-term to long-term considerations with an emphasis on strategic planning.

5. We are moving from a period of centralization to decentralization of power.

6. We are shifting from reliance on institutional help to more self-reliance.

7. We are moving from representative democracy to more participative democracy in politics as well as in the workplace.

8. We are giving up our dependence on traditional hierarchical structures in favor of informal networks of contacts.

9. We are moving geographically from the North to the South and West.

10. We are moving from a society with a limited number of personal choices to a multiple-option society.[38]

If Naisbitt is correct, these changes will have enormous impact on business corporations. Strategic planners will need to closely monitor the environment for any trends or issues which will have serious impact on the future of

		PROBABLE IMPACT ON CORPORATION	
	High	**Medium**	**Low**
PROBABILITY OF OCCURRENCE — High	High Priority	High Priority	Medium Priority
Medium	High Priority	Medium Priority	Low Priority
Low	Medium Priority	Low Priority	Low Priority

Figure 4.2   **Issues priority matrix.**
SOURCE: Adapted from L. L. Lederman, "Foresight Activities in the U.S.A.: Time for a Re-Assessment?" *Long-Range Planning* (June 1984), p. 46. Copyright © 1984 by Pergamon Press, Ltd. Reprinted by permission.

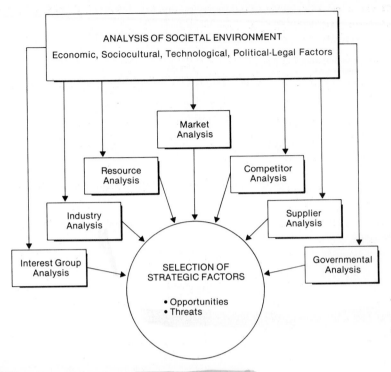

Figure 4.3 **Scanning the external environment.**

their corporation. To avoid information overload, planners should use an *issues priority matrix,* as shown in Fig. 4.2, to help them decide which issues to monitor closely (high priority) and which issues to merely scan (low priority).

As was noted earlier, changes in the societal environment tend to be reflected in pressures on the corporation from task environment groups. As shown in Fig. 4.3, a corporation's scanning of the environment will include analyses of all the relevant elements in the task environment—interest groups, its industry, resources, the marketplace, competitors, suppliers, and governments.

Porter, an authority on competitive strategy, contends that a corporation is most concerned with the intensity of competition within its industry. The level of this intensity is determined by basic competitive forces, which are depicted in Fig. 4.4. "The collective strength of these forces," he contends, "determines the ultimate profit potential in the industry, where profit potential is measured in terms of long-run return on invested capital."[39] Although Porter only mentions five forces, a sixth—other stakeholders—is added to

Task Environment

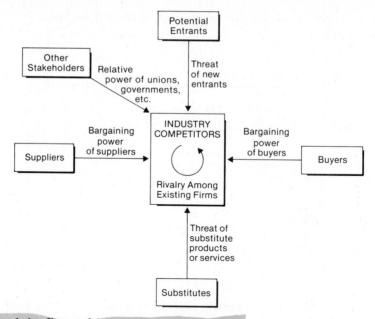

Figure 4.4   Forces driving industry competition.
SOURCE: Adapted with permission of The Free Press, a division of Macmillan, Inc. from
Competitive Strategy by M. E. Porter. Copyright © 1980 by The Free Press.

reflect the power of unions, governments, and other groups from the task
environment on industry activities.

A corporation must carefully scan the task environment to assess the importance to its success of each of the following six forces.[40]

1. *Threat of New Entrants:* New entrants to an industry typically bring to it
    new capacity, a desire to gain market share, and substantial resources
    and are, therefore, threats to an established corporation. The threat of
    entry depends on the presence of entry barriers and the reaction that
    can be expected from existing competitors. For example, there have
    been very few new automobile companies successfully established since
    the 1930s because of the high capital requirements to build production
    facilities and to develop a dealer distribution network.

2. *Rivalry among Existing Firms:* In most industries, corporations are mu-
    tually dependent. A competitive move by one firm can be expected to
    have a noticeable effect on its competitors and thus may cause retalia-
    tion or efforts to counter the move. For example, the entry of Philip
    Morris into the beer industry through the acquisition of Miller Brewing

increased the level of competitive activity to such an extent that a new product or promotion is now quickly followed by similar moves from other brewers.

3. *Threat of Substitute Products or Services:* In effect, all corporations in an industry are competing with industries that produce substitute products. According to Porter, "Substitutes limit the potential returns of an industry by placing a ceiling on the prices firms in the industry can profitably charge."[41] In the 1970s, for example, the high price of cane sugar caused soft drink manufacturers to turn to high fructose corn syrup as a sugar substitute. Sometimes a difficult task, the identification of possible substitute products or services means searching for products or services that can perform the same *function*, even though they may not appear to be easily substitutable. Videotape recorders, for example, are becoming substitutes for home motion picture projectors. The television screen thus substitutes for the portable projection screen.

4. *Bargaining Power of Buyers:* Buyers affect an industry through their ability to force down prices, bargain for higher quality or more services, and play competitors against each other. A buyer or a group of buyers is powerful if some of the following hold true:

- It purchases a large proportion of the seller's product or service.
- It has the potential to integrate backward by producing the product itself.
- Alternative suppliers are plentiful.
- Changing suppliers costs very little.

For example, to the extent that General Motors purchases a large percentage of Firestone's total tire production, GM's purchasing department can easily make all sorts of demands on Firestone's marketing people. This would be the case especially if GM could easily get its tires from Goodyear or General Tire at no extra trouble or cost. Increasing demands by large manufacturing companies for "just-in-time delivery" means that in order to get the orders, a small supplier dependent on the large firm's business must take over the warehousing functions previously handled by the large firm.

5. *Bargaining Power of Suppliers:* Suppliers can affect an industry through their ability to raise prices or reduce the quality of purchased goods and services. A supplier group is powerful if some of the following apply:

- The supplier industry is dominated by a few companies, but sells to many.

- Substitutes are not readily available.

- Suppliers are able to integrate forward and compete directly with their present customers. An example is the construction of oil refineries by Saudi Arabia.

- A purchasing industry buys only a small portion of the supplier group's goods and services.

For example, major oil companies in the 1970s were able to raise prices and reduce services because so many companies that purchased oil products had heavy energy needs and, in the short run, were unable to switch to substitute fuels, such as coal or nuclear power. Wishing to be less dependent on suppliers for the raw material so necessary to produce synthetic materials, Dupont chose to buy Conoco, a major oil company.

6. *Relative Power of Other Stakeholders:* Freeman recommends adding this sixth force to Porter's list to include a variety of stakeholder groups from the task environment.[42] Some of them are governments, unions, local communities, creditors (if not included with suppliers), trade associations, special interest groups, and stockholders. The importance of these stakeholders will vary by industry. For example, environmental groups successfully fought to pass bills in Maine, Michigan, Oregon, and Iowa outlawing disposable bottles and cans, thus requiring deposits for most drink containers. Although Porter contends that government influences the level of competitive activity through the previously mentioned five forces, it is suggested here that governments deserve a special mention because of their strong relative power in all industries.

Strategic Groups   In analyzing the level of competitive intensity within an industry, it is useful to categorize the various competitors for predictive purposes. According to Miles and Snow, competing firms within a single industry can be grouped on the basis of similar patterns of behavior into one of four basic types: the Defender, the Prospector, the Analyzer, and the Reactor. Each of these types has its own favorite strategy for responding to the environment. Each has its own combination of structure, culture, and processes consistent with that strategy. These general types have the following characteristics:

- *Defenders* are corporations with a limited product line that focus on improving the efficiency of their existing operations. Their focus makes them less likely to innovate in new areas. An example would be the Schlitz Brewing Company.

- *Prospectors* are corporations with fairly broad product lines that focus on product innovation and market opportunities. They tend to emphasize creativity over efficiency. An example would be the Miller Brewing Company.

- *Analyzers* are corporations that operate in two different product-market areas, one stable and one changing. In the stable area, efficiency is emphasized. In the changing area, innovation is emphasized. An example would be Anheuser-Busch (beer and snack food).

- *Reactors* are corporations that lack a consistent strategy-structure-culture relationship. They tend to respond (often ineffectively) to environmental pressures with piecemeal strategic changes. An example would be the Pabst Brewing Company.[43]

Lumping the competition into one of these four groups enables the strategic manager to not only monitor the effectiveness of certain strategic orientations, it also aids in the development of future industry scenarios (to be discussed later in this chapter).

Sources of Information

Studies have shown that much environmental scanning is done on an informal and individual basis. Information is obtained from a variety of sources such as customers, suppliers, bankers, consultants, publications, personal observations, subordinates, superiors, and peers. For example, scientists and engineers working in a firm's R&D lab may learn about new products and competitors' ideas at professional meetings; or speaking with supplier representatives' personnel in the purchasing department may uncover valuable bits of information about a competitor. A study of product innovation in the scientific instruments and machine tool industries found that 80% of all product innovations were initiated by the *customer* in the form of inquiries and complaints.[44] In these industries, the sales force and service departments must be especially vigilant.

Some of the main sources of information about an industry's environment are shown in Fig. 4.5. Because people throughout a corporation may obtain an extraordinary amount of data in any given month, top management must develop a system to get these data from those who obtained it to the people who can integrate it with other information to form a comprehensive environmental assessment.

As one would suspect, research suggests that corporations develop and implement more scanning procedures for following, anticipating, and responding to changes in the activities of *competitors* than for any other stakeholder in the environment.

There is danger in focusing one's scanning efforts too closely on one's

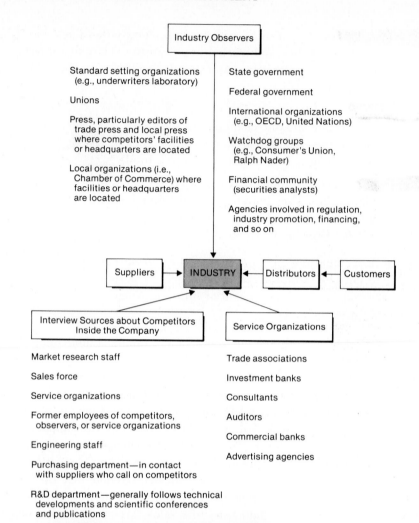

Figure 4.5 **Sources of data for industry analysis.**
SOURCE: Reprinted with permission of The Free Press, a division of Macmillan, Inc. from *Competitive Strategy* by M. E. Porter. Copyright © 1980 by The Free Press.

own industry, though. According to research by Snyder, "History teaches that most new developments which threaten existing business practices and technologies do not come from traditional industries."[45] For instance, *technology transfer,* the process of taking new technology from the laboratory to the marketplace, has become an important issue in recent decades. Consider just one example. With the development of the integrated circuit, electronics firms, such as Texas Instruments, were able to introduce high-volume, low-cost electronic digital watches. These firms' entry into the watch-making industry took well-established mechanical watchmakers by surprise. Timex,

Seiko, and especially the Swiss firms found that their market had changed overnight. Their production facilities, however, had not; and they spent a lot of money buying the new technology.

Most corporations rely on outside organizations to provide them with environmental data. Firms such as A. C. Nielsen Co. provide subscribers with bimonthly data on brand share, retail prices, percentages of stores stocking an item, and percentages of stock-out stores. These data can be used to spot regional and national trends as well as to assess market share. Information on market conditions, government regulations, competitors, and new products can be bought from "information brokers." Such firms as FIND/SVP, a New York company, get their data from periodicals, reference books, computer data banks, directors, and experts in the area. Other firms, like Chase Econometrics, offer various data bases plus a software package to enable corporate planners to gain computer access to a large number of key indicators. Typically, the largest corporations spend from \$20,000 to \$25,000 a year for database services. Close to 6,000 firms in the United States and Canada have established their own in-house libraries to deal with the growing mass of available information.[46]

Some companies, however, chose to get their information straight from their competitors through industrial espionage or other intelligence gathering techniques. For example, Hitachi Ltd, the large Japanese electronics firm, pleaded guilty in 1983 to conspiring to transport stolen IBM material to Japan.[47] In 1984, Procter & Gamble filed a patent-infringement suit against Nabisco Inc, Keebler Co., and Frito-Lay Inc., accusing them of *cookie espionage*. Procter & Gamble (P&G) claimed to have invented the process to make the "dual texture" cookies—crispy outside and soft inside. P&G charged that one competitor took aerial photographs of its cookie manufacturing plant during construction and that another learned the recipe by penetrating a restricted area where the secret technology was being used. The competitors denied all allegations.[48] Other legal, but still questionable, approaches to intelligence gathering are hiring people away from competitors, getting customers to put out phony bid requests, and analyzing a competitor's garbage, to name a few![49]

Once a business corporation has collected data about its current environmental situation, it must analyze present trends to learn if they will continue into the future. The strategic planning horizon for many large corporations is from five to ten years in the future. A long-term planning horizon is especially necessary for large, capital-intensive corporations, such as automobile or heavy-machinery manufacturers. These corporations require many years to move from an accepted proposal to a finished product. As a result, most

**4.4
FORECASTING**

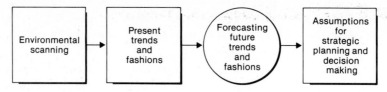

Figure 4.6   **The role of forecasting.**

corporations must make future plans on the basis of a forecast, a set of assumptions about what that future will look like. These assumptions may be derived from an entrepreneur's vision, from a head-in-the-sand hope that the future will be similar to the present, or from the opinions of experts. Figure 4.6 depicts the role of forecasting in the strategy formulation process.

The Danger of Assumptions

A forecast is nothing more than a leap of faith into the future. Environmental scanning provides reasonably hard data on the present situation, but intuition and luck are needed to predict the future. Nevertheless, many firms formulate and implement strategic plans with little or no realization that their success is based on a series of assumptions. Many long-range plans are simply based on projections of the current situation. One example of what can happen when corporate strategy rests on the very questionable assumption that the future will simply be an extension of the present is that of the Pacific Coal Corporation.

In 1981, the Pacific Coal Corporation decided to build a coal-export terminal near Portland, Oregon. One of a score of coal-export terminals proposed for the West Coast, the terminal was planned after the world's second oil crisis when Asian nations sought new supplies of steam coal for electric generating plants. West Coast ports, coal developers, and railroads expected a coal-export boom. Unfortunately, a global recession coupled with an unforeseen drop in oil prices reduced Asian energy demands. Construction of the $60 million Portland facility was suspended in March 1983 with only 80% completion. The facility, with a planned annual capacity of 12 million tons of coal, had no long-term contracts. "The situation is pretty bleak," stated another developer. "Our assessment of the future is it may be unlikely to turn around until the early 1990's—we may be talking about ten years."[50]

Techniques

As depicted in Table 4.4, various techniques are used to forecast future situations. Each has its proponents and critics. A recent study of nearly 500 of the world's largest corporations revealed *trend extrapolation* to be the most widely practiced form of forecasting—over 70% use this technique either occasionally or frequently.[51] Simply stated, extrapolation is the extension of present trends into the future. Like the Pacific Coal Corporation example, it

Table 4.4   Degree of Usage of Forecasting Techniques*

Technique	Top 1,000 U.S. Industrials (n=215)	Top 100 U.S. Industrials (n=40)	Top 300 U.S. Non-Industrials (n=85)	Top 500 Foreign Industrials (n=105)
Trend extrapolation	73%	70%	74%	72%
Statistical modeling (i.e., regression analysis)	48	61	51	45
Scenarios	57	67	67	61
Relevance trees	5	3	7	4
Simulation	34	45	38	27
Brainstorming	65	61	69	52
Trend impact analysis	34	33	31	29
Expert opinion/Delphi	33	42	24	35
Morphological analysis	2	0	0	5
Signal monitoring	15	19	14	18
Cross-impact analysis	12	22	11	5

SOURCE: H. E. Klein and R. E. Linneman, "Environmental Assessment: An International Study of Corporate Practices," *Journal of Business Strategy* (Summer 1984), p. 72. Copyright © 1984 by Warren, Gorham & Lamont, Inc. Reprinted by permission. All rights reserved.

* Figures reflect the percentage of respondents indicating either "frequent" or "occasional" use. Respondents had been asked to classify their frequency of technique use as "not used," "rarely used," "used occasionally," or "used frequently."

rests on the assumption that the world is reasonably consistent and changes slowly in the short run. Time series methods are approaches of this type which attempt to carry a series of historical events forward into the future. The basic problem with extrapolation is that a historical trend is based upon a series of patterns or relationships among so many different variables that a change in any one can drastically alter the future direction of the trend. As a rule of thumb, the further back into the past one can find relevant data supporting the trend, the more confidence one can have in the prediction. Nevertheless, even experts in forecasting admit: "Forecasts that cover a period of two years or more are typically very inaccurate."[52]

As shown in Table 4.4 brainstorming and statistical modeling are also very popular forecasting techniques. *Brainstorming* is a nonquantitative approach requiring simply the presence of people with some knowledge of the situation to be predicted. The basic ground rule is to propose ideas without first mentally screening them. No criticism is allowed. Ideas tend to build upon previous ideas until a consensus is reached. This is a good technique to use with operating managers who have more faith in "gut feel" than in more quantitative "number crunching" techniques.

Statistical modeling is a quantitative technique that attempts to discover causal or at least explanatory factors that link two or more time series together. Examples of statistical modeling are regression analysis and other econometric methods. Although very useful to grasp historic trends, statistical modeling, like trend extrapolation, is based on historical data. As the patterns of relationships change, the accuracy of the forecast deteriorates.[53]

Other forecasting techniques, such as *cross-impact analysis, trend impact analysis,* and *relevance trees* have not established themselves successfully as regularly employed tools. Research by Klein and Linneman reports that corporate planners found these techniques to be complicated, time-consuming, expensive, and academic. Usage was therefore concentrated among the very largest companies.[54]

Research further reports that *scenario-writing* appears to be the most widely used forecasting technique after trend extrapolation. Among corporations in the top Fortune 1,000 Industrials, the usage of scenarios increased from 22% in 1977 to 57% in 1981. Klein and Linneman predict increasing usage of this popular forecasting technique, but point out that "most companies follow a very informal scenario-writing approach with little reliance on rigorous methodologies."[55] The scenario may thus be merely a written description of some future state in terms of key variables and issues or it may be generated from other forecasting techniques in combination. A more complex version used by General Electric is depicted in Fig. 4.7 and is based upon a Delphi panel of experts, a trend impact analysis, and a cross-impact analysis. The *Delphi* technique involves an anonymous panel of experts who are asked individually to estimate the probability of certain events occurring in the future. Each member of the panel is given several opportunities to revise his/her estimate after seeing the anonymous responses from the other experts on the panel.

In his recent book *Competitive Advantage,* Michael Porter strongly recommends the use of scenarios because they: (1) allow a firm to move away from dangerous, single-point forecasts of the future in instances when the future cannot be predicted, and (2) encourage managers to make their assumptions explicit.[56] He recommends the use of *industry scenarios* which utilize variables from the societal environment as they affect the key stakeholders in a corporation's task environment. The process may operate as follows.[57]

1. *Examine possible shifts in the societal variables* (e.g., economic, sociocultural, technological, and political-legal). Begin with the obvious factors in Table 4.3 and plot them on the issues priority matrix depicted in Fig. 4.2.

2. *Identify uncertainties in each of the six forces from the task environment* (e.g., competitors, buyers, suppliers, likely substitutes, potential

entrants, and other key stakeholders) as depicted in Fig. 4.4. Make sure that all the high-priority societal issues identified in the first step are specified as they affect the appropriate forces in the task environment.

3. *Identify the causal factors behind the uncertainties.* These sources of uncertainty may be inside the industry (e.g., competitor behavior) or outside the industry (e.g., new regulations). It is likely that many of these causal factors were identified earlier when analyzing the societal environment. It is also likely that new ones surfaced when analyzing the task environment.

4. *Make a range of plausible assumptions about each important causal factor.* For example, if the price of oil is a causal factor, make reason-

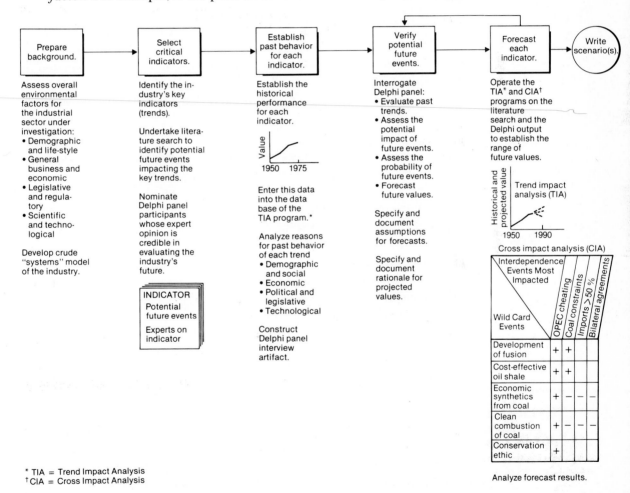

* TIA = Trend Impact Analysis
† CIA = Cross Impact Analysis

Figure 4.7   Scenario construction at General Electric.
SOURCE: General Electric Company. Used by permission.

able assumptions about its future level in terms of high, low, and most probable price.

5. *Combine assumptions about individual causal factors into internally consistent scenarios.* Put various combinations of the assumptions together into sets of scenarios. Since one assumption may affect another, ensure that the scenarios are internally consistent. For example, if a scenario includes the assumptions of high oil prices and a low level of inflation in the economy, that scenario is not internally consistent and should be rejected. It is an unlikely event because high oil prices tend to drive inflation upward.

6. *Analyze the industry situation that would prevail under each scenario.* For example, if one scenario assumes that generic (no-name) drugs will be more in demand than brand-name drugs, the situation in the drug industry will be very different than if one assumed that the demand for generic drugs will be negligible. For example, an industry dominated by generic drugs would mean low profit margins for all firms and a very heavy degree of competition. It is likely that a few firms would leave the drug industry.

7. *Determine the sources of competitive advantage under each scenario.* For example, in an industry dominated by generic drugs, the combination of low price backed up by low operating costs would provide competitive advantage to a firm. If brand-name drugs dominated, the combination of strong advertising, high-quality production, and heavy promotion would provide competitive advantage to the firm using them.

8. *Predict competitor behavior under each scenario.* As the industry moves toward a particular scenario each competitor will make some adjustment. Some may leave the industry. New competitors may enter. Estimate what each competitor is likely to do given its history and what is known about its management. Once this is done, management should be able to specify the *strategic factors* necessary for success in a variety of future scenarios. One may also attach probabilities to each of the developed scenarios in order to choose the ones most likely to occur.

4.5 SUMMARY AND CONCLUSION

Anyone concerned with how strategic decisions are made in large corporations should be aware of the impact of the external environment on top management and the board of directors. Long-run developments in the economic, technological, political-legal, and sociocultural aspects of the societal environment strongly affect the corporation's activities through the more immediate pressures in its task environment.

Business and commerce have lived an uneasy truce with society for centuries. Vacillating between heavy regulation and *laissez-faire* economics, business corporations are learning that they must be socially responsible if they are to operate with some autonomy. Top management and the board of directors must constantly balance the needs of one stakeholder in the corporation's task environment against the needs of another. They must work to ensure that their priorities do not get too far away from those valued by society.

Before strategy can be formulated, strategy makers must scan the external environment for possible opportunities and threats. They must identify which strategic factors to monitor, as well as assess which are likely to affect the corporation in the future. Then they must analyze the resulting information and disseminate it to the people involved in strategic planning and decision making.

Just as environmental scanning provides an understanding of present trends in the environment, forecasting provides assumptions about the future that are crucial for strategic management. Modern corporations primarily use the techniques of trend extrapolation, scenario-writing, brainstorming, and statistical modeling to predict their likely future environment. Even if the predictions prove to be wrong, the very act of scanning and forecasting the environment helps managers take a broader perspective. These techniques also help prevent the development of reactive managers who dare not take the time to plan for the future because they are caught up in the crises and problems of the present.

DISCUSSION QUESTIONS

1. Should U.S. corporations be allowed to operate in South Africa under an "apartheid"-oriented government?

2. How appropriate is the theory of *laissez-faire* in today's world?

3. Why should a business corporation be socially responsible?

4. What can a corporation do to ensure that information about strategic environmental factors gets to the attention of strategy makers?

5. To what extent do you agree with the conclusion that the ultimate profit potential of an industry depends on the collective strength of six key forces: the threat of new entrants, the rivalry among existing firms, the threat of substitutable products or services, the bargaining power of buyers, the bargaining power of suppliers, and the relative power of other stakeholders? Defend your view.

6. If most long-term forecasts are usually incorrect, why bother doing them?

7. Compare and contrast trend extrapolation with scenarios as forecasting techniques.

NOTES

1. E. C. Bursk, D. T. Clark, and R. W. Hidy, "The Oldest Business Code: Nearly 4000 Years Ago," *The World of Business,* vol. 1 (New York: Simon and Schuster, 1962), pp. 9–10.

2. F. E. Kast and J. E. Rosenzweig, *Organization and Management,* 2nd ed. (New York: McGraw-Hill, 1974), p. 28.

3. M. Weber, *The Protestant Ethic and the Spirit of Capitalism,* trans. Talcott Parsons (New York: Charles Scribner's Sons, 1958).

4. Kast and Rosenzweig, p. 35.

5. J. W. McGuire, *Business and Society* (New York: McGraw-Hill, 1963), p. 78.

6. Kast and Rosenzweig, pp. 37–39.

7. *New York Times* (April 23, 1962) as quoted by H. L. Gabel, G. A. Becker, and B. S. Seng, "Armco—The 1978 Wage and Price Guidelines," in T. L. Wheelen and J. D. Hunger, *Strategic Management and Business Policy,* 1st ed. (Reading, Mass.: Addison-Wesley, 1983), p. 397.

8. G. A. Steiner, *The New CEO* (New York: Macmillan Publishing, 1983), p. 6.

9. K. Hughes, *Corporate Response to Declining Rates of Growth* (Lexington, Mass.: Lexington Books, 1982), p. 14.

10. R. B. Reich, *The Next American Frontier* (New York: Times Books, 1983).

11. R. E. Freeman, *Strategic Management: A Stakeholder Approach* (Boston: Pitman Publishing Co., 1984), p. 25.

12. B. Z. Posner and W. H. Schmidt, "Values and the American Manager: An Update," *California Management Review* (Spring 1984), pp. 202–216.

13. "Pushing the Boundaries of Eminent Domain," *Business Week* (May 4, 1981), p. 174.

14. "Kennedy, Zulu Leader Discuss Investments," *Ames Tribune* (United Press International), Ames, Iowa, January 10, 1985, p. 20.

15. S. P. Sherman, "Scoring Corporate Conduct in South Africa," *Fortune* (July 9, 1984), pp. 168–172.
    M. Maremont, "Fire on Campus, Tremors in the Boardroom," *Business Week* (April 29, 1985), pp. 98–99.

16. "Three Mile Island's Lingering Ills," *Business Week* (October 22, 1979), p. 75.
    T. Redburn, "Stalled Nuclear Power Plant: PG&E Feels Powerless," *Los Angeles Times* (February 24, 1980), part 4, p. 1.
    J. H. Dobrzynski, W. B. Glaberson, R. W. King, W. J. Powell, Jr., and L. Helm, "Union Carbide Fights for Its Life," *Business Week* (December 24, 1984), pp. 52–56.

17. "Who Will Be Liable for Toxic Dumping?" *Business Week* (August 28, 1978), p. 32.

18. M. W. Walsh, "A. H. Robbins Seeks a Consolidated Trial for All Dalkon Punitive-Damage Claims," *Wall Street Journal* (October 23, 1984), p. 4.

19. L. Sorenson, "Chapter 11 Filing by Wilson Foods Roils Workers' Lives, Tests Law," *Wall Street Journal* (May 23, 1983), p. 25.

20. S. Soloman, "The Asbestos Fallout at Johns-Manville," *Fortune* (May 7, 1979), pp. 197–206.

21. "Test Case: A Defense Contractor Is Fined," *Time* (March 19, 1984), p. 47.
    F. Schwadel, "General Electric Pleads Guilty in Fraud Case," *Wall Street Journal* (May 14, 1985), p. 119.
    I. Ross, "How Lawless Are Big Companies?" *Fortune* (December 1, 1980), pp. 58–61.

22. W. M. Pride and O. C. Ferrell, *Marketing*, 2nd ed. (Boston: Houghton Mifflin, 1980), p. 720.

23. M. Friedman, "The Social Responsibility of Business Is to Increase Its Profits," *New York Times Magazine* (September 13, 1970), pp. 30, 126–127; and *Capitalism and Freedom* (Chicago: University of Chicago Press, 1963), p. 133.

24. W. D. Guth and R. Tagiuri, "Personal Values and Corporate Strategy," *Harvard Business Review* (September–October 1965), pp. 126–127.

25. Posner and Schmidt, pp. 203–205.

26. S. N. Brenner and E. A. Molander, "Is the Ethics of Business Changing?" *Harvard Business Review* (January–February 1977), p. 70.

27. A. B. Carroll, "A Three-Dimensional Conceptual Model of Corporate Performance," *Academy of Management Review* (October 1979), pp. 497–505.

28. L. Iacocca, *Iacocca: An Autobiography* (Toronto: Bantam Books, 1984), pp. 196–197.

29. K. E. Aupperle, A. B. Carroll, and J. D. Hatfield, "An Empirical Examination of the Relationship between Corporate Social Responsibility and Profitability," *Academy of Management Journal* (June 1985), p. 459.
    L. E. Preston, *Research in Corporate and Social Performance and Policy*, Vol. 3 (Greenwich, Conn.: Jai Publishing, 1981), p. 9.

30. "Control Data Starts a Painful Retrenchment," *Business Week* (October 22, 1984), pp. 94–96.

31. H. E. Klein and R. E. Linneman, "Environmental Assessment: An International Study of Corporate Practices," *Journal of Business Strategy* (Summer 1984), p. 67.

32. N. H. Snyder, "Environmental Volatility, Scanning Intensity and Organization Performance," *Journal of Contemporary Business* (September 1981), p. 7.

33. H. I. Ansoff, "Managing Strategic Surprise by Response to Weak Signals," *California Management Review* (Winter 1975), pp. 21–33.

34. F. J. Agvilar, *Scanning the Business Environment* (New York: Macmillan, 1967).

35. M. Javidan, "The Impact of Environmental Uncertainty on Long-Range

Planning and Practices of the U.S. Savings and Loan Industry," *Strategic Management Journal* (October–December 1984), pp. 381–392.

36. S. C. Jain, "Environmental Scanning in U.S. Corporations," *Long Range Planning* (April 1984), p. 119.

37. S. D. Atchison, "What's Giving Some Ski Resorts a Lift," *Business Week* (January 14, 1983), p. 32.

38. J. Naisbitt, *Megatrends* (New York: Warner Books, 1982).

39. M. E. Porter, *Competitive Strategy* (New York: Free Press, 1980), p. 3.

40. This summary of the forces driving competitive strategy is taken from M. E. Porter, *Competitive Strategy* (New York: Free Press, 1980), pp. 7–29.

41. Porter, p. 23.

42. R. E. Freeman, *Strategic Management: A Stakeholder Approach* (Boston: Pitman Publishing, 1984), p. 140–142.

43. R. E. Miles and C. C. Snow, *Organizational Strategy, Structure, and Process* (New York: McGraw-Hill Book Co., 1978).

44. R. T. Pascale, "Perspective on Strategy: The Real Story Behind Honda's Success," *California Management Review* (Spring 1981), p. 70.

45. Snyder, p. 16.

46. J. L. Roberts, "As Information Swells, Firms Open Libraries," *Wall Street Journal* (September 25, 1983), p. 25.

47. J. Drinkhall, "Hitachi Ltd. Pleads Guilty in IBM Case," *Wall Street Journal* (February 9, 1983), p. 4.

48. L. Renner, "Smart Cookies Stay Soft and Chewy on Store Shelves," *Des Moines Register* (September 16, 1984), p. 9E.

49. S. Flax, "How to Snoop on Your Competition," *Fortune* (May 14, 1984), pp. 28–33.
    R. Eells and P. Nehemkis, *Corporate Intelligence and Espionage* (New York: Macmillan, 1984).

50. N. Thorpe, "Grand Plans for Coal Ports Fade in West," *Wall Street Journal* (July 20, 1983), p. 27.

51. H. E. Klein and R. E. Linneman, "Environmental Assessment: An International Study of Corporate Practices," *Journal of Business Strategy* (Summer 1984), p. 72.

52. S. Makridakis and S. C. Wheelwright, "Introduction to Management Forecasting," *The Handbook of Forecasting* (New York: Wiley and Sons, 1982), p. 8.

53. Makridakis and Wheelwright, p. 6.

54. Klein and Linneman, p. 72.

55. Klein and Linneman, p. 73.

56. M. E. Porter, *Competitive Advantage* (New York: The Free Press, 1985), p. 447.

57. This process of scenario development is adapted from M. E. Porter, *Competitive Advantage* (New York: The Free Press, 1985), pp. 448–470.

Chapter 5

THE INTERNAL ENVIRONMENT

STRATEGIC MANAGEMENT MODEL

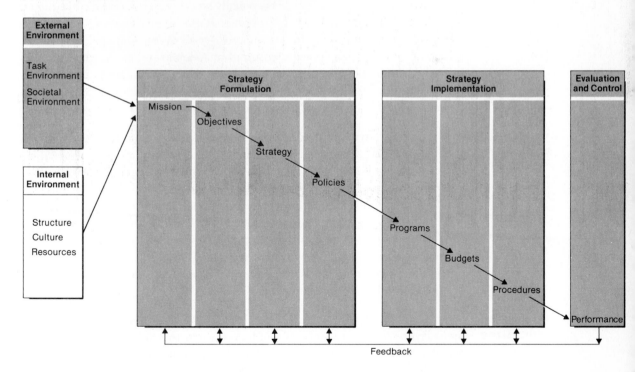

Strategic planning and decision making cannot be successful at the corporate level without an in-depth understanding of the strategic factors within the corporation. These factors are the internal *strengths* and *weaknesses* that act to either constrain or support a strategy. Part of a firm's internal environment, these factors are not within the short-run control of strategic managers. Instead they form the context within which work is accomplished. Strategic factors in a corporation's internal environment are *structure*, *culture*, and *resources*.

5.1 STRUCTURE

The structure of a corporation is often defined in terms of communication, authority, and work flow. It is the corporation's pattern of relationships, its "anatomy." It is a formal arrangement of roles and relationships of people so that the work is directed toward meeting the goals and accomplishing the mission of the corporation.[1] Sometimes it is referred to as the chain of command and is often graphically described in an organization chart.

Although there is an almost infinite variety of structural forms, certain types are predominant in modern complex organizations. These are simple, functional, divisional, matrix, and conglomerate structures.[2] Figure 5.1 illustrates some of these structures.

Simple Structure

Firms having a simple structure are usually small in size and undifferentiated laterally—that is, there are no functional or product categories. A firm with a simple structure is likely to be managed by an owner-manager who either does all the work or oversees a group of unspecialized people who do whatever needs to be done to provide a single product or service. A simple structure is appropriate if the owner-manager can grasp all the intricacies of the business and if the demand for the product or service is reasonably stable.

Functional Structure

In a functional structure, work is divided into subunits on the basis of such functions as manufacturing, finance, and sales. Functional structure enables a firm to take advantage of specialists and to deal with complex production or service-delivery problems more efficiently than it could if everyone performed an undifferentiated task. The functional structure is appropriate as long as top management is willing to invest a lot of energy in coordinating the many activities. The typical long vertical channels of communication and authority tend to make the firm rather inflexible to the requirements of a changing environment, but very successful when adaptability is not required and predictability is important.

Divisional Structure

When a corporation is organized on the basis of divisions, an extra management layer—division chiefs—is added between top management and functional managers. The standard functions are then designed around products,

I. SIMPLE STRUCTURE

II. FUNCTIONAL STRUCTURE

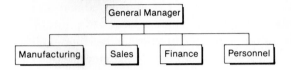

III. DIVISIONAL STRUCTURE*

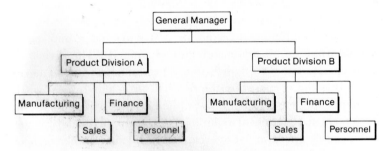

*Conglomerate structure is a variant of the division structure.

IV. MATRIX STRUCTURE

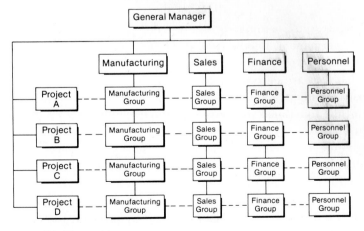

Figure 5.1   **Basic structures.**

clients, or territories.[3] A recent innovation in this area is the use of *strategic business units* (SBUs). Organizational groups composed of discrete, independent *product-market* segments are identified and given primary responsibility and authority to manage their functional areas. For example, instead of food preparation appliances being housed in three different divisions—such as large appliances, small appliances, and cookware—they can be merged into a single SBU serving the housewares market.

An SBU may be of any size or level, but it must have (1) a unique mission, (2) identifiable competitors, (3) an external market focus, and (4) control of its business functions.[4] Once a large corporation is organized on a divisional basis around strategic business units, there still may be too many SBUs for top management to effectively manage. In this case, an additional management layer—*group executives*—is added between top management and the division or SBU chiefs. The group executive is thus responsible for the management of a number of similar SBUs, such as housewares, building materials, and auto accessories. Approximately 70% of the Fortune 500 corporations are combining divisions or SBUs around group executives.[5] (For more information on SBUs, refer to Chapter 8.) The divisional structure is appropriate for a firm with many products serving many different markets. It gives the corporation the flexibility it needs to deal with a complex and changeable environment. It can be potentially inefficient, however, if there is much duplication of equipment and support staff. Furthermore, one division can be operating at overcapacity while in another division much of its facilities and staff are idle.

Matrix Structure   In matrix structures, functional and divisional areas are combined *simultaneously* at the same level of the corporation. Employees have two superiors, a project manager and a functional manager. The "home" department—that is, engineering, manufacturing, or sales—is usually functional and is reasonably permanent. People from these functional units are assigned on a temporary basis to one or more project units. The project units act like divisions in that they are differentiated on a product-market basis. Pioneered in the aerospace industry, the matrix structure was developed to combine the stability of the functional structure with the flexibility of a project organization. The matrix structure is very useful when the external environment (especially the technological and market aspects) is very complex and changeable. It does, however, result in conflicts revolving around duties, authority, and resource allocation.

Conglomerate Structure   A variant of a divisional structure organized by product, the conglomerate structure is typically an assemblage of separate firms having different products in different markets but operating together under one corporate umbrella. The divisions are independent of each other but share a dependence on central headquarters for financial resources and corporate planning. Its chief advantages to the corporation lie in the limitation of liability, a possible reduction in taxes, and, for the various divisions, the appearance of autonomy.[6] In addition, risks are spread over many different segments of the marketplace. The disadvantages of conglomerate structure derive from its heavy legalistic and financial orientation. In order to keep the legal advantages, the corporation cannot easily combine divisions to generate operating or marketing synergy. The investment orientation at the corporate level can easily prevent top management from understanding divisional problems in any sense other than financial. Furthermore, the ability to sell off a troubled division can lead to a short-run strategic orientation concerned only with the year-end bottom line.

An understanding of how a particular corporation is structured is very useful when formulating strategy. If the structure is compatible with a proposed change in strategy, it is a corporate strength. If, however, the structure is not compatible with either the present or proposed strategy, it is a definite weakness, and will act to keep the strategy from being implemented properly. Data General, for example, has had some serious problems because its growth strategy was incompatible with its centralized decision-making structure. Opportunities were not grasped quickly enough because all decisions had to be approved by the president.[7] In another example, a study by Fouraker and Stopford revealed that diversified corporations using a divisional structure were more likely to move into foreign operations than were centralized companies using a functional structure.[8]

5.2 CULTURE

A corporation's culture is the collection of beliefs, expectations, and values shared by the corporation's members and transmitted from one generation of employees to another. These create norms (rules of conduct) that define acceptable behavior of people from top management to the operative employee. Myths and rituals, often unrecorded, emerge over time to emphasize certain norms or values and to explain why a certain aspect of the culture is important. Like the retelling of the vision and perseverance of the founder(s) of the corporation, the myth is often tied closely to the corporate mission.

Corporate culture shapes the behavior of people in the corporation. Analysts Schwartz and Davis point this out: "Apparently, the well-run corporations of the world have distinctive cultures that are somehow responsible for their ability to create, implement, and maintain their world leadership positions."[9] Since these cultures have a powerful influence on the behavior of managers, they may strongly affect a corporation's ability to shift its strategic direction. For example, in 1975, the CEOs of two major oil companies changed the strategy of their respective firms from concentration in oil to diversification. They did so because they believed that their current business could neither support long-term growth nor deal with serious political threats. The strategy was announced, and elaborate implementation plans were developed and put into action. By 1980, however, both companies were again firmly concentrating in oil after five years of floundering in attempts to acquire and build new businesses. Both CEOs had been replaced. As *Business Week* reported, "Each of the CEOs had been unable to implement his strategy, not because it was theoretically wrong or bad but because neither had understood that his company's culture was so entrenched in the traditions and values of doing business as oilmen that employees resisted—and sabotaged—the radical changes that the CEOs tried to impose."[10]

Peters and Waterman, in their best-selling book *In Search of Excellence,* argue persuasively that the dominance and coherence of culture is an essential ingredient of the excellent companies they studied.

> The top performers create a broad, shared culture, a coherent framework within which charged-up people search for appropriate adaptations. Their ability to extract extraordinary contributions from very large numbers of people turns on the ability to create a sense of highly valued purpose. Such purpose invariably emanates from love of product, providing top-quality services, and honoring innovation and contribution from all.[11]

Peters and Waterman also state that poorer performing companies tend to have cultures that focus on internal politics instead of the customer and on "the numbers" instead of the product or the people who make it.

A recent study of thirty-four corporations by Denison supports the conclusions of Peters and Waterman. Denison found that companies with participative cultures (i.e., strong employee involvement in corporate decision making) not only have better performance records than those without such a culture, but that the performance difference widens over time. The evidence thus suggests a possible cause and effect relationship between culture and performance.[12]

Corporate culture fulfills several important functions in an organization:

- First, culture conveys a sense of identity for employees;

- Second, culture helps generate commitment by employees to something greater than themselves;

- Third, culture adds to the stability of the organization as a social system; and,

- Fourth, culture serves as a frame of reference for employees to use to make sense out of organization activities and to use as a guide for appropriate behavior.[13]

Corporate culture generally reflects the mission of firms. It gives a corporation a sense of *identity:* "This is who we are. This is what we do. This is what we stand for." The culture includes the dominant orientation of the company.[14] Some companies are *market-oriented.* Like IBM and John Deere they define themselves in terms of their customers and their customers' needs. For example, one of the secrets given for the success of Deere and Company during a period of agricultural recession is its rural roots. Unlike International Harvester, which has its headquarters in downtown Chicago, Deere has its headquarters in East Moline, Illinois, in the heart of an agricultural region responsible for two of the nation's major crops, corn and soybeans. Deere has "geographical awareness, because most of its executives live on a farm or near one . . ."[15] Other companies may be *materials-* or *product-oriented.* They define themselves in terms of the material they work on, the product they make, or the service they provide. As in the example given earlier of the two oil companies, they are first and foremost oil companies, steel companies, railroads, banks, or hospitals. This means that the people working for the company tend to identify themselves in the same way. They don't just work for a company; they *are* truckers, railroaders, bankers. For example, when he left Ford Motor Company, Lee Iacocca stated that he had no interest in pursuing possible offers from International Paper, Lockheed, or Tandy Corporation. Said Iacocca, ". . . cars were in my blood."[16] Other companies are *technology-oriented.* These companies define themselves in terms of the technology they are organized to exploit. Eastman Kodak, for example, ignored the development of xerography because of its strong commitment to the chemical film technology pioneered by George Eastman.[17] Similarly, high-tech firms in Silicon Valley think of themselves primarily as technological entrepreneurs.

An understanding of a corporation's (or division's) culture is thus imperative if the firm is to be managed strategically. A change in mission, objectives, strategies, or policies is not likely to be successful if it is in opposition to the accepted culture of the corporation. As was true for structure, if the culture is compatible with the change, it is an internal strength. But if the corporate culture is not compatible with the change, it is, under circumstances of a changing environment, a serious weakness. This does not mean that a manager should *never* consider a strategy that runs counter to the established culture. However, if such a strategy is to be seriously considered, top management must be prepared to attempt to change the culture as well, a task that will take much time, effort, and persistence.

William Newman, an authority in strategic management, points out that a practical way to develop a master strategy of the corporation is to "pick par-

5.3 RESOURCES

ticular roles or niches that are appropriate in view of competition and the company's resources."[18] Company resources are typically considered in terms of financial, physical, and human resources, as well as organizational systems and technological capabilities. Because these resources have functional significance, we can discuss them under the commonly accepted functional headings of marketing, finance, research and development, manufacturing/operations, human resources, and information systems. These resources, among others, should be audited to ascertain internal strengths and weaknesses.

Corporate-level strategy formulators must be aware of the many contributions each functional area can make to divisional and corporate performance. Functional resources include not only the people in each area but also that area's ability to formulate and implement under corporate guidance functional objectives, strategies, and policies. Thus they include the knowledge of analytical concepts and procedural techniques common to each area and the ability of the people in the area to utilize them effectively. These are some of the most valuable and well-known concepts and techniques: market segmentation, product life cycle, capital budgeting, financial leverage, technological competence, operating leverage, experience curve analysis, job analysis, job design, and decision support systems. There are many others, of course, but these are the basic ones. If used properly, these resources can improve overall strategic management.

Marketing

The primary task of the marketing manager from a corporation's point of view is to regulate the level, timing, and character of demand in a way that will help the corporation achieve its objectives.[19] The marketing manager is the corporation's primary link to the customer and the competition. The manager must therefore be especially concerned with the market position and marketing mix of the firm.

Market position deals with the question, "Who are our customers?" It refers to the selection of specific areas for marketing concentration, and can be expressed in terms of market, product, and geographical locations. Through market research, corporations are able to practice market segmentation with various products or services so that a family of products does not directly compete with each other. For example, Procter & Gamble Company positions Crest as a toothpaste for young children, whereas it positions Gleem as an adult toothpaste.

The *marketing mix* refers to the particular combination of key variables under the corporation's control that can be used to affect demand and to gain competitive advantage. These variables are *product, place, promotion,* and *price.* Within each of these four variables are several subvariables, listed in

Table 5.1   Marketing Mix Variables

Product	Place	Promotion	Price
Quality	Channels	Advertising	List price
Features	Coverage	Personal selling	Discounts
Options	Locations	Sales promotion	Allowances
Style	Inventory	Publicity	Payment periods
Brand name	Transport		Credit terms
Packaging			
Sizes			
Services			
Warranties			
Returns			

SOURCE: Philip Kotler, *Marketing Management: Analysis, Planning, and Control,* 4th ed. (Englewood Cliffs, N.J.: Prentice-Hall, 1980), p. 89. Copyright © 1980. Reprinted by permission of Prentice-Hall, Inc.

Table 5.1, which should be analyzed in terms of their effect upon divisional and corporate performance.

One of the most useful concepts in marketing insofar as strategic management is concerned is that of the *product life cycle*. As depicted in Table 5.2, the product life cycle is a graph showing time plotted against the dollar sales of a product as it moves from introduction through growth and maturity to decline. Table 5.2 lists the functional strategic objective at each developmental stage, as well as appropriate approaches for each stage in terms of design, pricing, promotion, and distribution. This concept enables a marketing manager to examine the marketing mix of a particular product or group of products given its position in its life cycle. Although marketing people agree that different products will have differently shaped life cycles, research concludes that a consideration of the product life cycle is an important factor in strategy formulation.[20]

Finance

The job of the financial manager is the management of funds. The manager must ascertain the best *sources* of funds, *uses* of funds, and *control* of funds. Cash must be raised from internal or external financial sources and allocated for different uses. The flow of funds in the operations of the corporation must be monitored. Benefits must be given to the sources of outside financing in the form of returns, repayments, or products and services. All these tasks must be handled in a way that complements and supports overall corporate strategy.

From a strategic point of view, the financial area should be analyzed to see how well it deals with funds. The mix of externally generated short-term and long-term funds in relation to the amount and timing of internally generated funds should be appropriate to corporate objectives, strategies, and

Table 5.2 Dynamic Competitive Strategy and the Market Life Cycle

	MARKET DEVELOPMENT (Introductory period for high learning products only)	RAPID GROWTH (Normal introductory pattern for a very low learning product)	COMPETITIVE TURBULENCE	SATURATION (MATURITY)	DECLINE
STRATEGY OBJECTIVE	Minimize learning requirements; locate and remedy offering defects quickly; develop widespread awareness of benefits; and gain trial by early adopters.	To establish a strong brand market and distribution niche as quickly as possible.	To maintain and strengthen the market niche achieved through dealer and consumer loyalty.	To defend brand position against competing brands and product category against other potential products, through constant attention to product-improvement opportunities and fresh promotional and distribution approaches.	To milk the offering dry of all possible profit.
OUTLOOK FOR COMPETITION	None is likely to be attracted in the early, unprofitable stages.	Early entrance of numerous aggressive emulators.	Price and distribution squeezes on the industry, shaking out the weaker entrants.	Competition stabilized, with few or no new entrants and market shares not subject to substantial change in the absence of a substantial perceived improvement in some brand.	Similar competition declining and dropping out because of decrease in consumer interest.
PRODUCT DESIGN OBJECTIVE	Limited number of models with physical product and offering designs both focused on minimizing learning requirements. Designs cost-and-use engineered to appeal to most receptive segment. Utmost attention to quality control and quick elimination of market-revealed defects in design.	Modular design to facilitate flexible addition of variants to appeal to every new segment and new use-system as fast as discovered.	Intensified attention to product improvement, tightening up of line to eliminate unnecessary specialties with little market appeal.	A constant alert for market pyramiding opportunities through either bold cost- and price-penetration of new markets or major product changes. Introduction of flanker products. Constant attention to possibilities for product improvement and cost cutting. Reexamination of necessity of design compromises.	Constant pruning of line to eliminate any items not returning a direct profit.

PRICING OBJECTIVE	To impose the minimum of value perception learning and to match the value reference perception of the most receptive segments. High trade discounts and sampling advisable.	A price line for every taste, from low-end to premium models. Customary trade discounts. Aggressive promotional pricing, with prices cut as fast as costs decline due to accumulated production experience. Intensification of sampling.	Increased attention to market-broadening and promotional pricing opportunities.	Defensive pricing to preserve product category franchise. Search for incremental pricing opportunities, including private label contracts, to boost volume and gain an experience advantage.	Maintenance of profit-level pricing with complete disregard of any effect on market share.
PROMOTIONAL GUIDELINES *Communications Objectives*	a) Create widespread awareness and understanding of offering benefits. b) Gain trial by early adopters.	Create and strengthen brand preference among trade and final users. Stimulate general trial.	Maintain consumer franchise, and strengthen dealer ties.	Maintain consumer and trade loyalty, with strong emphasis on dealers and distributors. Promotion of greater use frequency.	Phase out, keeping just enough to maintain profitable distribution.
Most valuable media mix	In order of value: Publicity. Personal Sales. Mass communications.	Mass media. Personal sales. Sales promotions, including sampling. Publicity.	Mass media. Dealer promotions. Personal selling to dealers. Sales promotions. Publicity.	Mass media. Dealer-oriented promotions.	Cut down all media to the bone—use no sales promotions of any kind.
DISTRIBUTION POLICY	Exclusive or selective, with distributor margins high enough to justify heavy promotional spending.	Intensive and extensive, with dealer margins just high enough to keep them interested. Close attention to rapid resupply of distributor stocks and heavy inventories at all levels.	Intensive and extensive, and a strong emphasis on keeping dealer well supplied, but with minimum inventory cost to him/her.	Intensive and extensive, with strong emphasis on keeping dealer well supplied, but at minimum inventory cost to him/her.	Phase out outlets as they become marginal.
INTELLIGENCE FOCUS	To identify actual developing use-systems and to uncover any product weaknesses.	Detailed attention to brand position, to gaps in model and market coverage, and to opportunities for market segmentation.	Close attention to product improvement needs, to market-broadening chances, and to possible fresh promotion themes.	Intensified attention to possible product improvements. Sharp alert for potential new inter-product competition and for signs of beginning product decline.	Information helping to identify the point at which the product should be phased out.

SOURCE: C. R. Wasson, *Dynamic Competitive Strategy and Product Life Cycles*, 3rd ed., (Austin, Tex.: Austin Press, 1978), pp. 256–257. Copyright © 1978 by Chester R. Wasson. Reprinted by permission.

NOTE: Strictly speaking, this is the cycle of the category market, and only a high-learning introduction passes through all the phases indicated above. The term *product life cycle* is sometimes applied indiscriminately to both brand cycles and category cycles. Most new brands are only emulative of other products already on the market, have a much shorter life cycle than the product category, and must follow a strategy similar to any low-learning product.

policies. The concept of *financial leverage* (the ratio of total debt to total assets) is very useful in describing the use of debt to increase the earnings available to common stockholders.[21] Financial leverage can be used to boost earnings per share. Although interest paid on debt reduces taxable income, the higher debt means there are fewer stockholders to share the profits. There are fewer stockholders because the corporation finances its activities by selling bonds or notes instead of stock. The debt, however, gives the firm a higher break-even point than it would have if the firm financed from internally generated funds only. High leverage may therefore be perceived as a corporate strength in times of prosperity and ever-increasing sales, or as a weakness in times of a recession and dropping sales. This is because leverage

Table 5.3   Costs and Benefits of Increasing Financial Leverage

Costs	Benefits
Increased financial risk:	Increased return on investment from an expanded investment program:
• Greater volatility of earnings and stock price	
• Increased probability of financial disruption of existing operations	• Ability to undertake projects with returns greater than the cost of capital
Increased potential for restrictive loan covenants:	• Strengthened competitive position (lower costs, increased product differentiation, higher market share, etc.)
• Reduced flexibility to respond financially to opportunity or competitive threats	
• Reduced autonomy for management	• Increased number of future investment options
Possibility of lower credit rating:	For a given ROI, increased return on equity because of financial leverage
• Higher interest rates	Increased sustainable rate of growth
• If rating falls below "A":	Reduced risk because of stronger competitive position
• Reduced institutional demand for common stock	Lower cost of capital:
• Possibly forced to private placement market during credit crises (to the extent not "insured" by bank lines)	• Tax deductibility of interest
Cost of larger bank lines to ensure against capital unavailability during credit crises	• Repayment of debt with inflated currency
Possible stimulation of excessive investment (i.e., investment in projects with returns less than the cost of capital)	

acts to magnify the effect on earnings *per share* of an increase or decrease in dollar sales. The costs and benefits of increasing financial leverage (that is, increasing the amount of debt used to fund new programs) is shown in Table 5.3.

The knowledge and use of *capital budgeting* techniques is an important financial resource. A good finance department will be able to analyze and rank possible investments in such fixed assets as land, buildings, and equipment in terms of additional outlays a corporation must make as well as the additional receipts that will result. Then it can rank investment proposals on the basis of some accepted criteria or "hurdle rate" (for example, years to pay back investment, rate of return, time to break-even point, etc.) and make a decision.

Break-even analysis is an analytical technique for studying the relations among fixed costs, variable costs, and profits. It is a device for determining the point at which sales will just cover total costs. Figure 5.2 shows a basic break-even chart for a hypothetical company. The chart is drawn on a unit basis, with volume produced shown on the horizontal axis and with costs and revenues measured on the vertical axis. Fixed costs are $80,000, as represented by the horizontal line; variable costs are $2.40 per unit. Total costs rise by $2.40, the amount of the variable costs, for each additional unit produced past $80,000, and the product is sold at $4.00 per unit. The total revenue line is a straight line increasing directly with production. As is usual, the slope of the total revenue line is steeper than that of the total cost line because, for every unit sold, the firm receives $4.00 of revenue for every

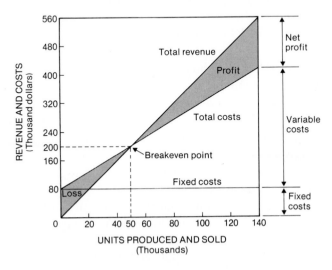

Figure 5.2   **Break-even chart.**

$2.40 paid out for labor and material. Up to the break-even point (the intersection of the total revenue and total cost lines), the firm suffers losses. After that point, the firm earns profits at an increasing amount as volume increases. In this instance, the break-even point for the firm is at a sales and cost level of $200,000 and a production level of 50,000 units.

The financial manager must be very knowledgeable of these and other more sophisticated analytical techniques if management is to implement functional strategies successfully, such as internal financing or leveraged buyouts (discussed in Chapter 7).

Research and Development

The R&D manager is responsible for suggesting and implementing a corporation's technological strategy in light of corporate objectives and policies. The manager's job therefore involves (1) choosing among alternative new technologies to use within the corporation, (2) developing methods of embodying the new technology in new products and processes, and (3) deploying resources so that the new technology can be successfully implemented.[22]

The term *research and development* is used to describe a wide range of activities. In some corporations R&D is conducted by scientists in well-equipped expensive laboratories where the focus is on theoretical problem areas. In other firms, R&D is heavily oriented toward marketing and is concerned with product or product-packaging improvements. In still other firms, R&D takes on an engineering orientation concentrating on quality control, the manufacturing of design specifications, and the development of improved production equipment. Most corporations will have a mix of basic, applied, and engineering R&D. The balance of these types of research is known as the *R&D mix* and should be appropriate to corporate strategy.

A corporation's R&D unit should be evaluated for *technological competence* in both the development and use of innovative technology. Not only should the corporation make a consistent research effort (as measured by reasonably constant corporate expenditures that result in usable innovations), it should also be proficient in managing research personnel and integrating their innovations into its day-to-day operation.

Corporations operating in technology-based industries must be willing to make substantial investments in R&D. For example, the computer and pharmaceutical industries spend an average of 7.2% and 6.7% respectively of their sales dollars for R&D. As shown in Table 5.4 other industries, such as steel and tobacco, spend less than 1%. General Electric, for example, spends a large amount of money on R&D. Michael Carpenter, vice-president of corporate business development and planning at GE, points out that much of the company's growth has developed internally out of its R&D efforts. He

Table 5.4   R&D Industry Expenditures

Industry		Sales (Million Dollars)	Profits (Million Dollars)	R&D Expenses		
				(Million Dollars)	Percent of Sales	Percent of Pretax Profits	Dollars per Employee
Aerospace	[17]	56,023	2,007	2,575	4.6	79.2	4,176
Appliances	[11]	10,304	345	192	1.9	30.7	1,362
Automotive:							
Cars, Trucks	[6]	140,366	5,081	4,906	3.5	61.8	3,968
Parts, Equipment	[15]	10,312	203	186	1.8	49.5	1,400
Building Materials	[16]	12,297	396	172	1.4	25.6	1,474
Chemicals	[44]	112,486	4,039	3,355	3.0	40.0	3,870
Conglomerates	[13]	56,827	2,039	1,480	2.6	43.5	1,840
Containers	[6]	12,900	418	103	0.8	18.9	794
Drugs	[29]	51,411	5,477	3,422	6.7	39.6	5,641
Electrical	[32]	53,648	3,473	1,690	3.2	31.7	2,317
Electronics	[74]	39,114	1,463	1,592	4.1	66.7	2,567
Food & Beverage	[31]	81,376	3,566	657	0.8	10.4	858
Fuel	[19]	387,557	18,578	2,367	0.6	6.1	2,910
Informational Processing:							
Computers	[33]	81,725	7,680	5,853	7.2	43.7	5,958
Office Equipment	[16]	13,686	711	730	5.3	66.4	4,169
Peripherals	[47]	6,461	392	445	6.9	68.3	4,524
Software, Services	[18]	1,962	182	145	7.4	44.9	5,105
Instruments	[66]	16,663	642	894	5.4	87.9	3,372
Leisure Time	[18]	22,343	425	1,133	5.1	110.9	3,978
Machinery:							
Farm, Construction	[19]	20,527	−353	702	3.4	NEG	3,047
Machine Tools, Industrial, Mining	[39]	13,171	51	396	3.0	422.0	2,101
Metals & Mining	[14]	19,968	−380	211	1.1	NEG	1,480
Miscellaneous Manufacturing	[95]	51,935	2,457	1,311	2.5	32.2	1,796
Oil Service & Supply	[23]	31,165	1,124	790	2.5	51.5	2,146
Paper	[15]	30,499	1,175	301	1.0	17.0	1,083
Personal & Home Care Products	[23]	32,031	1,951	789	2.5	22.8	2,869
Semiconductors	[15]	8,830	60	735	8.3	NEG	4,140
Steel	[7]	27,363	−1,974	174	0.6	NEG	803
Telecommunications	[17]	88,050	7,073	1,296	1.5	11.0	2,081
Textiles, Apparel	[14]	9,748	296	75	0.8	14.7	492
Tires, Rubber	[9]	22,786	617	517	2.3	46.0	1,751
Tobacco	[2]	4,816	461	19	0.4	2.2	242
All-Industry Composite	[803]	1,528,300	69,500	39,200	2.6	31.0	2,983

SOURCE: Adapted from "R&D Scoreboard," *Business Week* (July 9, 1984), pp. 65–78.

NOTE: Numbers in brackets represent the number of corporations in that industry grouping.

states: "We spend half as much money each year on R&D as all the money going into the venture capital industry . . . As a result GE has always been at the leading edge of technology."[23] Simply spending money on R&D or new projects does not mean, however, that the money will produce useful results. Between 1950 and 1979, the United States steel industry spent 20% more on plant maintenance and upgrading for each ton of production capacity added or replaced than did the Japanese steel industry. Nevertheless, U.S. steelmakers failed to recognize and adopt two "breakthroughs" in steel-making—the basic oxygen furnace and continuous casting. Their hesitancy to adopt new technology caused them to lose the world steel market.[24]

In addition to money, another important consideration in the effective management of research and development is the time factor. It is generally accepted that the time needed to obtain meaningful profits from the inception of a specific R&D program is typically seven to eleven years.[25] If a corporation is unwilling to invest the large amounts of money and time for its own program of research and development, it may be able to purchase or lease the equipment, techniques, or patents necessary to stay abreast of the competition. Ford Motor Company, for instance, invested $20 million during 1985 in American Robot Corporation in order to gain some manufacturing advantage over General Motors. Ford and American Robot planned to fully automate Ford's new electronic components plant near Toronto by 1987—well before GM would be able to complete a comparable facility. Ford's Chairman Donald E. Petersen reported that similar investments may follow: "If the best way to get technology is through acquisitions, we have an open-door policy."[26]

Those corporations that do purchase an innovative technology must, nevertheless, have the technological competence to make good use of it. Unfortunately, some corporations introduce the latest technology into their processes without adequately assessing the competence of their organization to handle it. For example, the U.S. Navy contracted with Tano Corporation to replace the existing manually operated propulsion controls of five amphibious assault vessels (at a cost of $6 million per ship) with new automatic, computer-controlled, electro-pneumatic systems. When in place the systems failed to operate as planned. A few months after installation, the Navy was forced to spend $30 million to have Tano take out the new automatic systems on all five ships and to replace them with the previously used manual systems. According to an executive from Tano, the removal was "a very unfortunate situation for us. We assumed that a certain level of technicians would be on the ships to operate this equipment. They weren't."[27]

The R&D manager must determine when to abandon present technology and when to develop or adopt new technology. After several years of studying progress and patterns in various technologies, Richard Foster of McKinsey and Company states that the displacement of one technology by another (*Technological Discontinuity*) is a frequent and strategically important phenomenon. For each technology within a given field or industry, the plotting of product performance against research effort/expenditures on a graph results in an S-shaped curve. Foster describes the process depicted in Fig. 5.3.

> Early in the development of the technology a knowledge base is being built and progress requires a relatively large amount of effort. Later, progress comes more easily. And then, as the limits of that technology are approached, progress becomes slow and expensive. *That* is when R&D dollars should be allocated to technology with more potential. That is also—not so incidentally—when a competitor who has bet on a new technology can sweep away your business or topple an entire industry.[28]

The presence of such a *technological discontinuity* in the world's steel industry during the 1960s may explain why the large capital expenditures by U.S. steel companies failed to keep them competitive with the Japanese firms adopting the new technologies. As Foster points out: "History has shown that as one technology nears the end of its S-curve, competitive leadership in a market generally changes hands."[29] The conclusion is that the

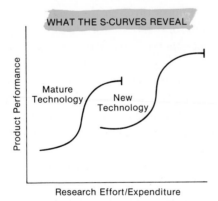

WHAT THE S-CURVES REVEAL

Product Performance (y-axis)

Mature Technology

New Technology

Research Effort/Expenditure (x-axis)

In the corporate planning process, it is generally assumed that incremental progress in technology will occur. But past developments in a given technology cannot be extrapolated into the future, because every technology has its limits. The key to competitiveness is to determine when to shift resources to a technology with more potential.

Figure 5.3 **Technological discontinuity.**
SOURCE: P. Pascarella, "Are You Investing in the Wrong Technology?" *Industry Week* (July 25, 1983), p. 38. Copyright © 1983 by Penton/IPC. All rights reserved. Reprinted by permission.

essence of managing technology well is the ability and willingness of all concerned to make timely transitions to new technologies.

Manufacturing/ Service

If the corporation is in business to transform tangible raw materials, like iron ore or petroleum, into usable products, like automobiles, machine parts, or plastic raincoats, the transformation process can be called *manufacturing*. If, however, the corporation is in the business of using people's skills and knowledge, such as those of doctors, lawyers, or loan officers, to provide services via hospitals, legal clinics, or banks, the work involved may be called *service*. These functions can be found in any corporation producing and providing either a tangible product or an intangible service. Many of the key concepts and techniques popularly used in manufacturing can therefore be applied to service businesses.

The primary task of the manufacturing or service manager is to develop and operate a system that will produce the required number of products or services, with a certain quality, at a given cost, within an allotted time. However, manufacturing plants vary significantly depending on the type of product made. In very general terms, manufacturing may be intermittent or continuous. In *intermittent systems* (job shops), the item normally goes through a sequential process, but the work and sequence of the process vary. At each center, the tasks determine the details of processing and the time required for them: "Work flows through the system in batches or special orders and commonly waits for a time before being processed at service facilities required by the products."[30] In contrast, *continuous systems* are those laid out as lines on which products can be assembled or processed. An example is an automobile assembly line.

The type of manufacturing system used by a corporation determines divisional or corporate strategy. It makes no sense, for example, to plan to increase sales by saturating the market with low-priced products if the corporation's manufacturing process was designed as an intermittent "job shop" system that now produces one-time-only products to a customer's specifications. Conversely, a plan to produce a number of specialty products may not be economically feasible if the manufacturing process was designed to be a mass-producing, continuous system using low-skilled labor or special purpose robots.

Continuous systems are popular because they allow a corporation to take advantage of manufacturing *operating leverage*. According to Weston and Brigham, "The degree of operating leverage is the percentage change in operating income that results from a percentage change in units sold."[31] For example, a highly labor-intensive firm has little automated machinery and thus a small amount of fixed costs. It has a fairly low break-even point, but its variable cost line has a relatively steep slope. Since most of the costs associated with the product are variable (many employees earning piece rate wages), its variable costs are higher than those of automated firms. Its advantage over other firms is that it can operate at low levels and still be profitable. Once it reaches break-even, however, the huge variable costs as a percentage of total costs keep the profit per unit at a relatively low level. Its low operating leverage prevents it from gathering the huge profits possible from a high volume of sales. In terms of strategy, this firm should look for a niche in the marketplace where it can produce and sell a reasonably small quantity of goods.

In contrast, a capital-intensive firm has a lot of money in fixed investments, such as automated processes and highly sophisticated machinery. Its labor force is relatively small but highly skilled, earning salaries rather than piece-rate wages. Consequently, it has a high amount of fixed costs. It also has a relatively high break-even point, but its variable cost line rises slowly. Its advantage over other firms is that once it reaches break-even, its profits rise faster than do those of less automated firms. In terms of strategy, this firm needs to find a high-demand niche in the marketplace where it can produce and sell a large quantity of goods. Its high operating leverage makes it an extremely profitable and competitive firm once it reaches its high break-even point. Changes in the level of sales have a magnified (leveraged) impact on profits. In times of recession, however, it is likely to suffer huge losses. During an economic downturn, the firm with less automation and thus less leverage is more likely to survive comfortably, since a drop in sales primarily affects variable costs. It is often easier to lay off labor than to sell off specialized plants and machines.

In terms of a service business, operations may also be continuous or intermittent. Continuous operations describe fairly similar services provided to the *same* clientele over a period of time (such as patients in a long-term care hospital), whereas intermittent operations describe somewhat different services provided to *different* clientele over a period of time (such as once-a-year auditing or income tax counseling by a CPA firm). Service firms that use continuous operations may be able to use operating leverage by substituting diagnostic machinery or videotape machines for highly paid professional personnel. Those using batch or intermittent operations may be able to substitute lower-paid support personnel for some of the more routine services performed by highly paid professionals.

A conceptual framework that many large corporations have used successfully is the *experience curve*.[32] The concept applied to manufacturing is that unit production costs decline by some fixed percentage (commonly 20%–30%) each time the total accumulated volume of production in units doubles. The actual percentage varies by industry and is based upon the time it takes a person to learn a new task, scale economies, product and process improvements, lower raw materials costs, and other variables. For example, in an industry where an 85% experience curve can be expected, a corporation might expect a 15% reduction in costs for every doubling of volume. The total costs per unit (adjusted for inflation) can be expected to drop from $100 when the total production is 10 units, to $85 ($100 × 85%) when production increases to 20 units, and to $72.25 ($85 × 85%) when it reaches 40 units.[33] To achieve these results often means making investments in R&D and fixed assets, thus resulting in higher operating leverage and less flexibility. Nevertheless, the manufacturing strategy is one of building capacity ahead of demand in order to achieve the lower unit costs of the experience curve. Price the product or service very low on the basis of some future point on the experience curve so as to preempt competition and increase market demand. The resulting high number of units sold and high market share should result in high profits given the low unit costs.[34] This idea of using the anticipated experience curve to price low in order to gain high market share and thus high profits underlies the Boston Consulting Group's portfolio matrix (discussed in Chapter 6).

The experience curve concept is commonly used in estimating the production costs of (1) a product never before made with the present techniques and processes or (2) current products produced by newly introduced techniques or processes. The concept was first applied in the airframe industry and may be applied in the service industry as well. While many firms have used experience curves extensively, an unquestioning acceptance of the industry norm (such as 80% for the airframe industry or 70% for integrated circuits) is very risky. The experience curve for an industry may not hold for a particular corporation for a variety of reasons.[35]

Recently, the use of large mass-production facilities to take advantage of experience curve economies has been criticized. The introduction of CAD/CAM (computer-assisted design and computer-assisted manufacturing) with robot technology means shorter learning times and the ability to economically manufacture products in small customized batches. Emphasizing *economies of scope* over *economies of scale,* a number of firms have introduced "flexible manufacturing."[36] The new flexible factories permit low-volume output of custom-tailored products at a profit. It is thus possible to have the cost advantages of continuous systems with the customer-oriented advantages of intermittent systems. For example, Deere's new tractor assembly plant in Waterloo, Iowa, can produce more than 5,000 variations of its tractors to suit its customers' needs.[37]

Human Resources   The primary task of the manager of human resources is to improve the match between individuals and jobs. The quality of this match influences job performance, employee satisfaction, and employee turnover.[38] Consequently, human resource management (HRM) is concerned with the selection and training of new employees, appraisal of employee performance, the assessment of employees' promotion potential, and recruitment and personnel planning for the future. HRM is also highly involved in wage and salary administration, labor negotiations, job design, and employee morale.

A good HRM department should be competent in the use of attitude surveys and other feedback devices to assess employee satisfaction with their jobs and with the corporation as a whole. HRM managers should also be knowledgeable in *job analysis* and competent in its use. Job analysis is a means of obtaining information for job descriptions about what needs to be accomplished by each job in terms of quality and quantity. Up-to-date job descriptions are essential not only for proper employee selection, appraisal, training, and development; wage and salary administration; and labor negotiations—but also for summarizing the human resources of a corporation in terms of employee-skill categories. Just as a corporation must know the number, type, and quality of its manufacturing facilities, it also must know the kinds of people it employs and the skills they possess. This knowledge is essential for the formulation and implementation of corporate strategy. The best strategies are meaningless if employees do not have the skills to carry them out or if jobs cannot be designed to accommodate the available workers. Honeywell, Inc., for example, uses *talent surveys* to ensure that it has the right mix of talents to implement its planned strategies.[39]

A good human resource manager should be able to work closely with the unions if the corporation is unionized. A recent development is the increasing desire by union leaders to work jointly with management in formulating and implementing strategic changes. For example, when General Electric announced its intention to close its Charleston, South Carolina, steam turbine generator plant in 1985, the United Electrical Workers proposed to management eleven alternative products the plant could produce. To save jobs, other unions are making the same argument. Jerome M. Rosow, president of the Work in America Institute, states that the involvement of union leaders in business decision making is a "major breakthrough which has great potential for improving the competitive edge of those companies."[40]

Human resource departments have found that to reduce employee dissatisfaction and unionization efforts (or conversely, to improve employee satisfaction and existing union relations), they must consider the *quality of work life* (QWL) in the design of jobs. Partially a reaction to the traditionally heavy emphasis upon technical and economic factors in job design, QWL emphasizes the human dimension of work. Corporations such as General Motors, General Foods, Procter & Gamble, Cummins Engine, and Shell Canada, Ltd., have been involved actively in improving QWL through extensive job and plant redesigning.[41] In general, quality of work life is "the degree to which members of a work organization are able to satisfy important personal needs through their experiences in the organization."[42] The knowledgeable human resource manager should therefore be able to improve the corporation's quality of work life by (1) introducing participative problem solving, (2) restructuring work, (3) introducing innovative reward systems, and (4) improving the work environment.[43] This will lead to hopefully a more participative corporate culture and thus higher performance.

The quality of work life becomes especially important in today's world of global communication and transportation systems. Advances in technology are copied almost immediately by competitors around the world. People, however, are not as willing to move to other companies in other countries. It is therefore argued that the only long-term resource advantage remaining to a corporation lies in the area of human resources. Paul Hagusa, president of the American subsidiary of Sharp Corporation of Japan, makes this point very clearly.

> Once there was a time when the Americans had very efficient machines and equipment, and Japan did not. At that time—regardless of the workers—those with the most modern machines had the competitive advantage. But now, one country soon has the same machinery as another. So, what makes the difference today is the quality of the people.[44]

Information Systems

The primary task of the management of information systems (MIS) department is to design and manage the information flow of the corporation in order to improve productivity and decision making. Information must be collected, stored, and synthesized in such a manner that it will answer important operating and strategic questions. This function is growing in importance for three reasons: (1) Corporations are growing in size and complexity. Managers must increasingly rely on second-hand, written information. (2) As corporations become more dispersed and decentralized, more sophisticated control techniques are needed to ensure that managers are operating according to agreed plans. (3) The widespread application and increasing low cost of the computer make it an ideal aid to information processing.[45]

Information systems can fulfill four major purposes.[46]

- *Provide a basis for analyzing early warning signals that can originate both externally and internally.* Any information system has a database. Like a library, the system collects, categorizes, and files the data so that the system can be used by other departments in the corporation.

- *Automate routine clerical operations.* Payroll, inventory reports, and other records can be generated automatically from the database and thus reduce the need for fileclerks.

- *Assist managers in making routine (programmed) decisions.* Scheduling orders, assigning orders to machines, and reordering supplies are routine tasks which can be automated through a detailed analysis of the company's work flow.

- *Provide the information necessary to make strategic (nonprogrammed) decisions.* Increasingly, personal computers coupled with sophisticated software are being used to analyze large amounts of information and to calculate likely payoffs from alternate strategies. In order to fulfill this purpose, decision suport systems are needed which allow more interaction by the user with the computer.

In assessing the corporation's strengths and weaknesses, it is important to note the level of development of the firm's information system. There are at least four distinct stages of development.[47] These are depicted in Table 5.5. Stage one, *initiation,* generally involves accounting applications. The information systems personnel are computer technicians who work to reduce clerical costs. Stage two, *growth,* emerges as applications spread beyond accounting into production and marketing. People now use the system to process information like budgets and sales forecasts. Stage three, *moratorium,* is a consolidation phase and calls for a stop to new applications. The spread of information systems is matched by increasing frustration in attempting to use it and by concern over the large costs of operating the system. Stage four, *integration,* stresses the acceptance of information systems as a major activity that must be integrated into the total corporation. Decision support systems are now developed to aid managers at all levels of the corporation. A stage-four system is a significant internal strength for a corporation.

The requirements of a well-designed information system include the following:[48]

1. The system must focus managers' attention on the critical success factors in their jobs.

2. The system must present information that is accurate and of high quality.

3. The system must provide the necessary information when it is needed to those who most need it.

4. The system must process raw data so that it can be presented in a manner useful to the manager.

A corporation's information system can be a strength in all three elements of strategic management: formulation, implementation, and evaluation and control. For example, it can not only aid in environmental scanning

Table 5.5   Stages of Development of Information Systems

	Stage One *Initiation*	Stage Two *Growth*	Stage Three *Moratorium*	Stage Four *Integration*
Application Focus	Accounting and cost reduction	Expansion of applications in many functional areas	Halt on new applications; emphasis on control	Integrating existing systems into the organization; decision support systems
Example Applications	Accounts payable, accounts receivable, payroll, billing	*Stage one plus:* cash flow, budgeting, forecasting, personnel inventory, sales, inventory control	*Stage two plus:* purchasing control, production scheduling	*Stage three plus:* simulation models, financial planning models, on-line personnel query system
MIS Staffing	Primarily computer experts and other skilled professionals	User-oriented system analysts and programmers	Entry of functional managers into MIS unit	Balance of technical and management specialists
Location of MIS in Structure	Embedded in accounting department	Growth in size of staff, still in accounting area	Separate MIS unit reporting to head financial officer	Same as stage three, or decentralization into divisions
What Top Management Wants from MIS	Speed computations with a reduction in clerical staff	Broader applications into operational areas	Concern over MIS costs and usefulness	Acceptance as a major organizational function, involved in planning and control
User Attitudes	Uncertainty; hands-off approach; anxiety over applications	Somewhat enthusiastic; minimum involvement in system design	Frustration and dissatisfaction over developed systems; concern over costs of developing and operating systems	Acceptance of MIS in their work; involvement in system design, implementation, and operation

and in controlling a corporation's many activities, it can also be used as a strategic weapon to gain competitive advantage. For example, American Hospital Supply (AHS), a leading manufacturer and distributor of a broad line of products for doctors, laboratories, and hospitals, has developed an order entry-distribution system that directly links the majority of its customers to AHS computers. The system has been successful because it simplifies ordering processes for customers, reduces costs for both AHS and the customer, and allows AHS to provide pricing incentives to the customer. As a result, customer loyalty is high and AHS's share of the market has become large.[49] Other examples are the automated reservations systems American Airlines and United Airlines make available to travel agents. Since the reservations systems feature either American or United most prominently in the listings, other airlines complain that American and United have an unfair advantage in attracting customers. The advantage appears to be real given that American and United have successfully obtained 65% of the market in automated reservations systems.[50]

5.4 SUMMARY AND CONCLUSION

Before strategies can be developed, top management needs to assess its internal corporate environment for strengths and weaknesses. It must have an in-depth understanding of the internal strategic factors, such as the corporation's structure, culture, and resources.

A corporation's *structure* is its anatomy. It is often described graphically with an organization chart. Corporate structures range from the simple structure of an owner-manager operated business to the complex series of structures of a large conglomerate. If compatible with present and potential strategies, a corporation's structure is a great internal strength. Otherwise, it may be a serious weakness that will either prevent a good strategy from being implemented properly or reduce the number of strategic alternatives available to a firm.

A corporation's *culture* is the collection of beliefs, expectations, and values shared by its members. A culture produces norms that shape the behavior of employees. Top management must be aware of this culture and include it in its assessment of strategic factors. Those strategies that run counter to an established corporate culture are likely to be doomed by the poor motivation of the workforce. If a culture is antagonistic to a strategy change, the implementation plan will also have to include plans to change the culture.

A corporation's *resources* include not only such generally recognized assets as people, money, and facilities, but also those analytical concepts and procedural techniques known and in use within the functional areas. Since most top managers view their corporations in terms of functional activities, it is simplest to assess resource strengths and weaknesses by functional area. Each area should be audited in tems of financial, physical, and human resources, as well as its organization and technological competencies and capabilities. Just as the knowledge of key functional concepts and techniques is a corporate strength, its absence is a weakness.

DISCUSSION QUESTIONS

1. In what ways can a corporation's structure act as an internal strength or weakness to those formulating corporate strategies?

2. Why should top management be aware of a corporation's culture?

3. What kind of internal factors help determine whether a firm should emphasize the production and sales of a large number of low-priced products or a small number of high-priced products?

4. What is the difference between operating and financial leverage? What are their implications to strategic planning?

5. Why is technological competence important in strategy formulation?

6. How can a knowledge of technological discontinuity help to improve a corporation's efficiency?

7. What are the pros and cons of using the experience curve to determine strategy?

8. Why should MIS be considered when analyzing a corporation's strengths and weaknesses?

NOTES

1. R. N. Osborn, J. G. Hunt, and L. R. Jauch, *Organization Theory: An Integrated Approach* (New York: John Wiley & Sons, 1980), p. 274.

2. R. H. Miles, *Macro Organizational Behavior* (Santa Monica, Calif.: Goodyear Publishing, 1980), pp. 28–34.

3. Osborn, Hunt, and Jauch, pp. 288–289.

4. M. Leontiades, "A Diagnostic Framework for Planning," *Strategic Management Journal* (January–March 1983), p. 14.

5. J. M. Stengrevics, "Managing the Group Executive's Job," *Organization Dynamics* (Winter 1984), p. 21.

6. Osborn, Hunt and Jauch, p. 293.

7. "Data General's Management Trouble," *Business Week* (February 9, 1981), pp. 59–61.

8. L. E. Fouraker and J. M. Stopford, "Organization Structure and the Multinational Strategy," *Administrative Science Quarterly* (June 1968), pp. 47–64.

9. H. Schwartz and S. M. Davis, "Matching Corporate Culture and Business Strategy," *Organizational Dynamics* (Summer 1981), p. 30.

10. "Corporate Culture," *Business Week* (October 27, 1980), p. 148.

11. T. J. Peters and R. H. Waterman, Jr., *In Search of Excellence* (New York: Harper & Row, 1982), pp. 293–294.

12. D. R. Denison, "Bringing Corporate Culture to the Bottom Line," *Organizational Dynamics* (Autumn 1984), pp. 5–22.

13. L. Smircich, "Concepts of Culture and Organizational Analysis," *Administrative Science Quarterly* (September 1983), pp. 345–346.

14. S. C. Wheelwright, "Manufacturing Strategy: Defining the Missing Link," *Strategic Management Journal* (January–March 1984), p. 79.

15. D. Muhm, "John Deere's Company: 145 Years of Farming History," *Des Moines Register* (November 11, 1984), p. 2F.

16. L. Iacocca, *Iacocca: An Autobiography* (Toronto: Bantam Books, 1984), p. 141.

17. T. Moore, "Embattled Kodak Enters the Electronic Era," *Fortune* (August 22, 1983), pp. 120–130.

18. W. H. Newman, "Shaping the Master Strategy of Your Firm," *California Management Review*, vol. 9, no. 3 (1967), p. 77.

19. P. Kotler, *Marketing Management,* 4th ed. (Englewood Cliffs, N.J.: Prentice-Hall, 1980), p. 22.

20. C. A. Anderson and C. P. Zeithaml, "Stage of the Product Life Cycle, Business Strategy, and Business Performance," *Academy of Management Journal* (March 1984), p. 22.

21. J. F. Weston and E. F. Brigham, *Managerial Finance,* 7th ed. (Hinsdale, Ill.: Dryden Press, 1981), pp. 555–569.

22. M. A. Maidique and P. Patch, "Corporate Strategy and Technological Policy" (Boston: Intercollegiate Case Clearing House, no. 9-769-033, 1978, rev. March 1980), p. 3.

23. R. J. Allio, "G.E. = Giant Entrepreneur?" *Planning Review* (January 1985), p. 21.

24. T. F. O'Boyle, "Steel's Management Has Itself to Blame," *Wall Street Journal* (May 17, 1983), p. 32.

25. E. F. Finkin, "Developing and Managing New Products," *Journal of Business Strategy* (Spring 1983), p. 45.

26. R. Brandt, M. Rothman, and A. Gabor, "Will Ford Beat GM in the Robot Race?" *Business Week* (May 27, 1985), p. 44.

27. "Navy Scraps $6 Million Computer Systems Sailors Couldn't Operate" (Charlottesville, Va.) *Daily Progress* (April 22, 1981), p. B11.

28. P. Pascarella, "Are You Investing in the Wrong Technology?" *Industry Week* (July 25, 1983), p. 37.

29. Pascarella, p. 38.

30. E. S. Buffa, *Modern Production/Operations Management,* 6th ed. (New York: John Wiley & Sons, 1980), p. 487.

31. Weston and Brigham, p. 231.

32. Buffa, p. 48.

33. A. C. Hax and N. S. Majuf, "Competitive Cost Dynamics: The Experience Curve," in A. C. Hax (ed.), *Readings on Strategic Management* (Cambridge, Mass.: Ballinger Publishing Co., 1984), pp. 49–60.

34. B. D. Henderson, *Henderson on Corporate Strategy* (Cambridge, Mass.: Abt Books, 1979), p. 11.

35. R. B. Chase and N. J. Aquilano, *Production and Operations Management,* rev. ed. (Homewood, Ill.: Richard D. Irwin, Inc., 1977), pp. 526–531.

36. J. D. Goldhar and M. Jelinek, "Plan for Economies of Scope," *Harvard*

Business Review (November–December 1983), pp. 141–148.
G. G. Anderson, "Planning for Restructured Competition," *Long Range Planning* (February 1985), p. 27.

37. J. Holusa, "Deere & Co. Leads the Way in 'Flexible' Manufacturing," *Des Moines Register* (January 29, 1984), p. 10F.

38. H. G. Heneman, D. P. Schwab, J. A. Fossum, and L. D. Dyer, *Personnel/Human Resource Management* (Homewood, Ill.: Richard D. Irwin, Inc., 1980), p. 7.

39. N. Tichy, "Conversation with Edson W. Spencer and Foster A. Boyle," *Organization Dynamics* (Spring 1983), p. 30.

40. J. Hoerr, "Now Unions Are Helping to Run the Business," *Business Week* (December 24, 1984), p. 69.
"A Bold Tactic to Hold On to Jobs," *Business Week* (October 29, 1984), pp. 70–72.

41. E. F. Huse, *Organization Development and Change,* 2nd ed. (St. Paul, Minn.: West Publishing Co., 1980), pp. 236–244.

42. J. L. Suttle, "Improving Life at Work—Problems and Perspectives," *Improving Life at Work: Behavioral Science Approaches to Organizational Change,* eds. J. R. Hackman and J. L. Suttle (Santa Monica, Calif.: Goodyear Publishing, 1976), p. 4.

43. D. A. Nadler and E. E. Lawler III, "Quality of Work Life: Perspectives and Directions," *Organization Dynamics* (Winter 1983), p. 27.

44. L. E. Calonius, "In a Plant in Memphis, Japanese Firm Shows How to Attain Quality," *Wall Street Journal* (April 29, 1983), p. 14.

45. R. F. Neuschel, *Management Systems for Profit and Growth* (New York: McGraw-Hill, 1976), p. 270.

46. R. G. Murdick, *MIS: Concepts and Designs* (Englewood Cliffs, N.J.: Prentice-Hall, 1980), p. 253.

47. R. L. Nolan, "Controlling the Costs of Data Services," *Harvard Business Review* (July–August 1977), p. 117.

48. R. H. Gregory and R. L. Van Horn, "Value and Cost of Information," in J. D. Cougar and R. W. Knapp (eds.), *Systems Analysis Techniques* (New York: Wiley, 1974), pp. 473–489.

49. R. I. Benjamin, J. F. Rockart, M. S. S. Morton, and J. Wyman, "Information Technology: A Strategic Opportunity," *Sloan Management Review* (Spring 1984), p. 5.

50. "Business Is Turning Data into a Potent Strategic Weapon," *Business Week* (August 22, 1983), p. 92.

PART THREE

STRATEGY FORMULATION

Chapter 6

STRATEGY FORMULATION: SITUATION ANALYSIS

STRATEGIC MANAGEMENT MODEL

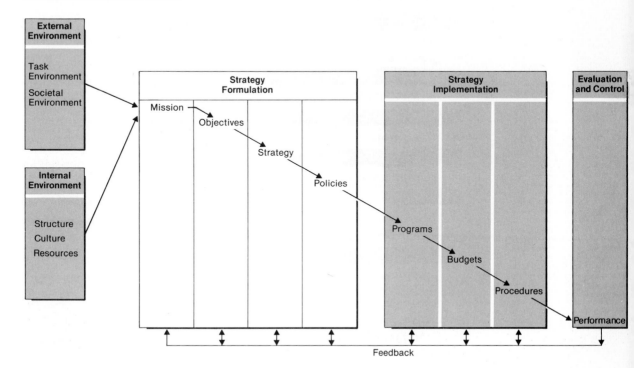

Strategy formulation is often referred to as strategic planning or long-range planning. Regardless of the term used, the process is primarily analytical, not action-oriented. The basic Strategic Management Model, shown first in Chapter 1, reflects the distinction between strategy formulation and strategy implementation. As shown in the model, the formulation process is concerned with developing a corporation's *mission, objectives, strategy,* and *policies.* In order to do this, corporate strategy makers must scan both the *external* and *internal environments* for needed information on strategic factors.

The Strategic Management Model does not show how the formulation process occurs. It merely describes the key *input variables* (internal and external environments) and the key *output factors* (mission, objectives, strategy, and policies). Chapters 6 and 7 therefore provide a more detailed discussion of the key activities in the process in order to supplement the Strategic Management Model.

In Chapter 2, a strategic decision-making process was introduced as a graphic representation of the strategic audit. It is also included in this chapter as Fig. 6.1.

The first six steps commonly found in strategy formulation are a series of interrelated activities:

1. *Evaluation* of (a) the corporation's current performance results in terms of return on investment, profitability, etc., and (b) the corporation's current mission, objectives, strategies, and policies.

2. *Examination* and *evaluation* of the corporation's strategic managers—board of directors and top management.

3. *Scanning* of the *external* environment to locate strategic opportunities and threats.

4. *Scanning* of the *internal* corporate environment to determine strategic strengths and weaknesses.

5. *Analysis* of the strategic factors from steps 3 and 4 to (a) pinpoint problem areas and (b) review and revise the corporate mission and objectives as necessary.

6. *Generation, evaluation,* and *selection* of the best alternative strategy appropriate to the analysis conducted in step 5.

Situation analysis is the first part of the strategy formulation process. Beginning with an evaluation of current performance and ending with the review and possible revision of mission and objectives, the process includes steps one through five. These steps are discussed in this chapter. Step six,

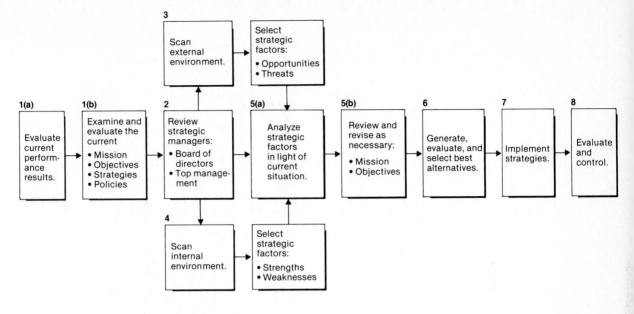

NOTE: Steps 1 through 6 are *strategy formulation.*
Step 7 is *strategy implementation.*
Step 8 is *evaluation and control.*

Figure 6.1   Strategic decision-making process.

the generation, evaluation, and selection of the best alternative strategy, is discussed in Chapter 7.

6.1 EVALUATION OF CURRENT RESULTS

After much research, Henry Mintzberg found that strategy formulation is typically not a regular, continuous process: "It is most often an irregular, discontinuous process, proceeding in fits and starts. There are periods of stability in strategy development, but also there are periods of flux, of groping, of piecemeal change, and of global change."[1] This view of strategy formulation as an irregular process may be explained by the tendency of most people to continue on a particular course of action until something goes wrong. In a business corporation, the stimulus for a strategy review lies, in most instances, in current performance results.

Performance results are generally periodic measurements of developments that occur during a given time period. At the corporate level, for example, the board and top management would be most concerned with overall measurements such as return on investment (ROI), profits after taxes, and earnings per share. The measurements for the current year would be compared to similar measurements from previous years to see whether a trend exists. At the business or divisional level, the manager might be concerned with the return on division assets or the net contribution to corporate profits. At the functional level, various managers would be concerned with total sales and market share, plant efficiency, or number of new patents.

Current performance results are compared with current objectives (desired results). If the results are equal to or greater than current objectives, most strategic managers are likely to assume that current strategies and policies are appropriate, as is. In this instance, only incremental changes to present objectives and strategy are likely to be recommended. The strategy formulation process may thus end rather abruptly with a summary statement suggesting that the corporation continue doing what it's already doing— only do it a little better next year. This is basically what occurred at Coca Cola Company a number of years ago. Hugh Schwarz, director of corporate planning at that time for Coca Cola, stated:

> If a person is happy with the present situation, he will not want to change. The very success of The Coca Cola Company works against its planning for change.[2]

If, however, the results of performance are less than what is desired, the formulation process begins in earnest. People at all levels are urged by the board and top management to question present objectives, strategies, and policies. Even the mission may be questioned. Are we aiming too high? Do our strategies make sense? Environmental scanning of both internal and external variables begins. What went wrong? Why? Questions such as these prompt top management to review the corporation's mission, objectives, strategies, and policies. Certainly Coca Cola's top management spent many hours during 1985 agonizing over their decision to change the traditional flavor of "Coke" to improve the brand's deteriorating market position. As discussed in Illustrative Example 6.1, General Foods Corporation and H&R Block both used a deteriorating situation to stimulate a strategy review.

EVALUATING CURRENT PERFORMANCE RESULTS: GENERAL FOODS AND H&R BLOCK

Illustrative Example 6.1

GENERAL FOODS CORPORATION

James Ferguson, CEO of General Foods, noticed in 1981 increasing stagnation in several of General Foods' businesses, such as cereals and pet foods. Even though General Foods' earnings had been increasing at an average annual rate over the last five years of 17%, the increase had come at the expense of product innovation and diversification. The corporation generated only enough new products between 1974 and 1980 to add $375 million to revenues in the 1980–81 fiscal year. Executive vice-president

(Continued)

Philip Smith commented, "Against a mass of $7 billion [estimated sales for the fiscal year ending March 31, 1981], $375 million is an inadequate addition." General Foods' top management reported that it wanted to make its businesses grow at a rate of 2 to 3% over time rather than the industry average of 1% per year. As a result, it began to develop a series of strategies focusing on diversification and growth.

H&R BLOCK

Founded by Henry and Richard Bloch in 1955, the Kansas City, Missouri-based H&R Block (spelled with a "k" to avoid mispronunciation) has built a very successful business out of helping people to complete their income tax forms. The company prepared 10% of all returns filed in the United States, so top management was concerned to see its growth in tax preparing level off and begin to decline in 1981. The number of forms processed by Block fell 3% from 1982 to 1983—the year the much simplified Form 1040EZ was introduced. The company was able to stay profitable chiefly by increasing prices. Nevertheless, its 1.6% (in 1982) and 6.5% (in 1983) increases in profits were far below the 15% annual growth goal set by Henry Bloch.

Believing that the company had reached a saturation point in its basic business, management decided that it had to do other things if the firm was to recapture its earlier profit growth rate. To become more than just a tax preparer, H&R Block decided to diversify into computer information services, employment services for temporary health and clerical workers, and legal advisory services. "You can't stand still," commented Jerome Grossman, executive vice president and chief operating officer. "You are either moving forward or going backward. This is an attempt to move forward."

SOURCES: "Changing the Culture at General Foods," *Business Week* (March 30, 1981), pp. 136–140. "Simpler Tax Forms Force H&R Block to Become Much More Than a Tax Preparer," *Des Moines Register* (April 22, 1984), p. 8F.

Evaluation of Mission

The breadth or narrowness of the corporate mission has an important effect upon performance.[3] The definition of the corporate mission determines the broad limits of a company's growth.[4] For example, amusement parks traditionally defined themselves as in-place carnivals. After floundering in the 1950s, many such businesses went bankrupt. The success of Disneyland in the 1960s caused many parks such as Cedar Point, Inc. in Sandusky, Ohio to redefine themselves as "theme" parks with entertainment "packages" of shows, rides, and nationally known performers. With the aging of the American population, that mission is being further broadened to include a wider spectrum of entertainment, including golf courses.

The concept of a corporate mission implies that throughout a corporation's many activities there should be a *common thread* or unifying theme and that those corporations with such a common thread are better able to direct and administer their many activities.[5] In acquiring new firms or in developing new products, such a corporation looks for "strategic fit," that is, the likelihood that new activities will mesh with present ones in such a way that the corporation's overall effectiveness and efficiency will be increased. There may be common distribution channels or similar customers, warehousing economies or the mutual use of R&D, better use of managerial talent or any of a number of possible synergistic effects.[6]

Evaluation of Objectives

As pointed out in Chapter 4, each stakeholder in a corporation's task environment will have its own way of measuring the corporation's performance. Stockholders may want dividends and price appreciation, whereas unions want good wages, stability of employment, and opportunities for advancement. Customers, distributors, creditors, suppliers, local communities, and other governments, to name only a few, have their own criteria to judge the corporation. The objectives and the priorities attached to them by the corporation are one way to recognize these outside forces and to deal with them in a logical fashion. Some of the possible objectives a corporation might pursue are the following:

- Profitability (net profits)

- Efficiency (low costs, etc.)

- Growth (increase in total assets, sales, etc.)

- Shareholder wealth (dividends plus stock price appreciation)

- Utilization of resources (ROE or ROI)

- Contributions to customers (quality/price)

- Contributions to employees (employment security, wages)

- Contributions to society (taxes paid, participation in charities)

- Market leadership (market share, reputation)

- Technological leadership (innovations, creativity)

- Survival (avoiding bankruptcy)

- Personal needs of top management (using the firm for personal purposes, such as providing jobs for relatives)

It is likely, however, that many small corporations have no formal objectives; rather, they have vague, verbal ones. It is even more likely that even though a corporation has specified, written objectives, they will not be ranked on the basis of priority.

Just as a number of firms have no formal objectives, many CEOs have "unstated, incremental, or intuitive strategies that have never been articulated or analyzed. . . ."[7] If pressured, these executives may state that they are following a certain strategy. This stated or "explicit" strategy is one with which few could quarrel, such as the development and acquisition of new product lines. Further investigation, however, may reveal the existence of a very different "implicit" strategy. For example, the prestige of a banker in one community is strictly a function of bank size. Top management, therefore, tends to choose strategies that will increase total bank assets rather than profits. An extremely profitable "small" bank is still just a "small" bank.

Often the only way to spot the implicit strategies of a corporation is to look not at what top management says, but at what it does. Implicit strategies can be derived from examining corporation policies, programs approved (and disapproved), and authorized budgets. Programs and divisions favored by budget increases and staffed by managers who are considered to be on the fast promotion track reveal where the corporation is putting its money and its energy.

It is, nevertheless, not always necessary for strategic planning to be a formal process for it to be effective. Small corporations, for example, may plan informally and irregularly.[8] The president and a handful of top managers may get together casually to resolve strategic issues and plan their next steps. They need no formal, elaborate planning system, for "The number of key executives involved in such decisions is usually small, and they are located close enough for frequent, casual get-togethers."[9]

In large, multidivisional corporations, however, the planning of strategy can become quite complex. A formalized system is needed to ensure that a hierarchy of objectives and strategy exists. Otherwise, top management becomes isolated from developments in the divisions and lower-level managers lose sight of the corporate mission.

6.2 EVALUATION OF STRATEGIC MANAGERS

As discussed in Chapter 3, the interaction of a corporation's board with its top management is likely to reflect one of four basic styles of strategic management: chaos, entrepreneurial, marionette, and partnership. Firms like Adolph Coors Company, Cannon Mills Company, and Tandy Corporation have for years been so dominated by their founders that their boards probably operated passively as an instrument of the founder. Once the founder dies and an outsider is brought in to head the firm, however, the board may take a more active role in representing the interests of the family. In such instances, the new CEO may be quite constrained by the board in terms of strategic options.

The strategic management style of such a corporation may thus change abruptly from entrepreneurial (where the founder dominates the board) to marionette management (where the board, made up of the founder's family and friends, dominates top management and makes the significant decisions).

In many instances where the board is only moderately involved in strategic management, the CEO has a free hand to set the direction of the corporation. Then the success or failure of a corporation's strategy must be evaluated in light of the CEO's managerial style.

For example, William Ylvisaker, chairman and CEO of Gould Inc., has a reputation of being "mercurial" and "cavalier" with his people. Credited with reshaping the stodgy battery maker into a high-tech electronics concern, "the unpredictable Mr. Ylvisaker bought and sold properties like someone playing Monopoly."[10] In contrast, Stephen Pistner, who took over the job of president of Montgomery Ward in 1981 and subsequently left in 1985 to join Rapid-American Corporation, has a reputation of being a strategic planner who "drives right for the meat of the situation" and builds strong management teams.[11] The personal style of J. Peter Grace heavily determines the strategic directions taken by W. R. Grace and Company. When Mr. Grace was on a business trip in California a few years ago, he stopped at a coffee shop called Coco's for breakfast. He liked the meal so much that, after some research, he bought the company that owned the restaurant chain![12]

Henry Mintzberg has pointed out that a corporation's objectives and strategies are strongly affected by top management's view of the world.[13] This view determines the approach or "mode" to be used in strategy formulation. He names three basic modes: entrepreneurial, adaptive, and planning. Characteristics of each mode are listed in Table 6.1.

- *Entrepreneurial mode*. Strategy is made by one powerful individual. The focus is on opportunities. Problems are secondary. Strategy is guided by the founder's own vision of direction and is exemplified by large, bold decisions. The dominant goal is growth of the corporation.

  As mentioned earlier, Gould Inc. under William Ylvisaker and W. R. Grace and Company under Peter Grace are examples of corporations being run in the entrepreneurial mode. Surprisingly, both are old, established firms with extremely dynamic and creative CEOs who have striven to change the character of their respective firms to match their vision of the future.

- *Adaptive mode*. Sometimes referred to as "muddling through," this strategy-formulation mode is characterized by reactive solutions to existing problems, rather than a proactive search for new opportunities. Much bargaining goes on concerning priorities of objectives. Strategy is

Table 6.1   **Characteristics and Conditions of the Three Modes**

Characteristic	Entrepreneurial Mode	Adaptive Mode	Planning Mode
Motive for decisions	Proactive	Reactive	Proactive and reactive
Goals of organization	Growth	Indeterminate	Efficiency and growth
Evaluation of proposals	Judgmental	Judgmental	Analytical
Choices made by	Entrepreneur	Bargaining	Management
Decision horizon	Long-term	Short-term	Long-term
Preferred environment	Uncertainty	Certainty	Risk
Decision linkages	Loosely coupled	Disjointed	Integrated
Flexibility of mode	Flexible	Adaptive	Constrained
Size of moves	Bold decisions	Incremental steps	Global strategies
Vision of direction	General	None	Specific
Condition for Use			
Source of power	Entrepreneur	Divided	Management
Objectives of organization	Operational	Nonoperational	Operational
Organizational environment	Yielding	Complex, dynamic	Predictable, stable
Status of organization	Young, small, or strong leadership	Established	Large

SOURCE: H. Mintzberg, "Strategy Making in Three Modes." Copyright © 1973 by the Regents of the University of California. Reprinted by permission of the Regents from *California Management Review*, vol. xvi, no. 2, p. 49.

fragmented and is developed to move the corporation forward in incremental steps.

This mode is typical of most universities, many large hospitals, a large number of government agencies, and a surprising number of large corporations. Western Union, for example, has for years successfully plodded along earning a small but predictable annual profit from businesses that largely were outgrowths of the telegraph. Only recently, when it tried to change modes and become more aggressive, did it fall on hard times.

• *Planning mode*. Analysts assume major responsibilities for strategy formulation. Strategic planning includes both the proactive search for new opportunities and the reactive solution of existing problems. Systematic comprehensive analysis is used to develop strategies that integrate the corporation's decision-making processes.

Sears, Roebuck and Company, in its strategic move into financial services, exemplifies this mode. Rather than simply working to improve their then-stagnant merchandising group, top management chose to capitalize on the firm's successes in insurance and real estate to take advantage of unique opportunities emerging in the financial services industry.

In the *entrepreneurial* mode, top management believes that the environment is a force to be used and controlled. In the *adaptive* mode, it assumes the environment is too complex to be completely comprehended. In the *planning* mode, it works on the assumption that systematic scanning and analysis of the environment can provide the knowledge necessary to influence the environment to the corporation's advantage. The specific planning mode used reflects top management's perception of the corporation's environment. If we categorize a corporation's top management according to one of these three planning modes, we can better understand how and why key decisions are made. Then if we look at these decisions in light of the corporation's mission, objectives, strategies, and policies, we can then determine whether the dominant planning mode is appropriate.

In addition, strategy-making modes may change as a corporation increases in size and complexity, or changes top management personnel. Tandy Corporation, for example, has changed from the entrepreneurial mode characteristic of the reign of its founder Charles Tandy to the more adaptive mode under his successor, Phil North. If Tandy Corporation continues to be successful, North's successor may move toward a more planning-oriented mode.[14]

6.3 SCANNING THE EXTERNAL ENVIRONMENT

At the point in the strategy formulation process where the external environment is scanned, strategic managers must examine both the societal and task environments for those strategic factors that are likely to strongly influence their corporation's success—factors that are, in other words, opportunities and threats. Long-run developments in the economic, technological, political-legal, and sociocultural aspects of the societal environment tend to affect strongly a corporation's activities by asserting more immediate pressures on the corporation's task environment. Such societal issues as consumerism, governmental regulations, environmental pollution, energy cost and availability, inflation-fed wage demands, and heavy foreign competition tend to emerge from stakeholders in the firm's task environment.

As discussed in Chapter 4, strategic managers should evaluate environmental issues in terms of the probability of their occurring and their probable impact on the corporation. In this manner, the possible societal issues listed in Table 4.3 can be placed on an issues priority matrix as shown in Fig. 4.2. Special emphasis may then be placed on monitoring these high-priority issues. Each of the six forces from the task environment depicted in Fig. 4.4, such as the threat of substitute products and services, also can be evaluated in this same manner and marked for special attention. Top management should then request its divisions and functional areas to report to it any significant developments in any of the high- or even medium-priority issues.

Before top management can properly address what possible future strategies are appropriate for the corporation, it must assess its own internal situation—the environment within the firm itself. Strategic decisions should not be made until top management understands the strengths and weaknesses in the division and functional areas.

Management audits can be very useful in this instance as a diagnostic aid. As mentioned in Chapter 5, the key internal variables to consider are the corporation's structure, culture, and resources. An example of a corporation (IBM) in which a basic weakness in a functional area seriously hurt the implementation of a reasonable strategy is given in Illustrative Example 6.2.

6.4 SCANNING THE INTERNAL ENVIRONMENT

INTERNAL WEAKNESS NEGATIVELY AFFECTS IMPLEMENTATION OF STRATEGIC DECISION AT IBM

Illustrative Example 6.2

In 1980, IBM began opening grandly decorated computer retail stores called IBM Product Centers in selected locations throughout the United States. Although the 81 stores achieved more than $100 million in sales during 1983, IBM decided to cancel its plans to add 100 additional stores during 1984. Burdened with start-up costs and high overhead, the stores were making far less than the 20% return IBM was accustomed to earning. It had become apparent that IBM's immense internal strengths in marketing to business customers did not transfer to standard retailing. Serious merchandising weaknesses translated into significant errors at the store level. Anxious not to appear cold and remote, IBM decorated its stores in bright red. To give its stores an image of class, IBM chose to avoid flashy, in-store displays, brochures, and racks of impulse items near the cash registers. It also staffed the stores entirely with the company's own career salespeople, few of whom had retailing experience. Using the approach that worked extremely well with its business customers, IBM stressed service over price-cutting and special offers. The retailing customers, however, were not impressed. The color of the stores caused mood problems. Commented Warren Winger, chairman of CompuShop, a Dallas-based retail chain, "Red doesn't just irritate bulls, it makes salesmen hostile and alarms customers." IBM's career salespeople intimidated first-time customers. The lack of store displays and competitive pricing caused customers to leave the stores disappointed and disillusioned. Jim Turner, the IBM vice president in charge of the stores, hinted that the Product Centers might change offerings to concentrate on selling office automation systems. In reviewing the retail stores' failure to generate the anticipated profits, Turner confessed: "The in-store merchandising—we never realized how important it was."

SOURCE: P. Petre, "IBM's Misadventures in the Retail Jungle," *Fortune* (July 23, 1984), p.80.

A current research effort to help pinpoint relevant strategic factors for business corporations is being made by the Strategic Planning Institute. Its *PIMS Program* (Profit Impact of Market Strategy) is composed of a data bank containing about 100 items of information on the strategic experiences of over 2,000 companies covering a four- to eight-year period. The research conducted with the data has been aimed at discovering the empirical "laws" that determine which strategy, under which conditions, produces what results in terms of return on investment and cash flows regardless of the specific product or services. To date, PIMS research has identified nine major strategic factors which account for around 80% of the variation in profitability across the businesses in the database.[15] In working with these factors, the Strategic Planning Institute has prepared profiles of high ROI companies as contrasted with low ROI companies. They found that the high rate of return companies had the following characteristics:

- Low investment intensity (the amount of fixed capital and working capital required to produce a dollar of sales)
- High market share
- High relative product quality
- High capacity utilization
- High operating effectiveness (the ratio of actual to expected employee productivity)
- Low direct costs per unit relative to competition[16]

These and other PIMS research findings are quite controversial. For example, PIMS research has reported consistently that a large market share should lead to greater profitability.[17] The reason appears to be that high market share results in low unit costs because of economies of scale. A company could therefore take advantage of the experience curve (discussed in Chapter 5) to gain share through low price. Unfortunately, a number of studies have found that high market share does not always lead to profitability. Firms selling products of high quality relative to the competition have been found to be very profitable even though they do not have large market share.[18] From a practitioner's point of view, the most important criticism of PIMS research is that the "significant predictors of performance (investment intensity, market share, relative product quality, capacity utilization, etc.) generally have tended to be variables outside of management's control, at least in the short run."[19] As a result of these and other limitations, one can conclude that we are still quite a distance away from discovering "univeral strategic laws." Nevertheless, the PIMS program is useful to help strategic managers identify some key internal strategic factors, such as investment intensity, market share, product quality, capacity utilization, operating effectiveness, and direct costs per unit. These factors can be measured and compared to other firms in the same industry to assess a corporation's relative strengths and weaknesses.

The analysis of the strategic factors in the strategic decision-making process calls for an integration and evaluation of data collected earlier from the scanning of the internal and external environments. External strategic factors are those opportunities and threats found in the present and future task and societal environments. Internal strategic factors are those important strengths and weaknesses within the corporation's divisional and functional areas. Step 5(a) in Fig. 6.1 requires that top management attempt to find a "strategic fit" between external opportunities and internal strengths.

6.5 ANALYSIS OF STRATEGIC FACTORS

S.W.O.T. is a term used to stand for a summary listing of a corporation's key internal *Strengths* and *Weaknesses* and its external *Opportunities* and *Threats*. These are the strategic factors to be analyzed in step 5(a) of Fig. 6.1. They should include not only those external factors that are most likely to occur and to have a serious impact on the company, but also those internal factors that are most likely to affect the implementation of present and future strategic decisions. In the case of Illustrative Example 6.2 discussing IBM, a S.W.O.T. analysis should reflect the great *opportunities* for profits emerging in the early 1980s for retail computer stores. It would also show the increasing *threat* from consumer-oriented Apple to dominate the developing personal computer market. S.W.O.T. analysis should also list IBM's impressive marketing, research, and personnel *strengths*. Nevertheless, an objective assessment of *weaknesses* should have highlighted IBM's lack of experience at the retail level and raised a "red flag" for management to seriously consider before choosing this particular strategy. Since IBM failed to note the seriousness of its retailing weaknesses, it was forced to (1) train its salespeople in retail selling, (2) install a point-of-sale computer system (which it had failed to do initially), and (3) change to a new store design with cozier colors and point-of-sale promotions.

S.W.O.T. Analysis

William Newman suggests that a corporation should seek to obtain a "propitious niche" in its strategy formulation process.[20] This niche is a corporation's specific competitive role. It should be so well-suited to the firm's internal and external environment that other corporations are not likely to challenge or dislodge it.

The finding of such a niche is not always easy. A firm's management must

Finding a Niche

always be looking for *strategic windows,* that is, market opportunities.[21] As in the case of Electronic Technology Corporation, presented in Illustrative Example 6.3, the first one through the strategic window (if the firm has the required internal strengths) can occupy a propitious niche and discourage competition. Zayre's decision to improve and emphasize its inner-city discount stores at a time when competitors were leaving inner-city locations in droves enabled it to build a niche successfully where none previously existed. Other examples are the many commuter airlines which sprouted throughout the country in the early 1980s after deregulation allowed major airlines to desert the smaller cities. Because these regional airlines fly smaller planes than the majors, their operating costs are lower and thus allow profits to well-managed firms.

A recent study of high-performing mid-sized growth companies found these successful corporations to have four characteristics is common:

- They innovate as a way of life.
- They compete on value, not price.
- They achieve leadership in *niche markets.*
- They build on their strengths by competing in *related niches.*[22]

The finding of a specific niche where a corporation's strengths fit well with environmental opportunities is therefore a desired outcome of situation analysis.

HIGH-TECH ELECTRONIC TECHNOLOGY CORPORATION AND *LOW-TECH* ZAYRE'S DISCOUNT STORES FIND PROPITIOUS NICHES

Illustrative Example 6.3

SILICON VALLEY IN CEDAR RAPIDS?

Just one year after its founding, Electronic Technology Corporation (ETC), is succeeding beyond its founder's fondest dreams. The firm manufactures semi-custom integrated circuits and sells to customers throughout the Midwest. Founder Scott Clark brought the idea to Iowa from the famed "Silicon Valley" of northern California where such companies are more common than hamburger stands. "When we began, our plan was to have a typical production order of $35,000," says Clark. "Within six months, we revised it to $90,000. And by September, orders were averaging $240,000. In fiscal year 1985, orders will average $400,000. . . . We can't grow fast enough to keep up." A significant reason for its success is its location in Cedar Rapids. Since an estimated 90% of the industry is located in Silicon Valley, about 5% on the East Coast, and the remainder

(Continued)

scattered throughout the United States, ETC leads the way in the upper Midwest. "We're between Chicago, Minneapolis, Milwaukee, St. Louis, and Kansas City. We're accessible and we're interested in our customers," states Clark. ETC offers its customers *service* and *security*. Clark says that it's not unusual for Silicon Valley engineers to stay with a company only a matter of months. When a company receives a big contract, it can hire the necessary design engineers from one of its competitors. "These guys jump from one job to another and think nothing of it. But what they do when they jump is take the secrets of the last company they did a contract for. They can offer it to a contractor's competitor. And that doesn't happen here. Our engineers come here planning to stay. They like the security of the job and they like being out of the rat race in California. We can guarantee our customers the security they must have," comments Clark. ETC's plans to expand over the next five years conjure up dreams of a Silicon Valley of the Midwest—located in Iowa. "I really believe it will happen," predicts Clark. "The business is here and our only real competitors are in California."

ZAYRE'S FINDS SUCCESS IN INNER-CITIES

In the late 1970s, Zayre Corporation was suffering from low earnings because of the "rummage sale" nature of its discount stores. Zayre responded by renovating its stores and improving its merchandise presentation and inventory. Unlike other discounters, who were leaving the inner-city in droves, Zayre decided to stay. The chain made a "significant commitment to become very good at something that [other retailers] were running away from," says President Malcolm L. Sherman. Inner-city Chicago stores were the first to be upgraded. By 1984, approximately 20% of Zayre's 276 stores were in or near black and Hispanic neighborhoods in Chicago, Pittsburgh, Atlanta, Indianapolis, and other cities. They are generally the chain's profit leaders. Zayre has few competitors in the inner-city. The inventory of the inner-city stores is tailored to the specific needs and tastes of area residents. The emphasis is on apparel. The inner-city stores stock more apparel than do suburban stores because inner-city residents "have fewer places to shop" and tend to have larger families, states Mr. Sherman. Its hiring and advertising practices also reflect the ethnic mix. Apparently, Zayre's concern for its inner-city customers is reciprocated by the people in the Zayre locations. When riots shook Miami's Liberty City in March, 1984, some residents of the area intervened to protect the store from troublemakers. "We had no damage," said Charles Howze, the inner-city store's manager.

SOURCES: J. Carlson, "Silicon Valley Comes to Iowa—and Sprouts," *Des Moines Register* (January 27, 1985), p. 6X. J. L. Roberts, "Zayre's Strategy of Ethnic Merchandising Proves To Be Successful in Inner-City Stores," *Wall Street Journal* (September 25, 1984), p. 37.

Portfolio Analysis

The business portfolio is the most recommended approach to aid the integration and evaluation of environmental data. Research suggests that "at least 200 of the Fortune 500 companies [and probably substantially more] are using the portfolio planning concept in some manner and informal discussions suggest a similar rate of adoption in Western Europe."[23]

All corporations, except the simplest and smallest, are involved in more than one business. Even though a corporation sells only one product, it may benefit from handling separately a number of distinct product-market segments. Procter & Gamble, for example, managed Prell Liquid and Prell Concentrate as two separate brands for a number of years because of their appeal to two separate and distinct market segments.

Portfolio analysis recommends that each product, strategic business unit (SBU), or division be considered separately for purposes of strategy formulation.[24]

There are a number of matrixes available to reflect the variables under consideration in a portfolio. SBUs or products can be compared for growth rate in sales, relative competitive position, stage of product/market evolution, market share, and industry attractiveness.

Four Cell BCG Growth-Share Matrix

The simplest matrix is the *growth-share matrix* developed by the Boston Consulting Group as depicted in Fig. 6.2. Each of the corporation's SBUs or products is plotted on the matrix according to both the growth rate of the industry in which it competes and its relative market share. A product's or SBU's relative competitive position is defined as its market share in the industry divided by that of the largest other competitor. The business growth rate is the percentage of market growth—that is, the percentage of increased sales of a particular product or SBU classification of products.

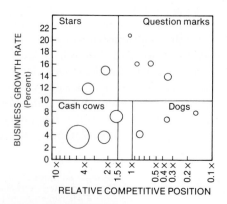

Figure 6.2   **The BCG portfolio matrix.**
SOURCE: B. Hedley, "Strategy and the Business Portfolio," *Long Range Planning* (February 1977), p. 12. Reprinted by permission.

The line separating areas of high and low relative competitive position is set at 1.5 times. Relative strengths of this magnitude are needed to ensure the dominant position needed to be a star or cash cow. On the other hand, a product or SBU should be 1 times or less to ensure its dog status.[25] Each product or SBU is represented in Fig. 6.2 by a circle. The area of the circle represents the relative significance of each SBU or product to the corporation in terms of assets used or sales generated.

The growth-share matrix has a lot in common with the product life cycle. New products are typically introduced in a fast-growing industry. These initially are termed *question mark* products. To gain enough market share to become a market leader and thus a *star,* money must be taken from more mature *cash cow* products to spend on the *question marks. Stars* are typically at the peak of their product life cycle and are usually able to generate enough cash to invest in keeping a high share of the market. Once the market growth rate slows, *stars* become *cash cows.* These products typically bring in far more money than is needed to sustain their market share. As these products move along the decline stage of their life cycle, they are "milked" for cash to invest in new *question mark* products. Those products unable to obtain a dominant market share by the time the industry growth rate inevitably slows become *dogs* which are either sold off or managed carefully for the small amount of cash they may generate.

Once a corporation's current position has been plotted on a matrix, a projection can be made of its future position, assuming no changes in strategy. Present and projected matrixes can thus be used to assist in the identification of major strategic issues facing the corporation.

Research on the growth-share matrix generally supports its assumptions and recommendations except for the advice that dogs should be promptly harvested or liquidated.[26] Products with a low share in declining industries may be very profitable if the products have niches where market demand remains stable and predictable.[27] If enough of the competition leaves the industry, a product's market share may increase by default until the dog becomes the market leader and thus a cash cow. All in all, the BCG growth-share matrix is a very popular technique. It is quantifiable and easy to use. The barnyard analogies of cash cows and dogs have become trendy buzzwords in management circles.

The growth-share matrix has been criticized for a number of reasons nevertheless:

- The use of highs and lows to make just four categories is too simplistic.

- The link between market share and profitability is not necessarily strong. Low share businesses can be profitable, too (and vice versa).

- The highest-growth rate markets may not always be the best.
- It only considers the product or SBU in relation to one competitor—the market leader. It misses small competitors with fast-growing market shares.
- Growth rate is only one aspect of industry attractiveness.
- Market share is only one aspect of overall competitive position.[28]

Nine Cell GE Business Screen A more complicated matrix is that developed by General Electric with the assistance of the McKinsey and Company consulting firm. As depicted in Fig. 6.3, it includes nine cells based on long-term industry attractiveness and business strength/competitive position. Interestingly, this nine-cell matrix is almost identical to the *Directional Policy Matrix* developed by Shell Oil and used extensively by European firms. Both use the same factors and both use nine cells. The GE Business Screen, in contrast to the BCG growth-share matrix, includes much more data in its two key factors than just business growth rate and comparable market share. For example, at GE, industry attractiveness is defined as a composite projection of—among other character-

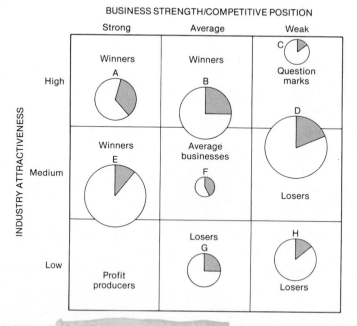

Figure 6.3 **General Electric's business screen.**

SOURCE: Adapted from *Strategic Management in GE*, Corporate Planning and Development, General Electric Corporation. Used by permission of General Electric Company.

istics—*market size, market growth rate, competitive diversity, competitive structure,* and *profitability.*[29] Business strength or competitive position can be a combination of, among others, *market share, facilities, technological position, image in marketplace,* and *caliber of management.* The individual products or SBUs are identified by a letter and plotted on the GE Screen. The area of the circles is in proportion to the size of the industry in terms of sales. The pie slices within the circles depict the market share of each product or SBU.[30]

The following four steps are recommended for plotting products or SBUs on the GE Business Screen.[31]

1. *Assess industry attractiveness.*

   a) Select general criteria to rate the industry. These criteria should be key aspects of the industry, such as its potential for sales growth and likely profitability. Table 6.2 lists fifteen criteria for one specific industry.

Table 6.2   **An Example of an Industry Attractiveness Assessment Matrix**

Attractiveness Criteria	Weight*	Rating**	Weighted Score
Size	0.15	4	0.60
Growth	0.12	3	0.36
Pricing	0.05	3	0.15
Market diversity	0.05	2	0.10
Competitive structure	0.05	3	0.15
Industry profitability	0.20	3	0.60
Technical role	0.05	4	0.20
Inflation vulnerability	0.05	2	0.10
Cyclicality	0.05	2	0.10
Customer financials	0.10	5	0.50
Energy impact	0.08	4	0.32
Social	GO	4	—
Environmental	GO	4	—
Legal	GO	4	—
Human	0.05	4	.20
	1.00		3.38

SOURCE: C. W. Hofer and D. Schendel, *Strategy Formulation: Analytical Concepts* (St. Paul, Minn.: West Publishing Co., 1978), p. 73. Copyright © 1978 by West Publishing Company. All rights reserved. Reprinted by permission.

* Some criteria may be of a GO/NO GO type. For example, many *Fortune 500* firms probably would decide not to invest in industries that are viewed negatively by our society, such as gambling, even if it were both legal and very profitable to do so.

** 1 (*very unattractive*) through 5 (*highly attractive*).

b) Weight each criterion according to management's perception of the criterion's importance to achieving corporate objectives. For example, because the key criterion of the corporation in Table 6.2 is profitability, it receives the highest weight, 0.20.

c) Rate the industry on each of these criteria from 1 (very unattractive) to 5 (very attractive). For example, if an industry is facing a long-term decline in profitability, this criterion should be rated 2 or less.

d) Multiply the weight for each criterion by its rating to get a weighted score. These scores are then added to get the weighted attractiveness score for the industry as a whole for a particular SBU.

2. *Assess business strength/competitive position.*

a) Identify the SBU's key factors for success in the industry. Table 6.3 lists seventeen such factors for a specific industry.

b) Weight each success factor (market share, for instance) in terms of its relative importance to profitability or some other measure of success within the industry. For example, since market share was believed to have a relatively small impact on most firms in the industry of Table 6.3, this success factor was given a weight of only 0.10.

c) Rate the SBU on each of the factors from 1 (very weak competitive position) to 5 (very strong competitive position). For example, as the products of the SBU of Table 6.3 have a very high market share, it received a rating of 5.

d) Multiply the weight of each factor by its rating to get a weighted score. These scores are then added to provide a weighted business strength/competitive position score for the SBU as a whole.

3. *Plot each SBU's current position.*   Once industry attractiveness and business strength/competitive position are calculated for each SBU, the actual position of all the corporation's SBUs should be plotted on a matrix like the one illustrated in Fig. 6.3. The areas of the circles should be proportional to the size of the various industries involved (in terms of sales), the company's current market share in each industry should be depicted as a pie-shaped wedge, and the circles should be centered on the coordinates of the SBU's industry attractiveness and business strength/competitive position scores.

To develop a range of scores for the *industry attractiveness* axis of the matrix, look back at Table 6.2. A highly attractive industry

Table 6.3   An Example of a Business Strength/Competitive Position Assessment Matrix for an SBU

Key Success Factors	Weight	Rating**	Weighted Score
Market share	0.10	5	.50
SBU growth rate	X*	3	—
Breadth of product line	.05	4	.20
Sales distribution effectiveness	.20	4	.80
Proprietary and key account advantages	X	3	—
Price competitiveness	X	4	—
Advertising and promotion effectiveness	.05	4	.20
Facilities location and newness	.05	5	.25
Capacity and productivity	X	3	—
Experience curve effects	.15	4	.60
Raw materials cost	.05	4	.20
Value added	X	4	—
Relative product quality	.15	4	.60
R&D advantages/position	.05	4	.20
Cash throw-off	.10	5	.50
Caliber of personnel	X	4	—
General image	.05	5	.25
	1.00		4.30

SOURCE: C. W. Hofer and D. Schendel, *Strategy Formulation: Analytical Concepts* (St. Paul, Minn.: West Publishing Co., 1978), p. 76. Copyright © 1978 by West Publishing Company. All rights reserved. Reprinted by permission.

* For any particular industry, there will be some factors that, while important in general, will have little or no effect on the relative competitive position of firms within that industry. It is usually better to drop such factors from the analysis than to assign them very low weights.

** 1 (*very weak competitive position*) through 5 (*very strong competitive position*).

should have mostly 5s in the rating column. An industry of medium attractiveness should have mostly 3s in the rating colum. An industry of low attractiveness should have mostly 1s in the rating column. Since the weights of the criteria used for each industry must sum to 1.00 regardless of the number of criteria used, the attractiveness axis of the GE Business Screen matrix should range from 1.00 (low attractiveness) to 5.00 (high attractiveness) with 3.00 as the midpoint.

Similarly, the range of scores for the *business strength/competitive position* axis of the GE Business Screen matrix should also range from 1.00 (weak) to 5.00 (strong) with 3.00 as the midpoint (average). This can be more clearly understood by again looking at Table 6.3.

Given that the criteria weights must sum to 1.00 regardless of the number of criteria used for each SBU, an SBU with a very strong competitive position might have all 5s in the rating column and thus a total weighted score of 5.00.

The resulting matrix shows the corporation's current portfolio situation. This situation is then contrasted with an ideal portfolio. Figure 6.4 depicts what Hofer and Schendel consider to be such a portfolio. It is considered ideal because it includes primarily winners, with enough winners and profit producers to finance the growth of developing (or potential) winners. In reality, however, even a successful firm would probably have a few question marks and perhaps a small loser.

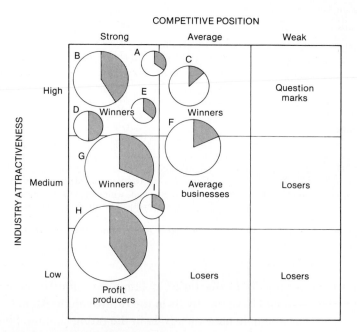

Figure 6.4   **An ideal multi-industry corporate portfolio.**

SOURCE: C. W. Hofer and D. Schendel, *Strategy Formulation: Analytical Concepts* (St. Paul, Minn.: West Publishing Co., 1978), p. 83. Copyright © 1978 by West Publishing Company. All rights reserved. Reprinted by permission.

NOTE: It is impossible to identify the orientation (i.e. growth, profit, or balance) of an ideal portfolio based solely on the information contained in the GE Business Screen, because the screen does not reflect all the information needed to do so. For instance, SBUs B, C, F, G, and H could be developing winners in very large markets or established winners in smaller markets. Likewise, SBUs A, D, E, and I could represent either developing potential winners in large markets or established winners in small markets. In the majority of instances, however, the pattern of SBU sizes and positions depicted in this figure would correspond to a balanced ideal portfolio.

4. *Plot the firm's future portfolio.*   An assessment of the current situation is complete only when the present portfolio is projected into the future. Assuming the present corporate and SBU strategies continue unchanged, top management should assess the probable impact likely changes to the corporation's task and societal environments will have on both future industry attractiveness and SBU competitive position. They should ask themselves whether future matrixes show an improving or deteriorating portfolio position. Is there a performance gap between projected and desired portfolios? If the answer is yes, there is a *strategic gap* that should be the stimulus to review the corporation's current mission, objectives, strategies, and policies.

Overall, the nine cell GE Business Screen is an improvement over the Boston Consulting Group growth-share matrix. It considers many more variables and does not lead to such simplistic conclusions. Nevertheless, it can get quite complicated and cumbersome. The calculations used in Tables 6.2 and 6.3 give the appearance of objectivity but are in reality subjective judgments that may vary from one person to another. Another shortcoming of this portfolio matrix is that it cannot effectively depict the positions of new products or SBUs in developing industries.

This matrix, based on the product life cycle, was developed by Hofer to depict the developing types of products or SBUs that cannot be easily shown on the GE Business Screen. Products or SBUs are plotted in terms of their competitive positions and their stages of product/market evolution.[32] As with the GE Business Screen, the circles represent the sizes of the industries involved with the pie wedges representing the market shares of the firm's SBUs or products. Present and future matrixes can be developed to identify strategic issues. In Fig. 6.5, for example, one could ask why product or SBU B does not have a greater share of the market, given its strong competitive position.[33]

Fifteen Cell Product/Market Evolution Matrix

6.6 REVIEW OF MISSION AND OBJECTIVES

A reexamination of a corporation's current mission and objectives must be done before alternative strategies can be generated and evaluated. The seriousness of this step is emphasized by Tregoe and Zimmerman.

When making a decision, there is an almost universal tendency to concentrate on the alternatives—the action possibilities—rather than on the objectives we want to achieve. This tendency is widespread because it is much easier to deal with alternative courses of action that exist right here

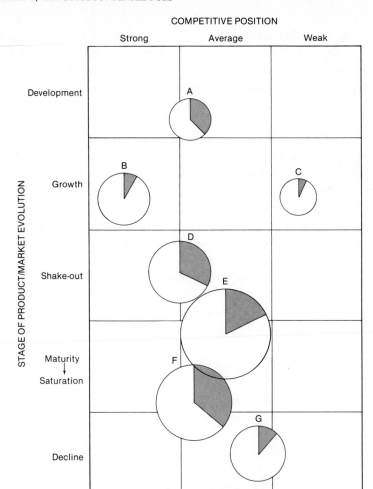

Figure 6.5   **Product/market evolution portfolio matrix.**

SOURCE: C. W. Hofer and D. Schendel, *Strategy Formulation: Analytical Concepts* (St. Paul, Minn: West Publishing Co., 1978), p. 34. From C. W. Hofer, "Conceptual Constructs for Formulating Corporate and Business Strategies" (Dover, Mass: Lord Publishing), no. BP-0041, p. 3. Copyright © 1977 by Charles W. Hofer. Reprinted by permission.

and now than to really think about what we want to accomplish in the future. Projecting a set of values forward is hard work. The end result is that we make choices that set our objectives for us, rather than having our choices incorporate clear objectives.[34]

Problems in corporate performance may derive from an inappropriate statement of mission, which may be too narrow or too broad. If the mission does not provide a common thread for a corporation's businesses, managers may be unclear about where the corporation is heading. Objectives and strategies may be in conflict with each other. Divisions may be competing against one another, rather than against outside competition—to the detriment of the corporation as a whole. According to Lorange, "Rapid changes in the environment suggest that the definition of businesses should be reviewed frequently, so that the relevance of the business definitions can be maintained."[35]

An example of a revision of a corporation's mission statement is that by American Telephone and Telegraph (AT&T). The revised mission was published in AT&T's 1980 annual report to the stockholders and had important implications for future corporate strategy:

> No longer do we perceive that our business will be limited to telephony or, for that matter, telecommunications. Ours is the business of information handling, the knowledge business. And the market that we seek is global.

A corporation's objectives may also be inappropriately stated. They may either focus too much on short-term operational goals or be so general that they provide little real guidance. Consequently, objectives should be constantly reviewed to ensure their usefulness.

6.7 SUMMARY AND CONCLUSION

This chapter describes the key activities involved in the process of formulating strategy. Following the strategic decision-making process introduced in Chapter 2, formulation is described as being composed of six distinct steps. Situation analysis incorporates five steps beginning with the evaluation of current performance results and ending with the review and revision of mission and objectives. Step six—the generation, evaluation, and selection of the best alternative strategy—is discussed in the next chapter.

Step 1—the evaluation of current performance results and the review of the corporation's mission, objectives, strategies, and policies—deals with the initial stimulus to start the formulation process. *Step 2,* the review of strategic managers, includes an evaluation of the competencies, level of involvement, and performance of the corporation's top management and board of directors. *Step 3,* scanning the external environment, focuses on collecting information, selecting strategic factors, and forecasting future events likely to affect the corporation's strategic decisions. *Step 4,* scanning the internal environment, deals with the assessment of internal strengths and weaknesses in terms of structure, culture, and resources. *Step 5(a),* analysis of strategic factors in light of the current situation, proposes S.W.O.T. analysis and portfolio analysis as techniques to locate a business' propitious niche. Matrixes developed by the Boston Consulting Group, General Electric, and Hofer are described as three ways to compare business strengths with industry attractiveness. *Step 5(b),* review and revision of the mission and objectives, completes the situation analysis by forcing a strategic manager to reexamine corporate purpose and objectives before initiating alternative strategies.

DISCUSSION QUESTIONS

1. Does strategy formulation need to be a regular continuous process? Explain.

2. Is it necessary that a corporation have a "common thread" running through its many activities in order to be successful? Why or why not?

3. What set of objectives might a typical university have?

4. What is likely to happen to an SBU that loses its propitious niche?

5. What value has portfolio analysis in the consideration of strategic factors?

6. Compare and contrast S.W.O.T. analysis with portfolio analysis.

7. Is the GE Business Screen just a more complicated version of the Boston Consulting Group growth/share matrix? Why or why not?

8. Is portfolio analysis used to formulate strategy at the corporate, divisional, or functional level of the corporation?

NOTES

1. H. Mintzberg, "Planning on the Left Side and Managing on the Right," *Harvard Business Review* (July–August 1976), p. 56.

2. P. Lorange, *Implementation of Strategic Planning* (Englewood Cliffs, N.J.: Prentice-Hall, 1982), p. 130.

3. J. A. Pearce, III, "The Company Mission as a Strategic Tool," *Sloan Management Review* (Spring 1982), pp. 15–24.
W. R. Stone and D. F. Heany, "Dealing with a Corporate Identity Crisis," *Long Range Planning* (February 1984), pp. 10–18.

4. B. E. Gup, *Guide to Strategic Planning* (New York: McGraw-Hill, 1980), p. 12.

5. H. I. Ansoff, *Corporate Strategy* (New York: McGraw-Hill, 1965), pp. 104–108.

6. A. A. Thompson, Jr., and A. J. Stricklin, III, *Strategic Management: Concepts and Cases,* 3rd ed. (Plano, Tex.: Business Publications, Inc., 1984), pp. 48–49.

7. K. R. Andrews, "Directors' Responsibility for Corporate Strategy," *Harvard Business Review* (November–December 1980), p. 30.

8. R. B. Robinson, Jr., and J. A. Pearce, III, "Research Thrusts in Small Firm Strategic Planning," *Academy of Management Review* (January 1984), pp. 128–137.

9. F. R. Vancil and P. Lorange, "Strategic Planning in Diversified Companies," *Harvard Business Review* (January–February 1975), p. 81.

10. J. Bussey, "Gould Reshapes Itself into High-Tech Outfit amid Much Turmoil," *Wall Street Journal* (October 3, 1985), p. 1.

11. S. Weiner, "Much of Old Montgomery Ward May Go as Pistner Seeks Profitability, New Image," *Wall Street Journal* (June 15, 1981), p. 23.

12. T. Hall, "For a Company Chief, When There's a Whim There's Often a Way," *Wall Street Journal* (October 1, 1984), p. 1.

13. H. Mintzberg, "Strategy-Making in Three Modes," *California Management Review* (Winter 1973), pp. 44–53.

14. J. Kirkpatrick, "Tandy Corp. Survives Loss of Legendary Entrepreneur," (Charlottesville, Va.) *Daily Progress* (July 8, 1981), p. B14.

15. S. Schoeffler, "The PIMS Program," in K. J. Albert (ed.), *The Strategic Management Handbook* (New York: McGraw-Hill, 1983), pp. 23.1–23.10.

16. G. Badler, "Strategizing for a Spectrum of Possibilities," *Planning Review* (July 1984), pp. 28–31.

17. Badler, p. 28.
R. G. Wakerly, "PIMS: A Tool for Developing Competitive Strategy," *Long Range Planning* (June 1984), p. 95.

18. C. Y. Woo, "Market-Share Leadership—Not Always So Good," *Harvard Business Review* (January–February 1984), pp. 50–54.
J. K. Newton, "Market Share—Key to Higher Profitability?" *Long Range Planning* (February 1983), pp. 37–41.

19. V. Ramanujan and N. Venkatraman, "An Inventory and Critique of Strategy Research Using the PIMS Database," *Academy of Management Review* (January 1984), p. 147.

20. W. H. Newman, "Shaping the Master Strategy of Your Firm," *California Management Review*, vol. 9, no. 3 (1967), pp. 77–88.

21. D. F. Abell, "Strategic Windows," *Journal of Marketing* (July 1978), pp. 21–26, as reported by K. R. Harrigan, "Entry Barriers in Mature Manufacturing Industries" in R. Lamb (ed.), *Advances in Strategic Management,* Vol. 2 (Greenwich, Conn.: Jai Press, 1983), pp. 67–97.

22. D. K. Clifford and R. E. Cavanagh, "The Winning Performance of Midsized Growth Companies," *Planning Review* (November 1984), pp. 18–23, 35.

23. R. A. Bettis and W. K. Hall, "Strategic Portfolio Management in the Multibusiness Firm," *California Management Review* (Fall 1981), p. 23.

24. B. Hedley, "Strategy and the Business Portfolio," *Long Range Planning* (February 1977), p. 9.

25. Hedley, pp. 12–13.

26. D. C. Hambrick, I. C. MacMillan, and D. L. Day, "Strategic Attributes and Performance in the BCG Matrix—A PIMS-Based Analysis of Industrial Product Businesses," *Academy of Management Journal* (September 1982), pp. 510–531.
D. C. Hambrick and I. C. MacMillan, "The Product Portfolio and Man's Best Friend," *California Management Review* (Fall 1982), pp. 84–95.

27. C. Y. Woo and A. C. Cooper, "The Surprising Case for Low Market Share," *Harvard Business Review* (November–December 1982), pp. 106–113.

28. C. W. Hofer and D. Schendel, *Strategy Formulation: Analytical Concepts* (St. Paul: West Publishing Co., 1978), pp. 31–32.
P. McNamee, "Competitive Analysis Using Matrix Displays," *Long Range Planning* (June 1984), pp. 98–114.
R. E. Walker, "Portfolio Analysis in Practice," *Long Range Planning* (June 1984), pp. 63–71.
J. A. Seeger, "Reversing the Image of BCG's Growth/Share Matrix," *Strategic Management Journal* (January–March 1984) pp. 93–97.

29. W. K. Hall, "SBUs: Hot, New Topic in the Management of Diversification," *Business Horizons* (February 1978), p. 20.

30. Hofer and Schendel, pp. 32–33.

31. Hofer and Schendel, pp. 72–87.

32. Similar to the Hofer model, but using twenty instead of fifteen cells is the Arthur D. Little (ADL) strategic planning matrix. For details see M. B. Coate, "Pitfalls in Portfolio Planning," *Long Range Planning* (June 1983), pp. 47–56.

33. Hofer and Schendel, pp. 33–34.

34. B. B. Tregoe and J. W. Zimmerman, "The New Strategic Manager," *Business* (May–June 1981), p. 19.

35. Lorange, p. 211.

Chapter 7

STRATEGY FORMULATION: STRATEGIC ALTERNATIVES

STRATEGIC MANAGEMENT MODEL

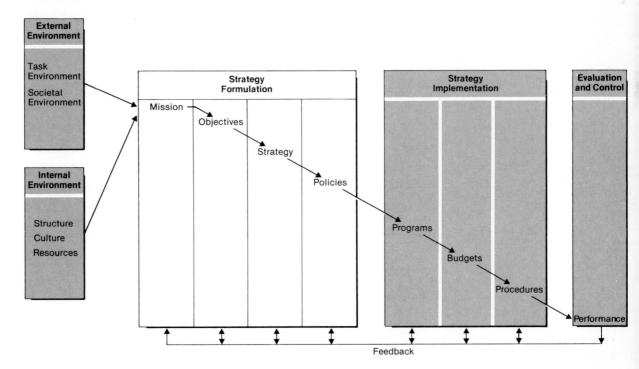

A key part of strategy formulation is the development of alternative courses of action that specify means by which the corporate mission and objectives are to be accomplished. As explained in Chapter 6 and depicted in Fig. 6.1, the generation, evaluation, and selection of the best strategic alternative is the sixth step of the strategic decision-making process. Once the best strategy is selected, appropriate policies must be established to define the ground rules for implementation. This chapter, therefore, will (a) explain the many alternative strategies available at the corporate, divisional, and functional levels of the corporation; (b) suggest criteria to use in the evaluation of these strategies; (c) explain how an optimal strategy is selected; and (d) suggest how strategy is translated into policies.

7.1 ALTERNATIVE STRATEGIES

There is no one set of strategies that can be used at all levels of a corporation. Most likely, a company will need both corporate and functional-level strategies. If it is in many different industries, the corporation will also have to develop divisional or SBU strategies for its families of related products or businesses.

Corporate Strategies

Prefaced by the broad question, "What should our corporation be like in the future?" top management should ask the following questions in order to develop strategic alternatives:[1]

1.   Should we stay in the same business(es)?

2.   Should we leave this business entirely or just some parts of it by merging, liquidating, and/or selling part of our corporation?

3.   Should we become more efficient or effective in the business(es) we are presently in?

4.   Should we try to grow in this business by (a) increasing our present size and market or (b) acquiring corporations in similar businesses?

5.   Should we try to grow primarily by expanding into other businesses?

6.   Should we use different strategies in different parts of the corporation?

If question 1 is answered yes, top management will probably choose a *stability* strategy. If question 2 or 3 is yes, *retrenchment* is a likely strategy. If either question 4 or 5 is yes, a *growth* strategy is appropriate. If question 6 is yes, top management should adopt a *combination* of strategies.

An analysis by Glueck of the strategic choices of 358 executives over a period of 45 years found the following frequency of usage of the four overall strategies:[2]

Stability:	9.2%
Growth:	54.4%
Retrenchment:	7.5%
Combination:	28.7%

The *stability* family of strategies is appropriate for a successful corporation operating in a reasonably predictable environment. Epitomized by a steady-as-she-goes philosophy, these strategies involve no major changes. A corporation concentrates its resources on its present businesses in order to build upon and improve its competitive advantage. It retains the same mission and similar objectives; it simply increases its level of achievement by approximately the same percentage each year. Its main strategic decisions concern improving the performance of functional areas. Some stability strategies are as follows:

No-change strategy   In this strategy, a corporation continues on its course only with an adjustment for inflation in its objectives. Rarely articulated as a definite strategy, the success of a no-change strategy depends on a lack of change in a corporation's internal or external environments. This strategy may evolve from a lack of interest in or need to engage in hard strategic analysis. After all, if everything is going along fine, why change anything?

Profit strategy   The profit strategy involves the sacrifice of future growth for present profits. The result is often short-term success coupled to long-term stagnation. By reducing expenditures for R&D, maintenance, or advertising, short-term profits increase and are reflected in the stockholders' dividends. If a corporation has a number of "cash cow" divisions, they can be "milked" of more cash than they spend. For example, when times were tough for railroads in the 1960s, a number of firms chose to meet expenses and prop up their annual dividends by cutting back on track maintenance. Unfortunately, difficulties continued into the 1970s, and the railroad track continued to deteriorate. On some sections, the trains were restricted to less than 20 miles per hour because of the poor track conditions! Obviously, the profit strategy is only useful to help a company get through a temporary difficulty. Unfortunately, the profit strategy is seductive and if continued long enough will lead to bankruptcy.

Pause strategy   After a period of prolonged fast growth, a corporation may become inefficient or unmanageable. The addition of new divisions through

Stability Strategies

acquisition or internal development can stretch management and resources thin. A pause strategy involves reducing the levels of a corporation's objectives so that it is able to consolidate its resources. The strategy is generally considered temporary—a way to get a corporate house in order. For example, after acquiring more than 150 companies and selling off about 75 of them since 1952, W. R. Grace and Company turned to consolidating organizationally its myriad holdings in chemicals, natural resources, and consumer goods.[3]

Proceed-with-caution strategy   This strategy results from a specific decision to proceed slowly because of important factors developing in the external environment. Top management may feel that a growth strategy is no longer feasible given, for instance, a sudden scarcity of needed raw materials, new governmental regulations, or a poor economic climate.

Growth Strategies   *Growth* strategies are extremely popular because most executives tend to equate growth with success. Those corporations that are in dynamic environments *must* grow in order to survive. Growth means greater sales and a chance to take advantage of the experience curve to reduce the per unit cost of products sold, thereby increasing profits. This becomes extremely important if a corporation's industry is growing quickly and competitors are engaging in price wars in order to gain larger shares of the market. Those firms that have not reached "critical mass" (that is, gained the necessary economy of large-scale production) will face large losses unless they can find and fill a small, but profitable, niche.

Growth is a very seductive strategy for two key reasons:

- A growing firm can cover up mistakes and inefficiences more easily than can a stable one. A growing flow of revenue into a highly leveraged corporation can create a large amount of "organization slack"[4] (unused resources) that can be used to quickly resolve problems and conflicts between departments and divisions.

- There are more opportunities for advancement, promotion, and interesting jobs in a growing firm. Growth, per se, is exciting and ego-enhancing for CEOs. A growing corporation tends to be seen as a "winner" or "on the move" by the marketplace and by potential investors.

Vertical integration strategy   The vertical integration strategy is the strategy of a corporation that enters one or more businesses that are necessary to the manufacture and distribution of its own products but that were previously purchased from other companies. These can range from the obtaining of raw materials to the merchandising of the product. *Backward integration* is the corporation's entry into the business of supplying some of its present raw materials. Henry Ford I achieved this when he built his own steel mill to supply Ford's assembly lines. *Forward integration* is the entry of the corporation into the business of distributing its product by entering marketing channels closer to the ultimate consumer. This is common in the tire industry where manufacturers, such as Firestone and Goodyear, own and manage their own retail outlets. More recently, IBM has opened retail stores in order to market its personal computers directly to the consumer. Backward and forward integration as well as other popular growth strategies are depicted in Fig. 7.1.

Vertical integration is quite common in the oil, rubber, basic metal, automobile, and forest products industries. As pointed out in Table 7.1, some of the advantages are lower costs and improved coordination and control. Although backward integration is usually more profitable than forward integration,[5] it can reduce a corporation's strategic flexibility by an

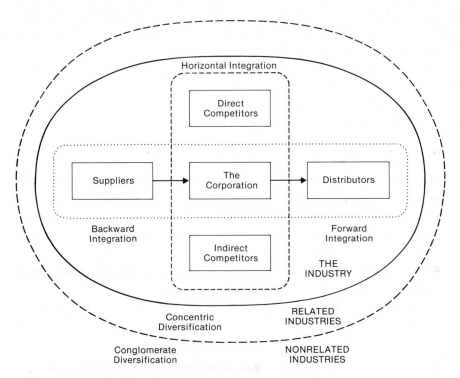

Figure 7.1   **Basic growth strategies.**
SOURCE: Suggested by C. W. Hofer as part of his presentation with J. J. Chrisman of "First Diversification and the Strategic Management Process: A New Perspective," a paper presented to the Academy of Management, Boston, Massachusetts, August 1984.

Table 7.1   Some Advantages and Disadvantages of Vertical Integration

Advantages	Disadvantages
Internal benefits	*Internal costs*
Integration economies reduce costs by eliminating steps, reducing duplicate overhead, and cutting costs (technology dependent)	Need for overhead to coordinate vertical integration increased costs
Improved coordination of activities reduces inventorying and other costs	Burden of excess capacity from unevenly balanced minimum efficient scale plants (technology dependent)
Avoid time-consuming tasks, such as price shopping, communicating design details, or negotiating contracts	Poorly organized vertically integrated firms do not enjoy synergies that compensate for higher costs
Competitive benefits	*Competitive dangers*
Avoid foreclosure to inputs, services, or markets	Obsolete processes may be perpetuated
Improved marketing or technological intelligence	Creates mobility (or exit) barriers
Opportunity to create product differentiation (increased value added)	Links firm to sick adjacent businesses
Superior control of firm's economic environment (market power)	Lose access to information from suppliers or distributors
Create credibility for new products	Synergies created through vertical integration may be overrated
Synergies could be created by coordinating vertical activities skillfully	Managers integrated before thinking through the most appropriate way to do so

SOURCE: K. R. Harrigan, *Strategic Flexibility: A Management Guide for Changing Times,* (Lexington, MA: Lexington Books, 1986), p. 162. Copyright © 1985, D. C. Heath & Co.

encumbrance of expensive assets that may be hard to sell and thus create an exit barrier to leaving that particular industry.[6]

A study by Harrigan reveals at least four types of vertical integration ranging from *full integration* to *long-term contracts.*[7] For example, if a corporation does not want to have the disadvantages of full vertical integration, it may choose either *taper* or *quasi-integration* strategies. With taper integration, a firm partially produces its own requirements and buys the rest from outside suppliers. In the case of quasi-integration, a company gets most of its requirements from an outside supplier which is under its partial control. IBM, for example, purchased 20% of the common stock of Intel Corporation in order to guarantee IBM's access to 16-bit microprocessors for its personal computers.[8]

Horizontal integration strategy   The acquisition by a corporation of another corporation in the same industry is called horizontal integration. The term is applied primarily to those corporations that predominantly operate in one industry, such as Ford Motor Company or Heileman Brewing Company. Since the acquiring firm is thus buying a competitor, such a transaction is liable to antitrust suits. The corporation's objective may be to become more efficient through larger economies of scale, to enter another geographic market, or simply to reduce competition for supplies and customers. Renault's acquisition of American Motors is one example of horizontal integration. United Airlines' acquisition in 1985 of Pan American World Airways' Pacific division was another example.

Diversification strategy   This is the strategy of adding *different* products or divisions to the corporation. There are two types of diversification—concentric and conglomerate.

Concentric diversification is the addition to a corporation of *related* products or divisions. The corporation's lines of business still possess some "common thread" that serves to relate them in some manner. The point of commonality may be similar technology, customer usage, distribution, managerial skills, or product similarity. An example of concentric diversification was the addition of "Eagle Snacks" to Anheuser-Busch's successful line of beers.

Conglomerate diversification, in contrast to concentric diversification, is the addition to the firm of *unrelated* products or divisions. Rather than keeping a common thread throughout their corporation, top managers who adopt this strategy are primarily concerned with a return on investment criterion: Will it increase the corporation's level of profitability? The addition may, however, be justified in terms of strategic fit. A cash-rich corporation with few opportunities for growth in its industry may, for example, move into another industry where opportunities are great, but cash hard to find. An example of this strategy was the purchase of Vydec Corporation, a maker of word processors, by Exxon Corporation, the oil company. Another instance of conglomerate diversification might be the purchase by a corporation with a seasonal and, therefore, uneven cash flow of a firm in an unrelated industry with complementing seasonal sales that will level out the cash flow.

Beginning with a classic study of Rumelt, researchers in the area have concluded consistently that diversification into other industries (unrelated or conglomerate) does *not* increase the profitability of a business corporation.[9] Peters and Waterman support the developing chorus in favor of concentric over conglomerate diversification.

> Our principal finding is clear and simple. Organizations that do branch out (whether by acquisition or internal diversification) but stick very close to their knitting outperform the others. The most successful of all are those diversified around a single skill—the coating and bonding technology at 3M, for example.

The second group, in descending order, comprises those companies that branch out into related fields—the leap from electric power generation turbines to jet engines (another turbine) from GE, for example.

Least successful, as a general rule, are those companies that diversify into a wide variety of fields. Acquisitions especially, among this group, tend to wither on the vine.[10]

Supporting this argument is the recent increase in spinoffs by conglomerate corporations of formerly acquired units. In the past few years ITT, RCA, Gulf & Western, Beatrice Foods, Quaker Oats, General Electric, Exxon, and R. J. Reynolds have sold off major nonrelated holdings.

Nevertheless, a study by *Fortune* magazine provides contrary results. The study compared the performance of the 39 largest conglomerates with the performance of the 226 largest nondiversified industrial companies on the Fortune 500 list. It found that although nondiversified companies did produce a higher median return on shareholder equity in 1978 and 1979 than did conglomerates, results were about equal in 1980. During the next three years (1981–1983), however, the conglomerates outperformed the nondiversified companies. In examining the results, Roy Little, founder of the huge conglomerate Textron, International, concluded:

> My basic concept of unrelated diversification is as sound as ever. The bad reputation the conglomerates acquired in the late 1960s and early 1970s just doesn't square with the facts today. . . . A well-run diversified company shouldn't ever lose money.[11]

The argument appears to be far from settled.

Mergers, acquisitions, and joint ventures   Corporations may engage in strategic mergers, acquisitions, and joint ventures in order to attain *synergy* (the 2 + 2 = 5 effect). Two corporations so involved are able to achieve more by working together than they could by acting separately. Different types of synergy are possible:

1. *Sales synergy* exists when many products use the same distribution channels.

2. *Operating synergy* exists when many products use the same manufacturing facilities and personnel, thereby distributing the overhead among more products.

3. *Management synergy* exists when managerial skills and abilities can be transferred from one corporation or industry to solving problems in another.

4. *Technological synergy* exists when R&D personnel and techniques can be combined for greater effectiveness.

A *merger* is a transaction involving two or more corporations in which stock is exchanged, but from which only one corporation survives. Mergers are usually between firms of somewhat similar size and are usually "friendly." The resulting firm is likely to have a name derived from its composite firms. One example is the merging of Allied Corporation and Signal Companies to form Allied Signal.

An *acquisition* is the purchase of a corporation that is completely absorbed as an operating subsidiary or division of the acquiring corporation. An example is the acquisition by U.S. Steel of Marathon Oil. Acquisitions are usually between firms of different sizes and can be either "friendly" or "unfriendly." A friendly acquisition usually begins with the acquiring corporation discussing its desires with the other firm's top management. In return for fair consideration after acquisition, the top management of the firm to be acquired agrees to work for the acquisition. Friendly acquisitions are thus very similar to mergers. Unfriendly acquisitions, in contrast, are often called "takeovers." The acquiring firm ignores the other firm's top management or board of directors and simply begins buying up the other firm's stock until it owns a controlling interest. The takeover target, in response, begins defensive maneuvers, such as buying up its own stock, calling in the Justice Department to initiate an anti-trust suit in order to stop the acquisition, or looking for a friendly merger partner (as Gulf Oil did with Standard Oil of California when Texas oilman T. Boone Pickens mounted a takeover effort to buy Gulf's stock).

Slang terms are very popular in mergers and acquisitions. For example, a "pigeon" (highly vulnerable target) or "sleeping beauty" (more desirable than a pigeon) may take a "cyanide pill" (taking on a huge long-term debt on the condition that the debt falls due immediately upon the firm's acquisition) in order to avoid being "raped" (forcible hostile takeover sometimes accompanied by looting the target's profitability) by a "shark" (extremely predatory takeover artist) using "hired guns" (lawyers, merger and acquisition specialists, and certain investment bankers).[12] To avoid takeover threats, a number of corporations have chosen to stagger the elections of board members (discussed in Chapter 3), prohibit two-tier tender offers (the offering of a higher price to stockholders who sell their shares first), prohibit "greenmail" (the buying back of a company's stock from a "shark" at a premium price), and require an 80% shareholder vote to approve a takeover. The ultimate countermeasure appears to be the *poison pill*, a procedure granting present shareholders the right to acquire at a substantial discount a large equity stake in an acquiring company whose offer does not have the support of the acquired company's board of directors. For an interesting application of a "takeover" strategy, see Illustrative Example 7.1.

USE OF TAKEOVER STRATEGY AT TYCO LABORATORIES, INC.

Illustrative
Example
7.1

Tyco Laboratories, Inc., a miniconglomerate based in New Hampshire, has adopted an interesting growth strategy. The stated aim of Tyco's president, Joseph S. Gaziano, is to make Tyco grow through acquisitions. Gaziano, according to Lynch, ". . . likes to muse that Tyco one day might be as well known as International Telephone and Telegraph Co.—with Mr. Gaziano ranked right up there with his idol, former ITT chairman Harold Geneen."

Tyco usually begins by buying the stock of another corporation on the open market. If the other firm objects, Mr. Gaziano becomes very aggressive. He once appeared at a takeover target's stockholders meeting and loudly demanded a meeting with the CEO. As in the case of his attempt to acquire Leeds and Northrup, he sometimes promises to fire the top executives, so his demand was tantamount to a threat. In 1979, Tyco acquired some shares of Trane Company, an air-conditioner manufacturer, for $43 each. So fearful was Trane of Gaziano's takeover tactics, it paid Tyco $50 per share to get its shares back. At the time, Trane's common stock was trading at less than $40 a share.

Tyco's attempt to acquire Ludlow Corporation took two and a half years to complete. Ludlow, a packaging and furniture concern, fought Tyco's advances at every step. At the beginning of his takeover attempt, Mr. Gaziano cited Ludlow's $22 million in cash as a reason for the bid. In order to avoid Tyco's grasp, Ludlow used the cash to acquire a packaging concern—a decision that has resulted in lower profits for Ludlow.

So far, Mr. Gaziano's use of the takeover strategy has been extremely profitable. Even in those attempts when a second bidder wins a takeover battle by paying a higher price, Tyco is able to sell the acquired stock at a much higher price than it paid for it. On three takeover attempts that failed, Tyco earned approximately $15 million.

SOURCE: M. C. Lynch, "Tyco's Successful Acquisition Still Leaves Questions about Gaziano's Grand Design," *Wall Street Journal* (August 27, 1981), p. 21.

A *joint venture* is the strategy of forming a temporary partnership or consortium for the purpose of gaining synergy. Joint ventures occur because the corporations involved do not wish to or cannot legally merge permanently. Joint ventures provide a way to temporarily fit the different strengths of partners together in order to achieve an outcome of value to both. For example, IBM, CBS, and Sears have formed a joint venture to develop and market *videotex*—the sending and receiving of words and pictures to at-home video screens by which people can order merchandise, do banking, and carry out other functions. A major innovation in the joint venture plan is to send the data to computers instead of to special-purpose video-screen terminals. CBS has experience with advertisers, news reporting, and publishing. Sears can use the venture to market its merchandise catalogue and financial services products electronically.[13] Joint ventures are extremely popular in international undertakings because of financial and political–legal constraints. They are also a convenient way for a privately owned and publicly owned (state-owned) corporation to work together. Joint ventures are discussed further in Chapter 10.

Mergers, acquisitions, and joint ventures are often combined with vertical and horizontal integration, and with diversification. As mentioned earlier, Henry Ford I vertically integrated backward by using his own and Ford Motor's cash to build a steel mill for his River Rouge Plant. Cincinnati Milacron diversified concentrically with its own resources into making industrial robots on the basis of its traditional excellence in manufacturing high-quality machine tools. In contrast, many corporations, such as DuPont and Philip Morris, grew externally; DuPont vertically integrated by acquiring Conoco to assure oil supplies for the manufacture of its petroleum-based synthetics; Philip Morris diversified concentrically in the acquisitions of Miller Brewing Company and Seven-Up Corporation so that it could apply its consumer marketing expertise to other industries.

Concentration strategy A corporation may choose to grow by concentrating all of its resources in the development of a single product or product line, single market, or single technology. Corporations such as McDonald's (fast food), Caterpillar (construction equipment), and Gerber (baby products) that concentrate their efforts on a single product line are able to stay ahead of competitors who dilute their effort in many industries. Gerber, for example, failed miserably when it tried to diversify into adult foods, mail-order insurance, and day-care centers. With a 71% share of the baby food market, Gerber decided that concentrating on selling a little more each year to a few more mothers was its best strategy.[14]

These firms can organize on a functional or geographical basis with no need for divisions. The very real advantages inherent in a concentration strategy may have been one reason why many large multi-industry, multi-product corporations have begun to reorganize themselves around strategic business units. Such concentration allows the corporation to put more time, energy, and resources into developing innovative product strategies through market penetration, market development, and product development. For an example of an effective use of the concentration strategy, see Illustrative Example 7.2.

CONCENTRATION STRATEGY AT CUMMINS ENGINE COMPANY

Illustrative Example 7.2

Cummins Engine Company has always been well known as a diesel-engine producer. Its real growth began after World War II, when truckers began clamoring for engines that cost less to run, lasted longer, and needed less maintenance than gasoline engines. In the late 1960s, however, top management at Cummins feared that the demand for diesel engines would slow. Noting the success of other corporations that tried diversification, Cummins acquired companies making products as unrelated as skis and computer software.

In the mid-1970s, top management reassessed the corporation. It had underestimated the demand for diesels. "We hadn't anticipated inflation or the beginning of the energy crisis," said Henry B. Schacht, Cummin's CEO and chairman. "The other businesses weren't bad, but we needed all of our capital to expand our diesel production." So in 1975 and 1976, Cummins divested itself of everything but its truck-engine line.

The crisis came in 1979. Cummins faced slumping demand for its engines. The economy was fading and the heavy truck industry was in recession. Top management made another strategic decision. They chose to stay in the diesel business and to devote the company's resources to its new engine line. This meant spending $900 million—nearly twice its net worth—to retool the engine line and develop new low-horsepower models to broaden its markets and to fend off Japanese and European competitors. Cummins cut the work force by 22% while pushing production to record levels. Break-even was reduced 31%; inventories were trimmed 40%. The union backed the strategy by signing a new contract three months ahead of schedule to keep up customer confidence in the firm.

The next four years were difficult ones for Cummins Engine. Truck-engine shipments dropped 36% in 1982. Earnings in 1983 were only $5.2 million. By 1984, sales and net income appeared to be improving at last. Mr. Schacht is optimistic about Cummin's single-product strategy. "We never felt we put the company in danger," he insists. Someday Cummins might try diversification again, he says, "but for quite a while, we think we can stick to our knitting."

SOURCE: H. S. Byrne, "Cummins Decides to Go with Its Strength as It Pins Hopes on Diesel Truck Engines," *Wall Street Journal* (July 3, 1984), p. 23.

Investment strategy Investment strategy is sometimes referred to as "grow to sell out." It is a way to maximize stockholder investment when the corporation is sold at an attractive price. An entrepreneur may build successfully a corporation for the purpose of selling it just at the point when competition becomes heavy and when further growth would require giving up control. The corporation is therefore viewed as an investment not only by the stockholders, but also by top management and the board of directors.

One example is that of Walter Cornett, an entrepreneur who started a nursing home chain, several medical supply companies, and a venture to raise Brahman bulls. Once each company became successful, Cornett sold it for a profit, paid the investors, and began a new company. The venture capitalists were interested in a quick return on their investment and Cornett was interested in starting (but not managing) a series of new businesses.[15]

Retrenchment strategies are relatively unpopular because retrenchment seems to imply failure—that something has gone wrong with previous strategies. With these strategies there *is* a great deal of pressure to improve performance. As with the coaches of losing football teams, the CEO is typically under pressure to do something quickly or be fired.

Retrenchment Strategies

Turnaround strategy   The turnaround strategy emphasizes improving operational efficiency. It is appropriate when a corporation's problems are pervasive, but not yet critical. Analogous to going on a diet, a turnaround strategy includes two initial phases. The first phase is *contraction,* the initial effort to reduce size and costs. It typically involves a general cutback in personnel and all noncritical expenditures. Hiring stops, and across-the-board reductions in R&D, advertising, training, supplies, and services are usual. The second phase is *consolidation,* the development of a program to stabilize the leaner corporation. An in-depth audit is conducted in order to identify areas where long-run improvements can be made in corporate efficiency. Plans are developed to streamline the corporation by reducing unnecessary overhead and to make functional activities "cost-effective." Financial expenditures in all areas must be justified on the basis of their contribution to profits. This is a crucial time for the corporation. If the consolidation phase is not conducted in a positive manner, many of the best people will leave the organization. If, however, all employees are encouraged to get involved in productivity improvements, the corporation likely may emerge from this strategic retrenchment period a much stronger and better organized company.

If the corporation successfully emerges from these two phases of contraction and consolidation, it is then able to enter a third phase, *rebuilding.* At this point, an attempt is made to once again expand the business.[16] For an example of an effective use of the turnaround strategy, see Illustrative Example 7.3.

TURNAROUND STRATEGY AT TORO COMPANY

Illustrative Example 7.3

Top management at Toro Company was astonished when a 1974 marketing survey showed the brand name of the little lawn-mower manufacturer ranked second only to Hershey chocolate in consumer recognition. They

(Continued)

rushed to transform Toro by broadening both its product lines and distribution system. By 1979 the company had 33,000 new chain-store outlets to sell a stream of new products, such as lightweight snow-throwers and chain saws. Sales of $358 million with earnings of $17.4 million both tripled 1974 levels. "The idea is to make the Toro name an umbrella under which we can market just about anything," said Chairman David T. McLaughlin.

Seeds for disaster had been planted. The pressure to increase sales led to a slide in product quality. New products were rushed to market in the late 1970s and early 1980s without the usual time-consuming development and testing phases. The distribution of mowers and snow-throwers through mass merchandisers like K-Mart and J. C. Penney infuriated Toro's traditional dealer network. Not only were the dealers forced to compete with their own products being sold at lower prices by discounters; they were being stuck with servicing the products the discounters sold! Some dealers refused to service machines they did not sell and actually told prospective customers not to buy a Toro.

The crisis arrived when the two snowless winters of 1979–80 and 1980–81 plunged the company into ten straight quarters of losses. In early 1981, as sales fell from $400 million to $247 million annually, McLaughlin resigned as chairman. Before leaving, he fired 125 managers including Toro's president, John Cantu. The dismissals were probably long overdue. One manager admitted that the firm's staff was that of a billion-dollar company—far too large for a small company like Toro.

Executive Vice-President Kendrick Melrose was named president. The fight for survival began. Dividends were suspended. Melrose acted to cut the work force in half, to 1,800 people; cut sales and administrative costs by 23%; consolidated production to five plants from eight; and suspended production of snow-throwers until sales caught up with inventories two years later. More importantly, Melrose worked to salvage the dealer network by stopping sales to discounters of equipment that required servicing. He also improved Toro's inventory-support program, giving independent dealers and distributors more protection from losses when their inventories exceeded a "normal year's" level.

"The toughest decision was to terminate half the employment force," admitted President Melrose. "The second toughest was to go to the half that remained and tell them that not only do we have fewer resources, but we still need greater productivity, and that they're going to have to make some financial sacrifices." That meant no incentive compensation for executives for at least four years, salary freezes and mandatory furlough days for office employees, and wage freezes or reductions for hourly workers. Stringent controls were set in place to keep management aware of inventory levels. "Now we can go through a year with little snow and still be fairly solid," says Mr. Melrose. Embarrassed by Toro's poor-quality image,

(Continued)

the new president re-dedicated the company to quality and appointed a vice-president for product excellence.

By 1985, the Minneapolis firm was a much slimmer, more carefully managed, and apparently healthier company. Fiscal 1984 earnings were $8.3 million on sales of $280 million compared with a modest profit in 1983. Sales have not returned to pre-disaster levels and probably will not for some time. Nevertheless, the dividend has been restored and top management is cautiously optimistic. To keep costs down, some manufacturing is done outside the U.S. Parts are being produced in South Korea, Taiwan, Japan, and Singapore. An assembly plant has opened near Winnepeg, Manitoba. Fabrication joint ventures are under way in New Zealand and Venezuela.

As a result of its successes, Toro management has switched from what it called "a defensive, survival mode" to "a more opportunistic direction." Mr. Melrose put two executive vice-presidents in charge of day-to-day operations so that he could focus on new ventures. According to Melrose, the company is "emphasizing businesses that deliver high margins and don't have a lot of vulnerability on the downside," such as turf irrigation and commercial lawn care equipment. "Long-range planning is something new at Toro," he says. "In the past we didn't spend much time thinking about the future. We thought only about how we're going to get out of the mess."

SOURCES: R. Gibson, "Toro Breaks Out of Its Slump after Taking Drastic Measures," *Wall Street Journal* (January 23, 1985), p. 7. "Toro: Coming to Life after Warm Weather Wilted Its Big Plans," *Business Week* (October 10, 1983), p. 118.

Divestment strategy   Divestment is appropriate when corporate problems can be traced to the poor performance of an SBU or product line or when a division or SBU is a "misfit," unable to synchronize itself with the rest of the corporation. This was the situation Exxon faced with its office systems division. The big oil company was unable to properly manage the acquired entrepreneurial units of Qwip, which made facsimile machines; Vydec, an early leader in word processors; and Qyx, which produced the first electronic typewriter. "Every move had to be reviewed and approved by oil men who just didn't understand the industry," said a former Exxon manager.[17]

Still another situation appropriate for divestment is that of a division's needing more resources to be competitive than a corporation is willing to provide. Some corporations, however, select divestment instead of the more painful turnaround strategy. With divestment, top management is able to do one of two things: (1) select a scapegoat to blame for all of the corporation's problems, or (2) generate a lot of cash in the sale, which can be used to reduce debt and buy time. The second rationale may explain why Pan American chose to sell the most profitable parts of its corporation, the Pan Am Building in New York and Intercontinental Hotels, while keeping its money-losing airline.[18]

Captive company strategy   Rarely discussed as a separate strategy, the captive strategy is similar to divestment; but instead of selling off divisions or product lines, the corporation reduces the scope of some of its functional activities and becomes "captive" to another firm. In this manner, it reduces expenses and achieves some security through its relationship with the stronger firm. An agreement is reached with a key customer that in return for a large number of long-run purchases, the captive company will guarantee delivery at a favorable price. Since 75% or more of its product is sold to a single purchaser, the captive company can reduce its marketing expenditures and develop long-run production schedules that reduce costs. If supplies ever become a problem for the captive company, it can call on its key customer to help put pressure on a reluctant supplier.

One interesting version of this strategy has developed out of the recent popularity of "just-in-time" deliveries. Emulating successful Japanese firms, General Motors is building a plant for its new Saturn company. It plans to require its key suppliers to build *satellite plants* around the Saturn facility for the sole purpose of manufacturing parts to Saturn specifications and delivering them to the Saturn assembly lines as they are needed. These satellite plants will thus be *captive* to General Motors.

Liquidation strategy   A strategy of last resort when other retrenchment strategies have failed, an early liquidation may serve stockholder interests better than an inevitable bankruptcy. To the extent that top management identifies with the corporation, liquidation is perceived as an admission of failure. Pride and reputation are liquidated as well as jobs and financial assets.

From their research of companies in difficulty, Nystrom and Starbuck conclude that top management very often does not perceive that crises are developing. When top managers do eventually notice trouble, they are prone to attribute the problems to temporary environmental disturbances and tend to follow profit strategies of postponing investments, reducing maintenance, halting training, liquidating assets, denying credit to customers, and raising prices. They adopt a weathering-the-storm attitude. "A major activity becomes changing the accounting procedures in order to conceal the symptoms."[19] Even when things are going terribly, there is a strong temptation for top management to avoid liquidation in the hope of a miracle. It is for this reason that a corporation needs a strong board of directors who can safeguard stockholder interests by telling top management when to quit.

Combination strategies can be composed of any number of variations of the preceding strategies. The main focus is on the conscious use of several overall strategies (stability, growth, retrenchment) in several SBUs at the same time or at different times in the future.[20]

Combination Strategies

Before the selection of a particular corporate strategy, top management must critically analyze the pros and cons of each feasible alternative in light of the corporation's situation. The tendency to select the most obvious strategy can sometimes lead to serious trouble in the long run. The orientation of most top management toward growth strategies has resulted in a high value being placed on acquisitions and mergers as preferred alternatives. In fact, a survey of 236 chief executive officers of the largest 1,000 U.S. industrial firms found that CEOs prefer diversification and acquisition over new product planning and development as a growth strategy.[21] A similar survey of chief financial officers found that the major motive for acquiring another firm was to generate fast growth.[22] Not surprisingly, W. T. Grimm and Company, a merger broker which keeps records on mergers, acquisitions, and divestitures, reported these transactions for the first nine months of 1984 to total $103.2 billion—more than $20 billion higher than the prior period for a full year![23]

Evaluation of Corporate Strategies

Nevertheless, it is estimated that because of poor planning, high prices, mismanaged consolidation, or bad luck, one-half to two-thirds of all acquisitions are ultimately failures.[24] The explanation may lie in top management's overestimating the benefits to be derived or from valuing too highly their own skills in managing a new business.

A number of techniques are available to aid strategic planners in estimating the likely effects of strategic changes. One of these was derived from the research project on the profit impact of market strategies (**PIMS**), which was discussed in Chapter 6. From the analysis of data from a large number of business corporations, key factors were identified in regression equations to explain large variations in ROI, profitability, and cash flow. As part of PIMS, reports are prepared for a participating corporation's business units showing how its expected level of ROI is influenced by each factor. A second report shows how ROI can be expected to change, both in the short and long runs, if particular changes are made in its strategy.[25]

Sometimes referred to as division strategy, business strategy focuses on improving the competitive position of a corporation's products or services within the specific industry or market segment that the division serves. It is a strategy developed by a division to complement the overall corporate strategy. Although many business strategies appear to be similar to corporate

Business (SBU) Strategies

strategies, they differ in terms of their orientation to a specific market and to a specific line of business or product.

Portfolio Strategies   The nine cell matrix discussed in Chapter 6 as the GE Business Screen or the Directional Policy Matrix may be used to identify suggested business level strategies. The combination of industry attractiveness and competitive strengths provides a matrix of strategies, as depicted in Fig. 7.2.

Depending on the cell in which a division or product is placed, the matrix recommends one of the following eight strategies:[26]

1. *Disinvest.* Products falling in this area will probably be losing money— not necessarily every year; but losses in bad years will outweigh the gains in good years. It is unlikely that any activity will surprise management by falling within this area because its poor performance should already be known.

2. *Phased withdrawal.* A product with an average-to-weak position with low, unattractive market prospects, or a weak position with average market prospects is unlikely to be earning any significant amounts of cash. The indicated strategy is used to realize the value of the assets on a controlled basis in order to make resources available for employment elsewhere.

3. *Cash generator.* A typical situation in this matrix area is that of a product moving toward the end of its life cycle, which is being replaced in the market by other products. No finance should be allowed for expansion; and the product, so long as it is profitable, should be used as a source of cash for other areas. Every effort should be made to maximize

BUSINESS STRENGTH/COMPETITIVE POSITION

		Strong	Average	Weak
INDUSTRY ATTRACTIVENESS	High	Leader	Try Harder	Double or Quit
	Medium	Leader / Growth	Growth / Proceed with Care	Phased Withdrawal
	Low	Cash Generator	Phased Withdrawal	Disinvest

Figure 7.2   **Portfolio strategies.**

profits, because activity concerning the product has no long-term future.

4. *Proceed with care.* In this position, some investment may be justified, but major investments should be made with extreme caution.

5. *Growth.* Investment should be made to allow the product to grow with the market. In general, the product will generate sufficient cash to be self-financing and will not be making demands on other corporate cash resources.

6. *Double or quit.* Tomorrow's breadwinners among today's R&D projects may come from this area. Putting the strategy simply, those with the best prospects should be selected for full backing and development. The rest should be abandoned.

7. *Try harder.* The implication is that the product can be moved toward the leader box by judicious application of resources. In these circumstances the division may wish to make available resources in excess of what the product can generate for itself.

8. *Leader.* The strategy should be to maintain a leading position. At certain stages this may imply that resources to expand capacity may be required, but that the cash required need not be met entirely from funds generated by the product, although its earnings should be above average.

The nine cell portfolio matrix can help a division or SBU develop appropriate alternative strategies. It is *not*, however, a push-button technique. It should be used sensibly and in conjunction with other methods. Portfolio analysis by its very nature tends to be somewhat simplistic. It may, for example, rule out what might be the very profitable strategy of being a minority producer in certain niche markets when industry attractiveness is very low.[27] When the eight portfolio strategies are considered in their most simplified form, they form the three popular strategies of *build, hold, or harvest.* Unfortunately, these are short-run cash-oriented terms that provide little, if any, guidance in developing a product line's business strength or competitive position.

Porter, an authority on business level strategies, proposes three generic strategies for outperforming other corporations in a particular industry: overall cost leadership, differentiation, and focus.[28]

Porter's Competitive Strategies

1. *Overall cost leadership.* This strategy requires "aggressive construction of efficient-scale facilities, vigorous pursuit of cost reductions from

experience, tight cost and overhead control, avoidance of marginal customer accounts, and cost minimization in areas like R&D, service, sales force, advertising, and so on."[29] Having a low-cost position gives an SBU a defense against rivals. Its lower costs allow it to continue to earn profits during times of heavy competition.

Backward vertical integration (a corporate-level strategy that can also be used at the divisional level) is one route to an overall low-cost position. For example, Humana, Inc., the hospital operator, has moved into the health insurance field as the low-cost competitor. It is able to underprice Blue Cross, Blue Shield because it controls the source of 60% of all medical bills, the hospital. "The one feature of our product that is clearly understood by employers is that because we own and operate hospitals, we can control costs," states William Werroven, chief operating officer of Humana's group health division.[30]

2. *Differentiation.* This strategy involves the creating of a product or service that is perceived throughout its industry as being unique. It may be accomplished through design or brand image, technology, features, dealer network, or customer service. Differentiation is a viable strategy for earning above-average returns in a specific business because the resulting brand loyalty lowers customer sensitivity to price.

Examples of the successful use of a differentiation strategy are Walt Disney Productions, Maytag appliances, Mercedes-Benz automobiles, and Beech-Nut Nutrition Corporation. Owned by Nestlé, Beech-Nut has chosen to attack Gerber's 70% share of the baby food market by launching *Stages,* a line of 123 baby foods. The Stages line of products is color-coded to correspond to different stages of an infant's development. "Baby food was just a commodity sold entirely on price," says Niels Hoyvald, Beech-Nut's president and CEO. "I wanted to set us apart." Even though Stages costs 10 to 30% more than comparable products offered by the competition, it has managed to earn 50% of the business in a few of the markets in which it competes. Profits are up nicely.[31]

3. *Focus.* Similar to the corporate strategy of concentration, this business strategy focuses on a particular buyer group, product line segment, or geographic market. The value of the strategy derives from the belief that an SBU that focuses its efforts is better able to serve its narrow strategic target more effectively or efficiently than can its competition. Focus does, however, necessitate a trade-off between profitability and overall market share.

The focus strategy has two variants: *cost focus* and *differentiation focus*. In cost focus, the company seeks a cost advantage in its target segment, while in differentiation focus, a company seeks differentiation in its target segment. "The target segments must either have buyers with unusual needs or else the production and delivery system that best serves the target must differ from that of the other industry segments."[32] A good example of cost focus is Hammermill Paper's move into low-volume, high-quality specialty papers. By focusing on the quality niche of the market, Hammermill is able to compete against larger companies which need high-volume production runs to reach breakeven. Johnson Products, in contrast, has successfully used a differentiation focus by manufacturing and selling hair care and cosmetic products to black consumers. This strategy was most successful when the large cosmetics companies ignored the product preferences of the black community.

Porter argues that a business unit must achieve one of these three "generic" business strategies to be successful. Otherwise, the business unit is *stuck in the middle* of the competitive marketplace with no competitive advantage and is doomed to below-average performance.[33] Research generally supports Porter's contention.[34] Before selecting one of these strategies for a particular corporate business or SBU, it is important to assess its feasibility in terms of divisional strengths and weaknesses. Porter lists some of the commonly required skills and resources, as well as organizational requirements, in Table 7.2.

It is interesting to note that the strategic groups of Miles and Snow discussed in Chapter 4 can be characterized by their usage of Porter's competitive strategies. *Defenders* tend to use overall cost leadership, whereas *prospectors* tend to follow a differentiation or focus strategy. *Reactors* are those companies with no real competitive strategy who are "stuck in the middle." *Analyzers* use whichever competitive strategy is most appropriate for each of their various product lines or businesses.

Functional-Area Strategies

The principal focus of functional-area strategy is to maximize corporate and divisional resource productivity. Given the constraints of corporate and divisional strategies, functional-area strategies are developed to pull together the various activities and competencies of each function to improve performance. For example, a manufacturing department would be very concerned with developing a strategy to reduce costs and to improve the quality of its output. Marketing, in comparison, typically would be concerned with developing strategies to increase sales.

Some of the many possible functional strategies are listed in the decision

Table 7.2   **Requirements for Generic Competitive Strategies**

Generic Strategy	Commonly Required Skills and Resources	Common Organizational Requirements
Overall cost leadership	Sustained capital investment and access to capital Process engineering skills Intense supervision of labor Products designed for ease in manufacture Low-cost distribution system	Tight cost control Frequent, detailed control reports Structured organization and responsibilities Incentives based on meeting strict quantitative targets
Differentiation	Strong marketing abilities Product engineering Creative flair Strong capability in basic research Corporate reputation for quality or technological leadership Long tradition in the industry or unique combination of skills drawn from other businesses Strong cooperation from channels	Strong coordination among functions in R&D, product development, and marketing Subjective measurement and incentives instead of quantitative measures Amenities to attract highly skilled labor, scientists, or creative people
Focus	Combination of the above policies directed at the particular strategic target	Combination of the above policies directed at the particular strategic target

SOURCE: Reprinted with permission of The Free Press, a division of Macmillan, Inc. from *Competitive Strategy* by M. E. Porter, pp. 40–41. Copyright © 1980 by The Free Press.

tree depicted in Fig. 7.3. These are some of the many functional-area strategy decisions that need to be made if corporate and divisional strategies are to be implemented properly by functional managers. For example, once top management decides to acquire another publicly held corporation, it must decide how it will obtain the funds necessary for the purchase. A very popular financial strategy is the *leveraged buyout*. In a leveraged buyout, a company is acquired in a transaction financed largely by borrowing. Ultimately, the debt is paid with money generated by the acquired company's operations or by sales of its assets. This is what happened when Westray Transportation, Inc., an affiliate of Westray Corporation, purchased Atlas Van Lines in 1984. Under the leveraged buyout plan Atlas stockholders received $18.35 for each share of stock outstanding and the company was taken private by Westray. The money was funded by Merrill Lynch Interfunding, Inc. and Acquisition Funding Corp. Westray then paid the debt from the operations of its new subsidiary, Atlas Van Lines.[35]

A functional area that has received a great deal of attention recently in

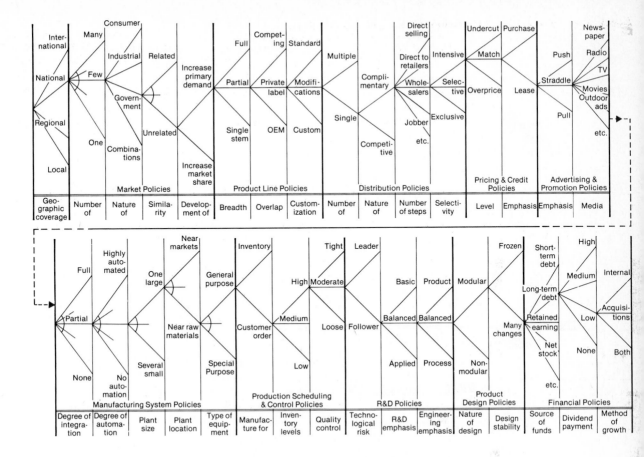

Figure 7.3   Functional strategy decision tree.
SOURCE: C. W. Hofer, "The Uses and Limitations of Statistical Division Theory" (Boston: Intercollegiate Case Clearing House), no. 9-171-653, 1971, p. 34. Copyright © 1971 by C. W. Hofer. Reprinted by permission.

terms of strategy is technology (R&D). Those corporations that are dependent on technology for their success are becoming concerned increasingly with developing R&D strategies that complement business level strategies.[36] As shown in Fig. 7.3, one of the R&D choices is to either be a *leader* or a *follower*. Porter suggests that the decision to become a technological leader or follower can be a way of achieving either overall low cost or differentiation.[37] This choice is described in more detail in Table 7.3.

Other functional strategies, such as the location and scale of manufacturing facilities, distribution channels, and the choice of push (promotion) versus pull (advertising) marketing emphasis can only be mentioned briefly in this book. For a detailed discussion of functional strategies, refer to ad-

Table 7.3   **Technological Leadership and Competitive Advantage**

	Technological Leadership	Technological Followership
Cost Advantage	Pioneer the lowest-cost product design Be the first firm down the learning curve Create low-cost ways of performing value activities	Lower the cost of the product or value activities by learning from the leader's experience Avoid R&D costs through imitation
Differentiation	Pioneer a unique product that increases buyer value Innovate in other activities to increase buyer value	Adapt the product or delivery system more closely to buyer needs by learning from the leader's experience

SOURCE: Reprinted with permission of The Free Press, a division of Macmillan, Inc. from *Competitive Advantage* by M. E. Porter, p. 181. Copyright © 1985 by Michael E. Porter.

vanced texts in each of the functional areas (e.g., *Marketing Planning and Strategy* by S. C. Jain, among others) or *Strategy, Policy, and Central Management* by Newman, Logan, and Hegarty.[38]

Strategies to Avoid

There are a number of strategies used at various levels that are very dangerous. They may be considered by managers because of a poor analysis or lack of creativity.[39]

1. *Follow the leader.* Imitating the strategy of a leading competitor may seem good, but it ignores a firm's particular strengths and weaknesses. Atari learned this when it attempted to move into the personal computer business against Apple and Commodore.

2. *Hit another home run.* If a corporation is successful because it pioneered an extremely successful product, it has a tendency to search for another superproduct that will ensure growth and prosperity. Like betting on "long shots" at the horse races, the probability of finding a second winner is slight. Polaroid spent a lot of money developing an "instant" movie camera, but the public ignored it.

3. *Arms race.* Entering into a spirited battle with another firm for increased market share may increase sales revenue, but will probably be more than offset by increases in advertising, promotion, R&D, and manufacturing costs. Since the deregulation of airlines, price wars and rate "specials" have contributed to low profit margins or bankruptcy for many major airlines.

4. *Do everything.* When faced with a number of interesting opportunities, there may be a tendency to take all of them. At first, a corporation may have enough resources to develop each into a project, but it soon runs short as the many projects demand large infusions of time, money, and

energy. Convinced that its brand name would serve as an effective umbrella for a whole series of new products, Toro Company quickly ran out of money and time (see Illustrative Example 7.3 on page 179).

5. *Losing hand.* A corporation may have invested so much in a particular strategy that top management is unwilling to accept the fact that the strategy is not successful. Believing that it has "too much invested to quit," the corporation continues to throw good money after bad. Pan American chose to sell its Pan Am Building and Intercontinental Hotels, the most profitable parts of the corporation, to keep its money-losing airline flying. It then agreed to pay $1.1 billion to Airbus Industries for 28 new jet planes.

7.2 SELECTION OF THE BEST STRATEGY

Once potential strategic alternatives have been identified and evaluated in terms of their pros and cons, top management must select one to implement. By this point, it is likely that a number of alternatives will have emerged as feasible. How is the decision made to determine the "best" strategy?

Choosing among a set of acceptable alternative strategies is often not easy. Each alternative is likely to have its proponents as well as critics. Steiner and Miner suggest using the twenty questions listed below before selecting one strategy over another. Perhaps the most important criterion to use is the ability of each alternative to satisfy agreed-upon objectives with the least use of resources and with the fewest number of negative side effects. It is therefore important to develop a tentative implementation plan in order to address the probable difficulties management is likely to face. Is the alternative worth the probable short-term as well as long-term costs?

TWENTY QUESTIONS TO USE IN EVALUATING STRATEGY

1. Does the strategy conform with the basic mission and purpose of the corporation? If not, a new competitive arena may be entered with which management is not familiar.

2. Is the strategy consistent with the corporation's external environment?

3. Is the strategy consistent with the internal strengths, objectives, policies, resources, and personal values of managers and employees? A strategy may not be completely in tune with all of these, but major dissonance should be avoided.

4. Does the strategy reflect the acceptance of minimum potential risk, balancing it against the maximum potential profit consistent with the corporation's resources and prospects?

(Continued)

5. Does the strategy fit a niche in the corporation's market not now filled by others? Is this niche likely to remain open long enough for the corporation to return capital investment plus the required level of profit? (Niches have a habit of filling up fast.)

6. Does the strategy conflict with other corporate strategies?

7. Is the strategy divided into substrategies that interrelate properly?

8. Has the strategy been tested with appropriate criteria (such as consistency with past, present, and prospective trends) and by the appropriate analytical tools (such as risk analysis, discounted cash flows, and so on)?

9. Has the strategy been tested by developing feasible implementation plans?

10. Does the strategy really fit the life cycles of the corporation's products?

11. Is the timing of the strategy correct?

12. Does the strategy pit the product against a powerful competitor? If so, reevaluate carefully.

13. Does the strategy leave the corporation vulnerable to the power of one major customer? If so, reconsider carefully.

14. Does the strategy involve the production of a new product for a new market? If so, reconsider carefully.

15. Is the corporation rushing a revolutionary product to market? If so, reconsider carefully.

16. Does the strategy imitate that of a competitor? If so, reconsider carefully.

17. Is it likely that the corporation can get to the market first with the new product or service? (If so, this is a great advantage. The second firm to market has much less chance of high returns on investment than the first.)

18. Has a really honest and accurate appraisal been made of the competition? Is the competition under- or overestimated?

19. Is the corporation trying to sell abroad something it cannot sell in the United States? (This is not usually a successful strategy.)

20. Is the market share likely to be sufficient to assure a required return on investment? (Market share and return on investment generally are closely related but differ from product to product and market to market.) Has this relationship of market and product been calculated?

SOURCE: Adapted with permission of Macmillan Publishing Company from *Management Policy and Strategy* by G. A. Steiner and J. B. Miner, pp. 219–221. Copyright © 1977 by Macmillan Publishing Company.

Detailed *scenarios* are often constructed using pro forma balance sheets and income statements to forecast the likely effect of each alternative strategy and its various programs on division and corporate return on investment. These scenarios are simply extensions of the industry scenarios discussed in Chapter 4. If, for example, industry scenarios suggest the probable emergence of a strong market demand for certain products, a series of alternative strategy scenarios can be developed. The alternative of acquiring another company having these products can be compared with the alternative of developing the products internally. Using three sets of estimated sales figures (optimistic, pessimistic, and most likely) for the new products over the next five years, the two alternatives can be evaluated in terms of their effect on future (pro forma or spread sheet) company financial statements. These scenarios can quickly become very complicated, especially if three sets of acquisition prices as well as development costs are also calculated. Nevertheless, this sort of detailed "what if" analysis is needed in order to realistically compare the projected outcome of each reasonable alternative strategy and its attendant programs, budgets, and procedures.

Regardless of the quantifiable pros and cons of each alternative, the actual decision will probably be influenced by a number of subjective factors that are difficult to quantify. Some of these factors are management's attitude toward risk, pressures from the external environment, influences from the corporate culture, and the personal needs and desires of key managers.

The attractiveness of a particular strategic alternative is partially a function of the amount of risk it entails. The risk is composed not only of the *probability* that the strategy will be effective, but also of the amount of *assets* the corporation must allocate to that strategy, and the length of *time* the assets will be unavailable for other uses. To quantify this risk, a number of people suggest the use of the *Capital Asset Pricing Model* (CAPM). CAPM is a financial method for linking the risk involved in a particular alternative with expected returns on a company's equity.[40]

The greater the amount of assets involved and the longer they are tied up, the more likely top management will demand a higher probability of success. This may be one reason why innovations seem to occur more often in small firms than in large, established corporations.[41] The small firm managed by an entrepreneur is willing to accept greater risk than would a large firm of diversified ownership. It is one thing to take a chance if you are the primary stockholder. It is something else if throngs of widows and orphans depend on your corporation's monthly dividend checks for living expenses.

The decision style of top management and the board of directors will heavily affect the way a decision is made. Thompson points out that there are two

Scenario Construction

Management's Attitude toward Risk

Decision Style

basic variables to each decision: (1) preferences about possible outcomes (the amount of agreement about the key objectives to be met), and (2) beliefs about cause/effect relationships (the amount of certainty that a specific means will cause a specific end).[42] These are depicted graphically in Fig. 7.4.

If there is total agreement among top management and the board about the corporation's mission and key objectives, one of two decision styles is likely to be used—computational or judgmental. A *computational* style is appropriate in those situations when there is a high degree of certainty about cause/effect relationships. The "best" alternative in this situation is either "obvious" or can be programmed on a computer using quantitative techniques. A *judgmental* style is typically used when there is no clear-cut connection between cause and effect. The ability of a specific strategy to achieve specific objectives is considered in terms of probabilities. This calls for executive judgment. This decision-making style is most likely to epitomize strategy makers who operate in what Mintzberg calls a "planning mode."

If, however, there is little agreement about the mission and key objectives of the corporation, one of two decision styles is likely to be used—compromising or inspirational. A *compromising* style is appropriate in those situations where there is a high degree of certainty about cause/effect relationships. The selection of the "best" strategy boils down to a compromise regarding which objectives top management and the board are willing to pursue. This style is characteristic of what Mintzberg calls the "adaptive

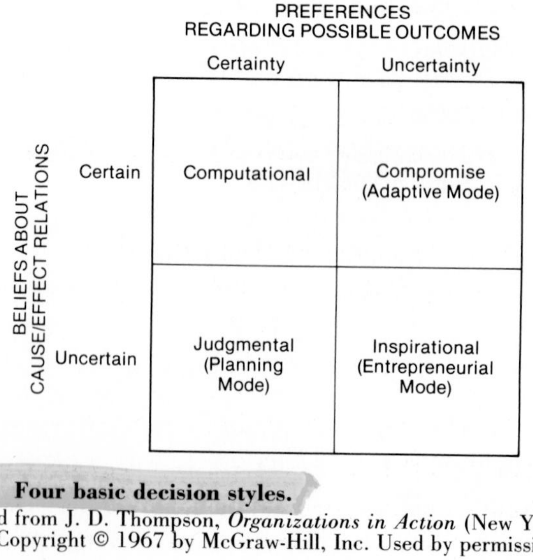

PREFERENCES
REGARDING POSSIBLE OUTCOMES

	Certainty	Uncertainty
Certain	Computational	Compromise (Adaptive Mode)
Uncertain	Judgmental (Planning Mode)	Inspirational (Entrepreneurial Mode)

BELIEFS ABOUT CAUSE/EFFECT RELATIONS

Figure 7.4   Four basic decision styles.

SOURCE: Adapted from J. D. Thompson, *Organizations in Action* (New York: McGraw-Hill, 1967), p. 134. Copyright © 1967 by McGraw-Hill, Inc. Used by permission.

mode." An *inspirational* style is likely to be used not only when there is no clear-cut connection between strategy and the accomplishment of objectives, but also when there is no agreement about which objective has priority. This style is characteristic of Mintzberg's "entrepreneurial mode." In this mode the founder of a corporation makes strategic decisions based on the personal need to achieve a vague goal such as success. To outsiders, such decisions may appear to be arbitrary and capricious.

The attractiveness of a strategic alternative will be affected by its perceived compatibility with the key stakeholders in a corporation's task environment. These stakeholders are typically concerned with certain aspects of a corporation's activities. Creditors want to be paid on time. Unions exert pressure for comparable wages and employment security. Governments and interest groups demand social responsibility. Stockholders want dividends. All of these pressures must be considered in the selection of the best alternative.

Pressures from the External Environment

As previously stated in Chapter 4, most strategy makers will probably lean toward satisfying pressures from stakeholders in their corporation's task environment in the following order:

1. Customers

2. Employees

3. Owners

4. General public

5. Stockholders

6. Elected public officials

7. Government bureaucrats[43]

Questions to raise in attempting to assess the importance to the corporation of these pressures are the following:

1. Which stakeholders are most crucial for corporate success?

2. How much of what they want are they likely to get under this alternative?

3. What are they *likely* to do if they don't get what they want?

4. What is the probability that they will do it?

By ranking the key stakeholders in a corporation's task environment and asking these questions, strategy makers should be better able to choose strategic alternatives that minimize external pressures.

**Pressures from
the Corporate
Culture**

As pointed out in Chapter 5, the norms and values shared by the members of a corporation do affect the attractiveness of certain alternatives. If a strategy is incompatible with the corporate culture, the likelihood of its success will be very low. Footdragging and even sabotage will result as employees fight to resist a radical change in corporate philosophy.

Precedents from the past tend to restrict the kinds of objectives and strategies that can be seriously considered. The "aura" of the founding father of a corporation lingers long past his lifetime because his values have been imprinted on the corporation's members. According to Cyert and March,

> Organizations have memories in the form of precedents, and individuals in the coalition are strongly motivated to accept the precedents as binding. Whether precedents are formalized in the shape of an official standard operating procedure or are less formally stored, they remove from conscious consideration many agreements, decisions, and commitments that might well be subject to renegotiation in an organization without a memory.[44]

In considering a strategic alternative, the strategy makers must assess its compatibility with the corporate culture. To the extent that there is little fit, management must decide if it should (1) take a chance on ignoring the culture, (2) manage around the culture by changing the implementation plan, (3) try to change the culture to fit the strategy, or (4) change the strategy to fit the culture.[45] If the culture will be strongly opposed to a possible strategy, it is foolhardy to ignore the culture. Further, a decision to proceed with a particular strategy without being committed to changing the culture or managing around the culture (both very tricky and time consuming) is dangerous. Nevertheless, restricting a corporation to only those strategies that are completely compatible with its culture may eliminate from consideration the most profitable alternatives. For an example of an attempt to change a corporate culture in order to implement a change in strategy, see Illustrative Example 7.4.

CHANGING THE CULTURE AT PROCTER & GAMBLE

*Illustrative
Example
7.4*

In choosing to emphasize overall low cost as the key competitive strategy for each of its product lines, Procter & Gamble under President Smale is attempting a turnaround strategy of large proportions. By firing people to boost overall management performance, Smale risks undermining the employee loyalty that has been one of the company's greatest strengths. Apparently some board members are unsettled by what they see as a conflict

(Continued)

between P&G's time-honored dedication to quality, high-performance products and its new emphasis on controlling costs. Similarly, the drive to move quickly and to take more risks with new products goes counter to the firm's traditional cautious style. Nevertheless, P&G must do something. Because its detergent and consumer paper goods markets are maturing, the company has been unable to attain its cherished goal of doubling its unit volume every ten years. The reason given is that consumers are increasingly responsive to price. The question remains, nonetheless: Will Smale be successful in changing P&G's corporate culture to implement a change from its traditional quality differentiation strategy to one of overall low cost?

SOURCE: "Why Procter & Gamble Is Playing It Even Tougher," *Business Week* (July 18, 1984), pp. 176–186.

Needs and Desires of Key Managers

Even the most attractive alternative may not be selected if it is contrary to the needs and desires of important top managers. A person's ego may be tied to a particular proposal to the extent that all other alternatives are strongly lobbied against. Key executives in operating divisions, for example, may be able to influence other people in top management in favor of a particular alternative so that objections to it are ignored.

An example of such a situation was described by John DeLorean when he was at Pontiac Division of General Motors in 1959. At that time, General Motors was developing a new rear-engined auto called Corvair. Ed Cole, the General Manager of Chevrolet Division, was very attracted to the idea of building the first modern, rear-engine American automobile. A number of engineers, however, were worried about the safety of the car and made vigorous attempts to either change the "unsafe" suspension system or keep the Corvair out of production. "One top corporate engineer told me that he showed his test results to Cole but by then he said, 'Cole's mind was made up.' "[46] By this time, there had developed quite a bit of documented evidence that the car should not be built as designed. However, according to DeLorean,

. . . Cole was a strong product voice and a top salesman in company affairs. In addition, the car, as he proposed it, would cost less to build than the same car with a conventional rear suspension. Management not only went along with Cole, it also told the dissenters in effect to "stop these objections. Get on the team, or you can find someplace else to work." The ill-fated Corvair was launched in the fall of 1959.

The results were disastrous. I don't think any one car before or since produced as gruesome a record on the highway as the Corvair. It was designed and promoted to appeal to the spirit and flair of young people. It was sold in part as a sports car. Young Corvair owners, therefore, were trying to bend their cars around curves at high speeds and were killing themselves in alarming numbers.[47]

In only a few years, General Motors was inundated by lawsuits over the Corvair. Ralph Nader soon published a book primarily about the Corvair called *Unsafe at Any Speed,* launching his career as a consumer advocate.

Strategic Choice Model   A technique found to be useful in methodically comparing various strategic alternatives is that of the Strategic Choice Model developed by Snyder.[48] As shown in Table 7.4, the model incorporates both the alternatives under consideration and the decision criteria considered most relevant by the strategic managers using the model.

The specific alternatives, criteria, and numbers given in Table 7.4 are those for a specific computer corporation and, of course, will vary depending upon the corporation and situation under consideration. The choice model is developed by going through the following seven steps:

1. List the feasible alternatives on the vertical axis. (Six are given in Table 7.4—for example, personal home computers and software development.)

Table 7.4   **Strategic Choice Model**

	Weighted Decision Criteria						
Alternatives	Internal Consistency (5×)	External Consistency (4×)	Short Run Return (3×)	Long Run Return (5×)	Marketability (4×)	Investment Feasibility (5×)	Total of Multiplied Weights
Personal home computers	4 = 20	5 = 20	3 = 9	5 = 25	3 = 12	4 = 20	106
Software development	5 = 25	5 = 20	4 = 12	5 = 25	5 = 20	4 = 20	122
Expansion/ retail stores	4 = 20	3 = 12	3 = 9	5 = 25	3 = 12	3 = 15	93
Management consulting	3 = 15	5 = 20	2 = 6	5 = 25	3 = 12	2 = 10	88
Computer networking	5 = 25	4 = 16	4 = 12	5 = 25	5 = 20	5 = 25	123
Communications satellite	2 = 10	4 = 16	1 = 3	5 = 25	2 = 8	3 = 15	77

SOURCE: N. H. Snyder, "A Strategic Choice Model," A Working Paper (Charlottesville, Va.: McIntire School of Commerce, University of Virginia), 1982. Used by permission.

2. List important internal and external considerations (decision criteria) along the horizontal axis. Although it is not done in Table 7.4, internal consistency can be subdivided into separate columns showing internal consistency with each functional area. Likewise, external consistency can be subdivided into external consistency with each element in the task environment. Obviously, other criteria in addition to those given in Table 7.4 can be listed for any particular situation.

3. Weight each decision criterion listed on the horizontal axis from 1 to 5 according to its importance to the firm. For example, the strategists who prepared Table 7.4 believed that long-run return on investment was more important than was short-run return. Thus, short-run return was weighted 3 and long-run return was weighted 5.

4. Evaluate each feasible alternative in terms of its effect on each criterion listed on the horizontal axis. The effect may be positive, neutral, or negative. Use a scale ranging from -5 (negative effect) to $+5$ (positive effect). The numerical weight of each criterion for each alternative is the left side of each "equation" at the intersection of each row and column. For example, in Table 7.4 software development is thought to have a positive effect $(+4)$ on the corporation's short-run return and an extremely positive effect $(+5)$ on its long-run return.

5. Multiply the numerical weight for each criterion in the horizontal axis (calculated in step 3) by the numerical weight on the left side of each equation (calculated in step 4). The resulting product of each multiplication is recorded on the right side of each "equation." For example, the value of software development on short-run return is $3 \times 4 = 12$.

6. Sum the products for each row. Record that total in the column on the far right. For example, we find the sum of the products for the "personal home computers" alternative by adding thus: $20 + 20 + 9 + 25 + 12 + 20 = 106$.

7. Find the "best" alternative; it has the highest numerical total. Given the decision criteria and weights stated in Table 7.4, "computer networking" is the best alternative. If the corporation has the resources to develop more than one alternative at a time, the model is of use in establishing the priority of each selected alternative.

The selection of the best strategic alternative is not the end of strategy formulation. Policies must now be established to define the ground rules for implementation. As defined earlier, policies are broad guidelines for making decisions. They flow from the selected strategy to provide guidance for deci-

**7.3
DEVELOPMENT
OF POLICIES**

sion making throughout the organization. Corporate policies are broad guidelines for divisions to follow in order to comply with corporate strategy. These policies are interpreted and implemented through each division's own objectives and strategies. Divisions may then develop their own policies that will be guidelines for their functional areas to follow.

One example of a corporate-level policy is that developed by Ford Motor Company. Concerned with the historic lack of cooperation between Ford U.S. and Ford of Europe, Ford's top management developed a company-wide policy requiring any new car design to be easily adaptable to any market in the world. Previous to this policy, Ford of Europe developed cars strictly for its own market, while engineers in the United States separately designed their own products. The policy was a natural result of Ford's emphasis on manufacturing efficiency and becoming more globally integrated as a corporation. One result of this new policy was the program to produce the European Sierra and its U.S. counterpart the Merkur. The cost to convert the European Sierra to meet all U.S. safety and emission standards was about one-fourth of what it would have cost to convert previous European models. The Taurus and Sable models have also been engineered for easy conversion to overseas markets, as well.[49]

Some policies will be expressions of a corporation's *critical success factors* (CSF). Critical success factors are those elements of a company that determine its strategic success or failure. They vary from company to company. IBM, for example, sees customer service as its critical success factor. McDonald's CSF is quality, cleanliness, and value. Hewlett-Packard is concerned with new product development.[50] Policies may therefore be guidelines for decision making based on a corporation's critical success factors. At Lazarus Department Store in Columbus, Ohio, for example, customer service is a critical success factor. Store policies state that the customer is *always* right. Even if a department manager believes that a customer bought a particular shirt from a competitor, the manager is bound by policy to accept the shirt and to give back money to the customer. Lazarus' top management believes that even though the store may be taken advantage of in the short run by a few people, the store will make up for it in the long run with good will and increased market share.

Policies tend to be rather long lived and may even outlast the particular strategy that caused their creation. Interestingly, these general policies, such as "The customer is always right" or "Research and development should get first priority on all budget requests," can become, in time, part of a corporation's culture. Such policies may make the implementation of specific strategies easier. They may also restrict top management's strategic options in the future. It is for this reason that a change in strategy should be followed quickly by a change in policies. It is one way to manage the corporate culture.

This chapter has focused on the last stage of the strategy formulation process: generating, evaluating, and selecting the best strategic alternative. It also has discussed the development of policies for implementing strategies.

7.4 SUMMARY AND CONCLUSION

There are three main kinds of strategies: corporate, business (divisional), and functional. Corporate strategies fall into four main families: stability, growth, retrenchment, and a combination of these. Epitomized by a steady-as-she-goes philosophy, *stability* strategies are (1) no change, (2) profit, (3) pause, and (4) proceed with caution. The very popular *growth* strategies are (1) vertical integration, (2) horizontal integration, (3) diversification, (4) merger, acquisition, and joint ventures, (5) concentration, and (6) investment. *Retrenchment* strategies are generally unpopular because they imply failure. They include (1) turnaround, (2) divestment, (3) captive company, and (4) liquidation. *Combination* strategies are composed of a number of these strategies.

Business or divisional strategies are described as the logical result of portfolio analysis. The nine cell portfolio matrix suggests eight recommended strategies based upon a division's or product line's situation in terms of industry attractiveness and business strengths. Porter's three generic competitive strategies—*overall cost leadership, differentiation,* and *focus*—are also suggested. Functional-area strategies are described briefly in terms of their effect upon maximizing corporate and divisional resource productivity.

The selection of the best strategic alternative from projected scenarios will probably be affected by a number of factors. Among them are management's attitude toward risk, pressures from the external environment, influences from the corporate culture, and the personal needs and desires of key managers. A Strategic Choice Model is recommended as a means of comparing feasible alternatives.

Corporate policies operate as broad guidelines for divisions to follow in order to assure their compliance with corporate strategy. Divisions may then generate their own internal policies for their functional areas to follow. These policies define the ground rules for strategy implementation and serve to align corporate activities in the new strategic direction.

DISCUSSION QUESTIONS

1. Is the profit strategy really a stability strategy? Why or why not?
2. Why is growth the most frequently used corporate-level strategy?
3. How does horizontal integration differ from concentric diversification?

4. In what situations at the corporate level might Porter's generic competitive strategies be useful?

5. Can corporate-level strategies also be used at the divisional or functional levels?

6. How can scenarios be used in conjunction with the Strategic Choice Model?

NOTES

1. W. F. Glueck, *Business Policy and Strategic Management,* 3rd ed. (New York: McGraw-Hill, 1980), p. 199.

2. Glueck, p. 290. Glueck uses the term *stable growth* instead of *stability.*

3. J. F. Berry, "Amazing Grace and Unbelievers," *Washington Post* (December 6, 1981), pp. F1 and F3.

4. R. M. Cyert and J. G. March, *A Behavioral Theory of the Firm* (Englewood Cliffs, N.J.: Prentice-Hall, 1963).

5. J. Vesey, "Vertical Integration: Its Effects on Business Performance," *Managerial Planning* (May–June 1978), pp. 11–15.

6. R. H. Hayes and W. J. Abernathy, "Managing Our Way to Economic Decline," *Harvard Business Review* (July–August 1980), pp. 72–73.
A. R. Burgess, "Vertical Integration in Petrochemicals—1. The Concept and Its Measurement," *Long Range Planning* (August 1983), p. 55.
K. R. Harrigan, "Exit Barriers and Vertical Integration," *Academy of Management Proceedings* (August 1983), p. 34.

7. K. R. Harrigan, *Strategies for Vertical Integration* (Lexington, Mass.: D. C. Heath–Lexington Books, 1983), pp. 16–21.

8. P. Richter, "Intel Corp. Rations Products, Scrambles to Meet Demand," *Des Moines Register* (April 22, 1984), p. 9F.

9. R. P. Rumelt, *Strategy, Structure, and Economic Performance* (Cambridge, Mass: Harvard University Press, 1974).
R. W. Hearn, "Fighting Industrial Senility: A System for Growth in Mature Industries," *Journal of Business Strategy* (Fall 1982), pp. 3–20.
M. Lubatkin, "Mergers and the Performance of the Acquiring Firm," *Academy of Management Review* (April 1983), p. 218.
C. A. Montgomery and H. Singh, "Diversification Strategy and Systematic Risk," *Strategic Management Journal* (April–June 1984), pp. 181–191.

10. T. J. Peters and R. H. Waterman, Jr., *In Search of Excellence* (New York: Harper & Row, 1982), pp. 293–294.

11. R. Little, "Conglomerates Are Doing Better Than You Think," *Fortune* (May 28, 1984), p. 60.

12. P. M. Hirsch, "Ambushes, Shootouts, and Knights of the Roundtable: The Language of Corporate Takeovers" (Paper presented to the 40th Meeting of the Academy of Management, Detroit, Mich., August 1980).

13. D. Kneale and L. Landro, "IBM, CBS and Sears Plan a Joint Venture in

At-Home Marketing through Videotex," *Wall Street Journal* (February 15, 1984), p. 3.

14. "Gerber: Concentrating on Babies Again for Slow, Steady Growth," *Business Week* (August 22, 1983), p. 80.

15. B. Morris, "Making a Killing," from Special Report on Small Business, *Wall Street Journal* (May 20, 1985), pp. 32c, 36c–37c.

16. D. C. Hambrick, "Turnaround Strategies," in W. D. Guth (ed.), *Handbook of Business Strategy* (Boston: Warren, Gorham & Lamont, 1985), pp. 10.1–10.32.

17. "Exxon Wants Out of the Automated Office," *Business Week* (December 17, 1984), p. 39.

18. D. Brand, "Pan Am to Sell Its Hotel Chain to Grand Met," *Wall Street Journal* (August 24, 1981), p. 6.

19. P. C. Nystrom and W. H. Starbuck, "To Avoid Organizational Crises, Unlearn," *Organizational Dynamics* (Spring 1984), p. 55.

20. Glueck, pp. 229–331.

21. R. Hise and S. McDonald, "CEOs' Views On Strategy: A Survey," *Journal of Business Strategy* (Winter 1984), pp. 81 and 86.

22. H. K. Baker, T. O. Miller, and B. J. Ramsperger, "An Inside Look at Corporate Mergers and Acquisitions," *MSU Business Topics* (Winter 1981), p. 51.

23. T. Metz, "Debate over Mergers Intensifies amid Record Surge of Transactions," *Wall Street Journal* (January 2, 1985), p. 6B.

24. S. Prokesch and W. J. Powell, "Do Mergers Really Work?" *Business Week* (June 3, 1985), p. 88.

25. S. Schoeffler, R. D. Buzzell, and D. F. Heany, "Impact of Strategic Planning on Profit Performance," *Harvard Business Review* (March–April 1974), pp. 144–145.

26. D. E. Hussey, "Portfolio Analysis: Practical Experience with the Directional Policy Matrix," *Long Range Planning* (August 1978), pp. 3–4.

27. K. R. Harrigan, *Strategies for Declining Businesses* (Lexington, Mass.: D. C. Heath–Lexington Books, 1980).
    K. R. Harrigan, "End-Game Strategies for Declining Industries," *Harvard Business Review* (July–August 1983), pp. 111–120.

28. M. E. Porter, *Competitive Strategy* (New York: Free Press, 1980), pp. 36–46.

29. Porter, 1980, p. 35.

30. J. B. Hull, "Hospital Chains Battle Health Insurers, But Will Quality Care Lose in the War?" *Wall Street Journal* (February 5, 1985), p. 35.

31. J. Fierman, "Beech-Nut Bounces Up in the Baby Market," *Fortune* (December 24, 1984), p. 56.

32. M. E. Porter, *Competitive Advantage* (New York: Free Press, 1985), p. 15.

33. Porter, 1985, p. 16.

34. G. G. Dess and P. S. Davis, "Porter's Generic Strategies as Determinants of Strategic Group Membership and Organizational Performance," *Academy of Management Journal* (September 1984), p. 484.

35. J. Zaslow, "Atlas Van Lines Agrees to Buyout for $71.6 Million," *Wall Street Journal* (June 25, 1984), p. 10.

36. A. L. Frohman and D. Bitondo, "Coordinating Business Strategy and Technical Planning," *Long Range Planning* (December 1981), pp. 58–67.

37. Porter, 1985, p. 181.

38. S. C. Jain, *Marketing Planning* and *Strategy* (Cincinnati: South-Western Publishing Co., 1981).
W. H. Newman, J. P. Logan, and W. H. Hegarty, *Strategy, Policy, and Central Management,* 9th ed. (Cincinnati: South-Western Publishing Co., 1985).

39. A. A. Thompson, Jr., and A. J. Strickland, III, *Strategy and Policy* (Plano, Tex.: Business Publications, 1981), pp. 106–107.

40. D. R. Harrington, "Stock Prices, Beta, and Strategic Planning," *Harvard Business Review* (May–June 1983), pp. 157–164.
M. B. Coate, "Pitfalls in Portfolio Planning," *Long Range Planning* (June 1983), pp. 53–54.

41. Peters and Waterman, pp. 115–116.

42. J. D. Thompson, *Organizations in Action* (New York: McGraw-Hill, 1967), p. 134.

43. B. Z. Posner, and W. H. Schmidt, "Values and the American Manager: An Update," *California Management Review* (Spring 1984), p. 206.

44. R. M. Cyert and J. G. March, "A Behavioral Theory of Organizational Objectives," *Management Classics,* eds. M. T. Matteson and J. M. Ivancevich (Santa Monica, Calif.: Goodyear Publishing, 1977), p. 114.

45. H. Schwartz and S. M. Davis, "Matching Corporate Culture and Business Strategy," *Organizational Dynamics* (Summer 1981), p. 43.

46. J. P. Wright, *On a Clear Day You Can See General Motors* (Grosse Point, Mich.: Wright Enterprises, 1979), p. 54.

47. Wright, p. 55.

48. N. H. Snyder, "A Strategic Choice Model," a Working Paper (Charlottesville, Va.: McIntire School of Commerce, University of Virginia, 1982).

49. M. Edid and W. J. Hampton, "Now That It's Cruising, Can Ford Keep Its Foot on the Gas?" *Business Week* (February 11, 1985), pp. 48–52.

50. A. L. Mendlow, "Setting Corporate Goals and Measuring Organizational Effectiveness—A Practical Approach," *Long Range Planning* (February 1983), p. 72.

PART FOUR

STRATEGY IMPLEMENTATION AND CONTROL

- Chapter 8 STRATEGY IMPLEMENTATION
- Chapter 9 EVALUATION AND CONTROL

$$\mathcal{C}hapter\ 8$$

STRATEGY IMPLEMENTATION

STRATEGIC MANAGEMENT MODEL

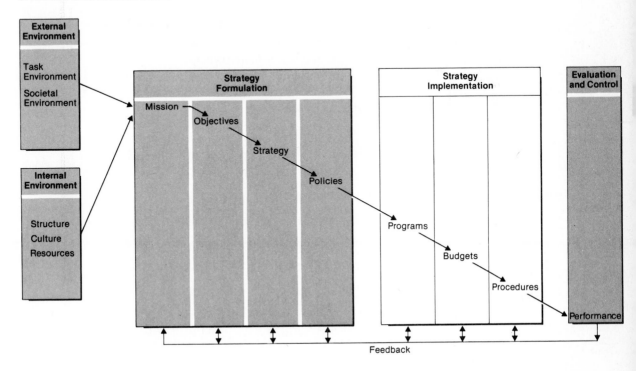

Once a strategy and a set of policies have been formulated, the focus of strategic management shifts to implementation. Corporate strategy makers must consider these three questions:

Who are the people who will carry out the strategic plan?

What must be done?

How are they going to do what is needed?

These questions and similar ones should have been addressed initially when the pros and cons of strategic alternatives were anlayzed. They must also be addressed now before appropriate implementation plans can be made. Unless top management can answer these basic questions in a satisfactory manner, even the best planned strategy will be unlikely to have the desired results.

For example, Fisher-Price's plan to expand from durable toys into children's playwear was a well-conceived strategy but failed in its introduction because of a strike and production problems at its partner's plant in Jamaica. Clothing arrived in stores six weeks late or not at all. Some retailers received shirts and no pants. Both Fisher-Price and the purchasing stores took a loss on the new line of clothes.[1]

Alexander's survey of ninety-three company presidents and divisional managers revealed the following ten problems experienced by over half of the group when attempting to implement a strategic change. These problems are listed in order of frequency of occurrence.

1. More time needed for implementation than originally planned.
2. Unanticipated major problems.
3. Ineffective coordination of activities.
4. Crises that distracted attention away from implementation.
5. Insufficient capabilities of the involved employees.
6. Uncontrollable external environmental factors.
7. Inadequate leadership and direction by departmental managers.
8. Inadequate training and instruction of lower-level employees.
9. Poor definition of key implementation tasks and activities.
10. Inadequate monitoring of activities by the information system.[2]

As shown in Fig. 8.1, poor implementation of an appropriate strategy may result in failure of the strategy. An excellent implementation plan, however, will not only cause the success of an appropriate strategy; it may also

STRATEGY FORMULATED

	Appropriate	Inappropriate
Excellent	*Success* Targets for growth, share, profits are met.	*Rescue or Ruin* Good execution may save a poor strategy or may hasten failure.
Poor	*Trouble* Poor execution hampers good strategy. Management may conclude strategy is inappropriate.	*Failure* Cause of failure hard to diagnose. Poor strategy marked by inability to execute.

STRATEGY IMPLEMENTED

Figure 8.1 **Interaction of strategy formulation and implementation.**
SOURCE: Reprinted by permission of the *Harvard Business Review.* An exhibit from "Making Your Marketing Strategy Work" by Thomas V. Bonoma (March/April 1984). Copyright © 1984 by the President and Fellows of Harvard College; all rights reserved.

rescue an inappropriate strategy. This is why an increasing number of chief executives are turning their attention to the problem of implementation. Now more than ever before, they realize that the successful implementation of a strategy depends on having the right organization structure, resource allocation, compensation program, information system, and corporate culture.[3]

8.1 *WHO* IMPLEMENTS STRATEGY?

Depending on how the corporation is organized, those who implement corporate strategy may be a different set of people from those who formulate it. In most large, multi-industry corporations, the implementers will be everyone in the organization except top management and the board of directors. Vice-presidents of functional areas and directors of divisions or SBUs will work with their subordinates to put together large-scale implementation plans. From these plans, plant managers, project managers, and unit heads will put together plans for their specific plants, departments, and units. As a result, every operational manager down to the first-line supervisor will be involved in some way in implementing corporate, divisional, and functional strategies.

It is important to note that most of the people in the corporation who are crucial to successful strategy implementation probably had little, if anything, to do with the development of the corporate strategy. As a result, they may be entirely ignorant of the vast amount of data and work that went into the formulation process. Unless changes in mission, objectives, strategies, and policies and their importance to the corporation are communicated clearly to all operational managers, there may be a lot of resistance and footdragging. In those instances when top management formulates strategy that challenges the corporation's culture, lower-level managers may even sabotage the implementation. These managers may hope to influence top management to abandon its new plans and return to the old ways.

8.2 *WHAT* MUST BE DONE?

The managers of divisions and functional areas work with their fellow managers to develop *programs, budgets,* and *procedures* for the implementation of strategy. A *program* is a statement of activities or steps needed to accomplish a single-use plan, the purpose of which is to make the strategy action-oriented. For example, top management may have chosen forward vertical integration as its best strategy for growth. The corresponding divisional strategy might be to purchase existing retail outlets from another firm rather than to build and develop its own outlets. Various programs—such as the following—would have to be developed to integrate the new stores into the corporation:

1. An advertising program ("Jones Surplus is now a part of Ajax Continental. Prices are lower. Selection is better.")

2. A training program for newly hired store managers as well as for those Jones Surplus managers the corporation has chosen to keep.

3. A program to develop reporting procedures that will integrate the stores into the corporation's accounting system.

4. A program to modernize the stores and to prepare them for a "grand opening."

Once these and other programs are developed, the budget process begins. A *budget* is a statement of a corporation's programs in terms of dollars. The detailed cost of each program is listed for planning and control purposes. Planning a budget is the last real check a corporation has on the feasibility of its selected strategy. An ideal strategy may be found to be completely impractical only after specific implementation programs are costed in detail. A good example was President Reagan's 1981 attempt to implement his strategy of reducing taxes, increasing defense spending, and balancing the federal budget without hurting the poor or the old. In theory, everyone agreed. In practice, conflict reigned. No member of Congress was willing to cut Social Security, the school lunch program, or any of a number of other social programs.

Once program, divisional, and corporate budgets are approved, procedures must be developed to guide the employees in their day-to-day actions. Sometimes referred to as Standard Operating Procedures, *procedures* are a system of sequential steps or techniques specified to perform a particular task or job. They typically detail the various activities that must be carried out to complete a corporation's programs. In the case of the corporation that decided to acquire another firm's retail outlets, new operating procedures must be established for, among others, in-store promotions, inventory ordering, stock selection, customer relations, credits and collections, warehouse distribution, pricing, paycheck timing, grievance handling, and raises and promotions. These procedures ensure that the day-to-day store operations will be consistent over time (that is, next week's work activities will be the same as this week's) and consistent among stores (that is, each store will operate in the same manner as the others). McDonald's, for example, has done an excellent job of developing very detailed procedures (and policing them!) to ensure that its policies are carried out to the letter in every one of its fast food retail outlets.

8.3 *HOW* IS STRATEGY TO BE IMPLEMENTED?

Up to this point, both strategy formulation and implementation have been discussed in terms of planning. Programs, budgets, and procedures are simply more detailed plans for the eventual implementation of strategy. The total management process includes, however, several additional activities crucial to implementation, such as organizing, staffing, directing, and controlling. Before *plans* can lead to actual performance, top management must ensure that the corporation is appropriately *organized*, programs are adequately *staffed*, and activities are being *directed* toward achieving desired objectives. These activities are reviewed briefly in this chapter. Top management must also ensure that there is progress toward objectives according to plan; this is a *control* function that will be discussed in Chapter 9.

Organizing

It is very likely that a change in corporate strategy will require some sort of change in the way a corporation is structured and in the kind of skills needed in particular positions. In a classic study of large American corporations, such as DuPont, General Motors, Sears Roebuck, and Standard Oil, Chandler concluded that changes in corporate strategy lead to changes in organization structure. He also concluded that American corporations follow a pattern of development from one kind of structural arrangement to another as they expand. According to him, these structural changes occur because inefficiences caused by the old structure have, by being pushed too far, become too obviously detrimental to live with: "The thesis deduced from these several propositions is then that structure follows strategy and that the most complex type of structure is the result of the concatenation [linking together] of several basic strategies."[4] Chandler therefore proposed the following as the sequence of what occurs:

1. New strategy is created.
2. New administrative problems emerge.
3. Economic performance declines.
4. New appropriate structure is invented.
5. Profit returns to its previous level.

Structure Follows Strategy   Chandler found that in their early years, corporations such as DuPont tend to have a centralized organizational structure that is well suited to their producing and selling a limited range of products. As they add new product lines, purchase their own sources of supply, and create their own distribution networks, they become too complex for highly centralized structures. In order to remain successful, this type of successful organization needs to shift to a decentralized structure with several semi-autonomous divisions.

In his book, *My Years with General Motors,* Alfred P. Sloan detailed how General Motors conducted such structural changes in the 1920s.[5] He saw decentralization of structure as centralized policy determination coupled with decentralized operating management. Once a strategy was developed for the total corporation by top management, the individual divisions, such as Chevrolet, Buick, etc., were free to choose how they would implement that strategy. Patterned after DuPont, GM found the decentralized multidivisional structure to be extremely effective in allowing the maximum amount of freedom for product development. Return on investment was used as a financial control.

Research generally supports Chandler's proposition that structure follows strategy (as well as the reverse proposition from Chapter 5 that structure influences strategy).[6] The recent decision by General Motors to restructure its automobile divisions into the three large-car divisions of Buick, Cadillac, and Oldsmobile and the two small-car divisions of Chevrolet and Pontiac is another example of how implementing strategic decisions may often require structural changes.

There is some evidence, however, that a change in strategy may not necessarily result in a corresponding change in structure if the corporation has very little competition. If a firm occupies a monopolistic position, with tariffs in its favor or close ties to a government, it can raise prices to cover internal administrative inefficiencies. This is an easier path for these firms to take than going through the pain of corporate reorganization.[7]

Although it is agreed that organizational structure must vary with different environmental conditions, which, in turn, affect an organization's strategy, there is no agreement about an optimal organizational design.[8] What was appropriate for DuPont and General Motors in the 1920s may not be appropriate today. Firms in particular industries do, however, tend to organize themselves in a similar fashion. For example, automobile manufacturers tend to emulate General Motors' decentralized division concept, whereas consumer-goods producers tend to emulate the brand-management concept pioneered by Procter & Gamble Company. The general conclusion seems to be that firms following similar strategies tend to adopt similar structures.[9]

Research by Burns and Stalker concluded that a "mechanistic" structure with its emphasis on the centralization of decision making and bureaucratic rules and procedures appears to be well suited to organizations operating in a reasonably stable environment. In contrast, however, they found that successful firms operating in a constantly changing environment, such as those in the electronics and aerospace industries, find that a more "organic" structure, with the decentralization of decision making and flexible procedures, is more appropriate.[10] Studies by Lawrence and Lorsch support this conclusion. They found that successful firms in a reasonably stable environment, such as the container industry, coordinate activities primarily through fairly centralized corporate hierarchies, which place some reliance on direct contact by managers as well as on paperwork directives. Successful firms in more dynamic environments, such as the plastics industry, coordinate activities through integrative departments and permanent cross-functional teams as well as through the hierarchical contact and paperwork.[11] These differences in the use of structural integrating devices are detailed in Table 8.1.

Organic and Mechanistic Structure

Table 8.1 Integrating Mechanisms in Three Different Industries

	Plastics	*Food*	*Container*
Percent new products in last 20 years	35%	15%	0%
Integrating devices	Rules. Hierarchy. Goal setting. Direct contact. Teams at 3 levels. Integrating departments.	Rules. Hierarchy. Goal setting. Direct contact. Task forces. Integrators.	Rules. Hierarchy. Goal setting. Direct contact.
Percent integrators/ managers	22%	17%	0%

SOURCE: J. Galbraith, *Designing Complex Organizations* (Reading, Mass.: Addison-Wesley, 1973), p. 111. Copyright © 1973 by Addison-Wesley Publishing Co. Reprinted by permission.

The container industry is most stable; foods, intermediate; plastics, the least stable.

Strategic Business Units

A successful method of structuring a large and complex business corporation was developed in 1971 by GE. Referred to as *strategic business units* or SBUs, organizational groups composed of discrete, independent product-market segments served by the firm were identified and given primary responsibility and authority to manage their own functional areas. Recognizing that its structure of decentralized operating divisions was not working efficiently (massive sales growth was not being matched by profit growth), GE's top management decided to reorganize. They restructured nine groups and forty-eight divisions into forty-three strategic business units, many of which crossed traditional group, divisional, and profit center lines. For example, food preparation appliances in three separate divisions were merged into a single SBU serving the "housewares" market.[12] The concept thus is to decentralize on the basis of strategic elements rather than on the basis of size or span of control.

General Electric was so pleased with the results of its experiment in organizational design that it reported ". . . the system helped GE improve its profitability, and return on investment has been rebuilt to a healthier level. In the last recession, General Electric's earnings dropped much less than the overall decline for the industry generally."[13] As a result, other firms such as General Foods, Mead Corporation, Eastman Kodak, Campbell Soup, Union Carbide, and Armco Steel, have implemented the strategic business unit concept. General Foods introduced the concept by organizing certain products on the basis of menu segments like breakfast food, beverage, main meal, dessert, and pet foods.

Typically, once a corporation organizes itself around SBUs, it combines similar SBUs together under a group or sector (mentioned earlier in Chapter 5). In 1985, Eastman Kodak, for example, reorganized into seventeen business units under three operating groups. This type of reorganization on the basis of markets is a way to develop a *horizontal strategy* based upon competitive considerations which cut across divisional boundaries. The group or sector executive therefore is responsible for developing and implementing a horizontal strategy to coordinate the various goals and strategies of related business units.[14] This can help a firm compete with *multipoint competitors*—that is, firms that compete with each other not only in one business unit but in a number of related business units.[15] For example, Procter & Gamble, Kimberly-Clark, Scott Paper, and Johnson and Johnson compete with each other in varying combinations of consumer paper products from disposable diapers to facial tissue. If (purely hypothetically), Johnson and Johnson had just developed a toilet tissue with which they chose to challenge

Procter & Gamble's high-share Charmin brand in a particular district, they might charge a low price for their new brand to build sales quickly. Procter & Gamble might not choose to respond to this attack on its share by cutting prices on Charmin. Because of Charmin's high-market share, Procter & Gamble would lose significantly more sale dollars in a price war than would Johnson and Johnson with Johnson and Johnson's initially low-share brand. Procter & Gamble might thus wish to retaliate by challenging Johnson and Johnson's high-share baby shampoo with Procter & Gamble's own low-share brand of baby shampoo in a different district. Once Johnson and Johnson had perceived the response by Procter & Gamble, it might choose to stop challenging Procter & Gamble's Charmin brand of toilet tissue in one district so that Procter & Gamble would stop challenging Johnson and Johnson's baby shampoo in a different district.

As pointed out in Chapter 5, the matrix structure simultaneously combines the stability of the functional structure with the flexibility of the project organization. It is likely to be used within an SBU when the following three conditions exist:

Matrix Structure

- There is a need for cross-fertilization of ideas across projects or products.
- Resources are scarce.
- There is a need to improve the ability to process information and to make decisions.[16]

The matrix structure is appealing but must be carefully managed. To the extent that the goals to be achieved are vague and the technology used is poorly understood, there is likely to be a continuous battle for power between project and functional managers.[17]

Those corporations that emphasize the latest technology as part of their missions, objectives, and strategies are finding that their structure tends to lag behind their technology. Keen suggests there is a lag time before a technology can be fully exploited because more change is expected than a system can handle. An infrastructure needs to be built within a corporation to deal with the implications and impact of rapid technological change.[18] Frohman makes a similar argument: "Many aspects of an organization—from technical talent to reward systems, from climate to equipment—affect the payoff a company will receive from its investments in technology."[19]

Organizing for Innovation

Large corporations that wish to encourage innovation and creativity within their firms must choose a type of structure that will give the new business unit an appropriate amount of freedom with headquarters still having

		Unrelated	3. Special Business Units	6. Independent Business Units	9. Complete Spin-Off
OPERATION RELATEDNESS		Partly Related	2. New Product Business Department	5. New Venture Division	8. Contracting
		Strongly Related	1. Direct Integration	4. Micro New Ventures Department	7. Nurturing and Contracting
			Very Important	Uncertain	Not Important

STRATEGIC IMPORTANCE

Figure 8.2 **Organization designs for corporate entrepreneurship.**
SOURCE: Reprinted from R. A. Burgelman, "Designs for Corporate Entrepreneurship in Established Firms." Copyright © 1984 by the Regents of the University of California. Reprinted by permission of the Regents from *California Management Review*, vol. xxvi, no. 3, p. 161.

some degree of control. In Fig. 8.2, Burgelman proposes that the particular organization design should be determined by the *strategic importance* of the new business to the corporation and the *relatedness* of the unit's operations to those of the corporation.[20] The combination of these two factors results in nine organizational designs for corporate entrepreneurship (or *intrapreneurship,* as it is called by Pinchot).[21]

1. *Direct integration.* High strategic importance and operational relatedness mean that the new business must be a part of the corporation's mainstream. Product "champions"—people who are respected by others in the corporation and who know how to work the system—are needed to manage these projects. When he was with Ford Motor Company, Lee Iacocca, for example, championed the Mustang.

2. *New product business department.* High strategic importance and partial operational relatedness require a separate department organized around an entrepreneurial project in the division where skills and capabilities can be shared.

3. *Special business units.* High strategic importance and low operational relatedness require the creation of a special new business unit with specific objectives and time horizons. General Motor's new Saturn unit is one example of this approach.

4. *Micro new ventures department.* Uncertain strategic importance and high operational relatedness seem typical for "peripheral" projects which are likely to emerge in the operating divisions on a continuous basis. Each division thus has its own new ventures department.

5. *New venture division.* When the new business has uncertain strategic importance and is only partly related to present corporate operations, it belongs in a new venture division. It brings together projects which may exist in various parts of the corporation or can be acquired externally to build sizable new businesses. Allied Corporation, for example, established a new ventures unit to try to commercialize technologies the company had neglected. It invests $20 million a year in the unit's new businesses in the hope that one will be successful.[22]

6. *Independent business units.* Uncertain strategic importance coupled with no relationship to present corporate activities may make external arrangements attractive. As in the case of Monsanto, the corporation owns Fisher Controls but controls it through membership on a separate Fisher Controls' board of directors. Monsanto's executive vice-president, Earle Harbison, serves as chairman of the separate board and presses Fisher to grow overseas and to achieve what he calls "an Arabian Nights of product development."[23]

7. *Nurturing and contracting.* When an entrepreneurial proposal may not be important strategically to the corporation but is strongly related to present operations, top management may help the entrepreneurial unit "spin off" from the corporation. This allows a friendly competitor to capture a small niche instead of one of the corporation's major competitors. For example, Tektronix, a maker of oscilloscopes, formed a unit to act as an in-house venture capitalist to its own employees by swapping the parent company's operational knowledge for equity in the new company. The arrangement is intended to provide Tektronix with a better return on its R&D expenditures and to help it maintain ties with innovative employees who want to run their own companies.[24]

8. *Contracting.* As the required capabilities and skills of the new business are less related to those of the corporation, the parent corporation may spin off the unit yet keep some relationship through a contractual arrangement with the new firm. The connection is useful in case the new firm develops something of value to the corporation.

9. *Complete spin off.* If both strategic importance and operational relatedness are negligible, the corporation is likely to completely sell off the unit to another firm or to the present employees in some form of ESOP (Employee Stock Ownership Plan). Or the corporation may sell off the unit through a leveraged buyout (executives of the unit buy the unit from the parent company with money from a third source to be repaid out of the unit's anticipated earnings).[25]

Organizing for innovation has become especially important for those corporations in "high tech" industries that wish to recapture the entrepreneurial spirit but are really too large to do so. Apple Computer, for example, turned to a small group to help develop its portable computer Lisa. IBM has formed "independent business units," each with its own mini-board of directors. One such IBU produced the company's successful personal computer. Even Levi Strauss and Company, the clothing manufacturer, is encouraging "in-house entrepreneurs" by financing new fashion-apparel businesses.

Rather than attempting such in-house innovation, a number of corporations are investing venture capital in existing small firms. Wang, for example, purchased a minority interest in InteCom, Inc., a maker of telephone switching equipment. General Motors did the same with Teknowledge, Inc. GM hopes Teknowledge will develop a diagnostic software program to prescribe repairs for troubled cars. This form of minority equity ownership is really quasi-vertical integration and raises a question of organizational identity. In such corporations, it becomes difficult to tell when one firm begins and the other leaves off.

Stages of Corporate Development

A key proposition of Chandler's was that successful corporations tend to follow a pattern of structural development as they grow and expand. Further work by Thain, Scott, and Tuason specifically delineates three distinct structural stages.[26]

Stage I is typified by the entrepreneur, who founds the corporation to promote an idea (product or service). The entrepreneur tends to make all the important decisions personally, and is involved in every detail and phase of the organization. The Stage I corporation has a structure allowing the entrepreneur to directly supervise the activities of every employee (see Fig. 8.3). The corporation in Stage I is thus characterized by little formal structure. Planning is usually short range or "fire-fighting" in nature. The typical managerial functions of planning, organizing, directing, staffing, and controlling are usually performed to a very limited degree, if at all. The greatest strengths of a Stage I corporation are its flexibility and dynamism. The drive of the entrepreneur energizes the corporation in its struggle for growth. Its greatest weakness is its extreme reliance on the entrepreneur to decide general strategies as well as detailed procedures. If the entrepreneur falters, the corporation usually flounders.

Stage I described Polaroid Corporation, whose founder Dr. Edwin Land championed *Polarvision*, a financially disastrous instant movie system, while ignoring industrial and commercial uses. Growing concern by stockholders over declines in sales and net income resulted in Dr. Land's resignation from his top management position in 1980 and from the board of directors in

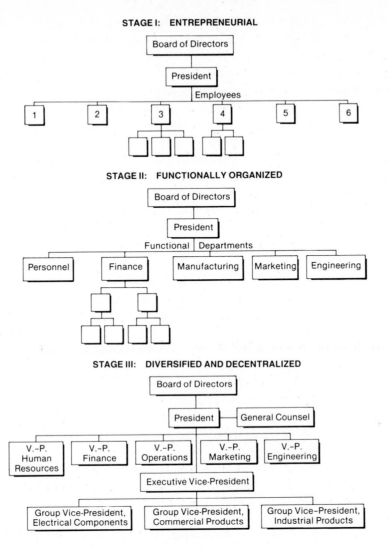

Figure 8.3   Stages of corporate development.

1982. In 1983, analysts reported that Polaroid was in the throes of a "mid-life crisis," worrying about its mortality and the loss of Dr. Land's inspiring vision.[27] Polaroid Corporation was, in effect, a Stage II corporation being managed by Dr. Land as if it still were a Stage I corporation.

At *Stage II,* the entrepreneur is replaced by a team of managers with functional specializations (see Fig. 8.3). The transition to this state requires a substantial managerial style change for the chief officer of the corporation, especially if the chief officer was the Stage I entrepreneur. Otherwise, having additional staff members yields no benefits to the corporation. At this juncture, the corporate strategy favors protectivism by trying to dominate the industry, often through vertical or horizontal integration. The great strength of a Stage II corporation lies in its concentration and specialization in one industry. Its great weakness is that all of its eggs are in one basket.

McDonald's, the world's largest food service company, is a Stage II corporation that is concentrating on fast food. Fred Turner, chairman of the board, commented in 1984 on the company's specialization in one industry:

> My view is that we can maintain a growth rate in the teens through this decade. And if you believe that, it makes the question of diversification beside the point.[28]

The *Stage III* corporation focuses on internal operating efficiencies. These corporations grow by diversifying their product lines and expanding to cover wider geographical areas. These corporations move to a divisional structure with a central headquarters (see Fig. 8.3). Headquarters attempts to coordinate the activities of its operating divisions through performance and results-oriented control and reporting systems, and by stressing corporate planning techniques. The divisions are not tightly controlled, but are held responsible for their own performance results. Therefore, to be effective, there has to be a decentralized decision process. The greatest strength of a Stage III corporation is its almost unlimited resources. Its most significant weakness is that it is usually so large and complex that it tends to become relatively inflexible.[29] General Electric, DuPont, and General Motors are Stage III corporations.

These descriptions of the three stages of corporate development are supported by research.[30] The differences among the stages are specified in more detail by Thain in Table 8.2.

In his study, Chandler noted that the empire builder was rarely the person who created the new structure to fit the new strategy, and that, as a result, the transition from one stage to another is often a painful one. This was true of General Motors Corporation under the management of William Durant, Ford Motor Company under its founder Henry Ford, and Polaroid Corporation under Edwin Land. Thain, in Table 8.3, summarizes the internal and external blocks to movement from one stage to another.

Table 8.2 Key Factors in Top Management Process in Stage I, II, and III Companies

Function	Stage I	Stage II	Stage III
1. Size-up: Major problems	Survival and growth dealing with short-term operating problems.	Growth, rationalization, and expansion of resources, providing for adequate attention to product problems.	Trusteeship in management and investment and control of large, increasing, and diversified resource. Also, important to diagnose and take action on problems at division level.
2. Objectives	Personal and subjective.	Profits and meeting functionally oriented budgets and performance targets.	ROI, profits, earnings per share.
3. Strategy	Implicit and personal; exploitation of immediate opportunities seen by owner-manager.	Functionally oriented moves restricted to "one product" scope; exploitation of one basic product or service field.	Growth and product diversification; exploitation of general business opportunities.
4. Organization: Major characteristic of structure	One unit, "one-man show."	One-unit, functionally specialized group.	Multiunit general staff office and decentralized operating divisions.
5. (a) Measurement and control	Personal, subjective control based on simple accounting system and daily communication and observation.	Control grows beyond one man; assessment of functional operations necessary; structured control systems evolve.	Complex formal system geared to comparative assessment of performance measures, indicating problems and opportunities and assessing management ability of division managers.
5. (b) Key performance indicators	Personal criteria, relationships with owner, operating efficiency, ability to solve operating problems.	Functional and internal criteria such as sales, performance compared to budget, size of empire, status in group, personal relationships, etc.	More impersonal application of comparisons such as profits, ROI, P/E ratio, sales, market share, productivity, product leadership, personnel development, employee attitudes, public responsibility.
6. Reward-punishment system	Informal, personal, subjective; used to maintain control and divide small pool of resources to provide personal incentives for key performers.	More structured; usually based to a greater extent on agreed policies as opposed to personal opinion and relationships.	Allotment by "due process" of a wide variety of different rewards and punishments on a formal and systematic basis. Company-wide policies usually apply to many different classes of managers and workers with few major exceptions for individual cases.

SOURCE: D. H. Thain, "Stages of Corporate Development," *The Business Quarterly* (Winter 1969), p. 37. Copyright © 1969 by *The Business Quarterly*. Reprinted by permission.

221

Table 8.3   Blocks to Development

a) Internal Blocks Stage I to II	Stage II to III
Lack of ambition and drive.	Unwillingness to take the risks involved.
Personal reasons of owner-manager for avoiding change in status quo.	Management resistance to change for a variety of reasons including old age, aversion to risk taking, desire to protect personal empires, etc.
Lack of operating efficiency.	
Lack of quantity and quality of operating personnel.	Personal reasons among managers for defending the status quo.
Lack of resources such as borrowing power, plant and equipment, salesmen, etc.	Lack of control system related to appraisal of investment of decentralized operations.
Product problems and weaknesses.	Lack of budgetary control ability.
Lack of planning and organizational ability.	Organizational inflexibility.
	Lack of management vision to see opportunities for expansion.
	Lack of management development, i.e., not enough managers to handle expansion.
	Management turnover and loss of promising young managers.
	Lack of ability to formulate and implement strategy that makes company relevant to changing conditions.
	Refusal to delegate power and authority for diversification.

b) External Blocks Stage I to II	Stage II to III
Unfavorable economic conditions.	Unfavorable economic, political, technological, and social conditions and/or trends.
Lack of market growth.	
Tight money or lack of an underwriter who will assist the company "to go public."	Lack of access to financial or management resources.
	Overly conservative accountants, lawyers, investment bankers, etc.
Labor shortages in quality and quantity.	Lack of domestic markets necessary to support large diversified corporation.
Technological obsolescence of product.	"The conservative mentality," e.g., cultural contentment with the status quo and lack of desire to grow and develop.

SOURCE: D. H. Thain, "Stages of Corporate Development," *The Business Quarterly* (Winter 1969), pp. 43–44. Copyright © 1969 by *The Business Quarterly*. Reprinted by permission.

Although it has been suggested that an additional phase in a corporation's development is the multinational or "global" stage,[31] this could be viewed as just a variation of the Stage III, multidivisional corporation. A truly multinational or global corporation usually has decentralized investment centers based on geography rather than on product line or strategic business unit. (Refer to Chapter 10 for additional information on multinational corporations.)

Organizational Life Cycle

A more recent approach to better understanding the development of corporations is that of the organizational "life cycle."[32] Instead of considering stages in terms of structure, this approach places the primary emphasis on the dominant issue facing the corporation. The specific organizational structure, therefore, becomes a secondary concern. These stages are *Birth* (Stage I), *Growth* (Stage II), *Maturity* (Stage III), *Decline* (Stage IV), and *Death* (Stage V). The impact of these stages on corporate strategy and structure is summarized in Table 8.4. Note that the first three stages of the organizational life cycle are basically the same as the three stages of corporate development mentioned previously. The only significant difference is the addition of the decline and death stages to complete the cycle.

The Stage IV firm became widespread in the Western world during the 1970s as many corporations in basic industries such as steel and automobiles seemed to lose their vitality and competitiveness. Most of the product lines of a Stage IV firm are at the mature or declining phase of their product life cycle. Sales are stagnant and actually declining if adjusted for inflation. An emphasis on company-wide cost-cutting further erodes future competitiveness. The major objective changes from stability to survival. Retrenchment coupled with pleas for government assistance is the only feasible

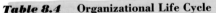

Table 8.4   Organizational Life Cycle

	Stage I	*Stage II*	*Stage III*	*Stage IV*	*Stage V*
Dominant Issue	Birth	Growth	Maturity	Decline	Death
Popular Strategies	Concentration in a niche	Horizontal and vertical integration	Concentric and conglomerate diversification	Profit strategy followed by retrenchment	Liquidation or bankruptcy
Likely Structure	Entrepreneur-dominated	Functional management emphasized	Decentralization into profit or investment centers	Structural surgery	Dismemberment of structure

strategy. Chrysler Corporation was a good example of a Stage IV corporation in the early 1980s.

Unless a corporation is able to resolve the critical issues facing it in Stage IV (as Chrysler was able to do), it is likely to move into Stage V, corporate death. This is what happened in the mid-1980s to AM International (previously known as the Addressograph-Multigraph Corporation), Baldwin-United, and Osborne Computers, as well as many other firms. The corporation is forced into bankruptcy. As in the cases of Rolls Royce and Penn Central, both of which went bankrupt in the 1970s, a corporation may nevertheless rise like a phoenix from its own ashes and live again. The company may be reorganized or liquidated, depending upon the individual circumstances. In some liquidations, the corporation's name is purchased, and the purchasing corporation places that name on some or all of its products. For example, Wordtronix, a maker of stand-alone word processors, acquired in 1983 the Remington Rand trademark, even though Remington Rand no longer made typewriters. Top management planned to change the Word-tronix name to Remington Rand to give its machines some name recognition in the marketplace.[33]

It is important to realize that not all corporations will move through these five stages in order. Some corporations, for example, may never move past Stage II. Others, like General Motors, may go directly from Stage I to Stage III. A large number will go from Stage I into Stages IV and V. Ford, for example, was unable to move from Stage I into Stage II as long as Henry Ford, I was in command. Its inability to realign itself no doubt contributed to its movement into Stage IV just before World War II. After the war, Henry Ford, II's turnaround strategy successfully restructured the corporation as a Stage II firm.

Staffing

The implementation of new strategy and policies often calls for a different utilization of personnel. If growth strategies are to be implemented, new people need to be hired and trained. Experienced people with the necessary skills need to be found for promotion into newly created managerial positions. For example, if a firm has decided to integrate forward by opening its own retail outlets, one key concern is the ability of the corporation to find, hire, and train store managers. If a corporation adopts a retrenchment strategy, however, a large number of people may need to be laid off or fired; and top management, as well as the divisional managers, need to specify criteria used to make these personnel decisions. Should employees be fired on the basis of low seniority or on the basis of poor performance? Sometimes corporations find it easier to close an entire division rather than choosing which individuals to fire. The University of Michigan followed this approach in

1981 when it cut back expenses by dropping its entire Geography Department.

Some authorities have suggested that the type of general manager needed to effectively implement a new divisional, corporate, or SBU strategy varies depending upon the desired strategic direction of that business unit.[34] Illustrative Example 8.1 tells how this approach was followed by the board of AM International in selecting the corporation's chief executive officer.

AM INTERNATIONAL MATCHES THE MANAGER WITH THE STRATEGY

Illustrative Example 8.1

The board of directors of AM International followed the theory that the general manager should match the firm's desired strategy when it both hired and fired Joe B. Freeman as the corporation's chief executive officer. Hired originally when the company filed for Chapter 11 bankruptcy in April 1982, Freeman worked hard to turn the firm around. He concentrated on cutting costs, boosting sales, and soothing both creditors and employees. By January 1984, the corporation was beginning to show a profit—and Joe B. Freeman was fired by the board. Looking back on the experience, Freeman admitted that some of the problem had been with his analytically oriented accounting background.

> The company had reached a new phase. My skills had been successful in bringing it to this phase but the board wanted a person with a different set of skills to lead it. . . . [The board wanted] an orientation toward business strategy and people skills. . . . I chose to devote most of my time to managing the company, to working with the creditors, and didn't spend much time on the image side with shareholders and directors.

SOURCE: R. Johnson, "AM International's Ex-Chief Freeman Tells How His Success Got Him Fired," *Wall Street Journal* (August 27, 1984), p. 21.

Depending on the situation of a specific division as determined by the GE Business Screen Matrix (Fig. 6.3), the "best" or most appropriate division manager may need to have a specific mix of skills and experiences. Some of these suggested "types" are depicted in Fig. 8.4.

One research study of business executives found that strategic business units with a "build" strategy as compared to SBUs with a "harvest" strategy tend to be headed by managers with a greater willingness to take risks and a higher tolerance for ambiguity.[35] Another study also found that managers with a certain mix of behaviors, skills, and personality factors tend to be linked with a different strategy than those with a different mix. For example,

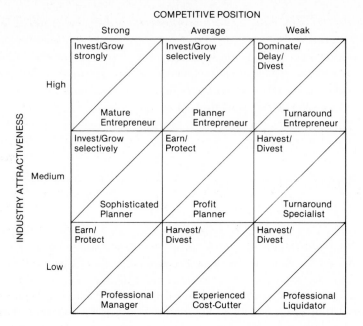

Figure 8.4   **The types of general managers needed to strategically manage different types of businesses.**
SOURCE: Adapted from C. W. Hofer and M. J. Davoust, *Successful Strategic Management* (Chicago: A. T. Kearney, Inc., 1977), pp. 45 and 82. Used by permission.

SBUs with a stability strategy tend to be run by a manager with a conservative style, a production or engineering background, and experience with controlling budgets, capital expenditures, inventories, and standardization procedures.[36] In summary, there is growing support for matching executive "types" with the dominant strategic direction of a business unit. Unfortunately, there is little help available to select the most appropriate manager when a corporation or SBU does not have a specific strategy formulated for that manager to implement.

There are a number of ways to ensure a continuous development of people for important managerial positions. One approach is to establish a sound *performance appraisal system* to identify good performers with managerial potential. A number of large organizations have started to use *assessment centers* to evaluate a person's suitability for a management position. Popularized by AT&T in the mid-1950s, corporations such as Standard Oil of Ohio and GE now use them.[37] Since each is specifically tailored to its corporation, these assessment centers are unique. They use special interviews, management games, in-basket exercises, leaderless group discussions, case analyses, decision-making exercises, and oral presentations to assess the potential of employees for higher-level positions. People are promoted into specific positions based on their performance in the assessment center. Many assessment centers have proved to be highly predictive of subsequent managerial performance.[38]

The implementation of strategy should not only be concerned with the selection of strategic managers, but also with the selection of the appropriate mix of professional, skilled, and unskilled labor. At IBM, for example, top management decided in 1984 to emphasize software development in order to reach its corporate growth objectives. Key divisions were then directed to expand their programming staffs by 20% per year for the next ten years.[39]

Directing

To effectively implement a new strategy, appropriate authority and responsibility must be delegated to the operational managers. People should be motivated to act in desired ways. Further, the actions must be coordinated to result in effective performance. Managers should be stimulated to find creative solutions to implementation problems without getting bogged down in conflict. When the proper people have been placed in the proper positions, a corporation needs a system to direct them toward the proper implementation of corporate, business, and functional strategies. Sometimes this is informally accomplished through a strong corporate culture with well-accepted norms and values regarding teamwork and commitment to the company's objectives and strategies. New employees are "socialized" into the culture through a series of planned training experiences.[40] Even if such a culture is not in place, activities can be directed toward accomplishing strategic goals through programs such as Management By Objectives (MBO) and incentive management.

Management By Objectives

Management By Objectives (MBO) is one organization-wide approach to help assure purposeful action toward desired objectives. MBO links organizational objectives and the behavior of individuals. Since it is a system that links plans with performance, it is a powerful implementation technique.

Although there is some disagreement about the purpose of MBO, most authorities agree that this approach involves (1) establishing and communicating organizational objectives, (2) setting individual objectives that help implement organizational ones, and (3) periodically reviewing performance as it relates to the objectives.[41] MBO provides an opportunity to connect the objectives of people at each level to those at the next higher level: "If carried out logically and ideally, the goals at each level would be contributing most directly toward overall organizational objectives. . . . MBO provides a potential method of integrating the physical, financial, and human resource plans of the organization to the goals that an individual is expected to achieve."[42] MBO, therefore, acts to tie together corporate, business, and functional objectives as well as the strategies developed to achieve them.

This forms a hierarchy of objectives similar to the hierarchy of strategy discussed earlier in Chapter 1. The MBO process is depicted in Fig. 8.5.

Research on corporate MBO programs is mixed but tends to support the belief that MBO should result in higher levels of performance than other approaches that do not include performance goals, relevant feedback, and joint supervisor/subordinate goal setting.[43] Galbraith and Nathanson point out that the existence of an MBO program at Dow-Corning permits its matrix structure (as discussed in Chapter 5) to function effectively: "Because people work against goals and problems, rather than against each other, they have less need for hierarchy and tie-breaking."[44] At Dow-Corning, the agreed-upon objectives are used to help reach consensus and thus reduce the potential for the conflict inherent in a matrix-style organization.

Incentive Management   To ensure that there is a congruence between the needs of the corporation as a whole and the needs of the employees as individuals, managers should develop an incentive system that rewards desired performance. Research confirms the conventional wisdom that when pay is tied to performance, it motivates higher productivity, strongly affecting both absenteeism and work quality.[45] Corporations have, therefore, developed various types of incen-

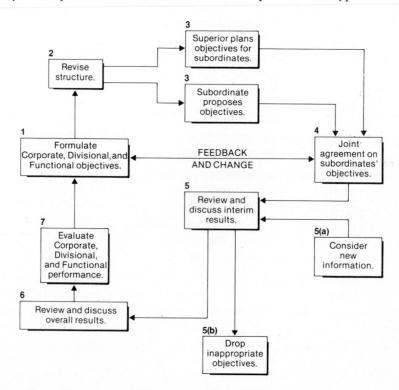

Figure 8.5   **The process of Management By Objectives.**

tives for executives that range from stock options to cash bonuses. All these incentive plans should be linked in some way to corporate and divisional strategy. Performance appraisal and incentive systems are discussed in more detail under Evaluation and Control in Chapter 9.

8.4 SUMMARY AND CONCLUSION

This chapter explains the implementation of strategy in terms of (1) *who* the operational managers are who must carry out strategic plans, (2) *what* they must do in order to implement strategy, and (3) *how* they should go about their activities. Vice-presidents of functional areas and directors of divisions or SBUs work with their subordinates to put together large-scale implementation plans. These plans include *programs, budgets,* and *procedures* and become more detailed as they move down the corporate "chain of command."

Strategy is implemented by management through planning, organizing, staffing, and directing activities.

Planning results in fairly detailed programs, budgets, and procedures.

Organizing deals with the design of an appropriate structure for the corporation. Research generally supports Chandler's proposal that changes in corporate strategy tend to lead to changes in organizational structure. The growing use of strategic business units, matrix structures, and entrepreneurial units reflects a need for more flexible structures to manage increasingly diversified corporations. Not only should a firm work to make its structure congruent with its strategy, it should also be aware that there is an organizational life cycle composed of stages of corporate development through which a corporation is likely to move.

Staffing focuses on finding and developing appropriate people for key positions. Without capable and committed managers and staff, strategy can never be implemented satisfactorily. To this end, performance appraisal systems and assessment centers are used by a number of large corporations.

Directing deals with organization-wide approaches that direct operational managers and employees to effect the implementation of corporate, business, and functional strategies. One such approach is Management By Objectives (MBO), which links organizational objectives and the behavior of operational managers. Its ability to tie planning with performance makes it a powerful implementation technique. The proper use of incentives, when integrated with a goal-centered approach such as MBO, is another method of directing effort toward achieving desired results.

DISCUSSION QUESTIONS

1. Japanese corporations typically involve many more organizational levels and people in the development of implementation plans than do U.S. corporations. Is this appropriate? Why or why not?

2. To what extent should top management be involved in strategy implementation?

3. Does structure follow strategy or does strategy follow structure? Why?

4. What can be done to encourage innovation in large corporations?

5. Should corporations select a certain type of person to be a general manager of a division depending on the strategic situation of that particular division? Why or why not?

NOTES

1. *Wall Street Journal* (December 27, 1984), p. 15.

2. L. D. Alexander, "Towards an Understanding of Strategy Implementation Problems," *Proceedings, Southern Management Association* (November 1982), p. 147.

3. P. Miesing, "Integrating Planning with Management, " *Long Range Planning* (October 1984), pp. 118–124.
"The Future Catches Up with a Strategic Planner," *Business Week* (June 27, 1983), p. 62.

4. A. D. Chandler, *Strategy and Structure* (Cambridge, Mass.: MIT Press, 1962), p. 14.

5. A. P. Sloan, Jr., *My Years with General Motors* (Garden City, N.Y.: Doubleday, Anchor Books, 1972).

6. J. R. Galbraith and D. A. Nathanson, *Strategy Implementation: The Role of Structure and Process* (St. Paul, Minn.: West Publishing Co., 1978), p. 47.
P. H. Grinyer and M. Yasai-Ardekani, "Strategy, Structure, Size, and Bureaucracy," *Academy of Management Journal* (September 1981), pp. 471–486.
P. Lorange, *Implementation of Strategic Planning* (Englewood Cliffs, N.J.: Prentice-Hall, 1982), p. 109.
L. G. Hrebiniak and W. F. Joyce, *Implementing Strategy* (New York: Macmillan, 1984), pp. 65–92.

7. Galbraith and Nathanson, p. 139.

8. D. R. Dalton, W. D. Todor, M. J. Spendolini, G. J. Fielding, and L. W. Porter, "Organization Structure and Performance: A Critical Review," *Academy of Management Review* (January 1980), pp. 49–64.

9. Hrebiniak and Joyce, p. 70.

10. T. Burns and G. M. Stalker, *The Management of Innovation* (London: Tavistock Publications, 1961).

11. P. R. Lawrence and J. W. Lorsch, *Organization and Environment* (Homewood, Ill.: Richard D. Irwin, Inc., 1967), p. 138.

12. William K. Hall, "SBUs: Hot New Topic in the Management of Diversification," *Business Horizons* (February 1978), p. 19.

13. "Evolving the GE Management System," *General Electric Monogram* (November–December 1977), p. 4.

14. M. E. Porter, *Competitive Advantage* (New York: The Free Press, 1985), pp. 395–398.

15. Porter, p. 322.

16. Hrebiniak and Joyce, pp. 85–86.

17. J. L. Brown and N. M. Agnew, "The Balance of Power in a Matrix Structure," *Business Horizons* (November–December 1982), pp. 51–54.

18. P. G. W. Keen, "Communications in the 21st Century: Telecommunications and Business Policy," *Organizational Dynamics* (Autumn 1981), pp. 54–67.

19. A. L. Frohman, "Technology as a Competitive Weapon," *Harvard Business Review* (January–February 1982), p. 97.

20. R. A. Burgelman, "Designs for Corporate Entrepreneurship," *California Management Review* (Spring 1984), pp. 154–166.

21. G. Pinchot, *Intrapreneuring, or Why You Don't Have to Leave the Corporation to Become an Entrepreneur* (New York: Harper & Row, 1985) as reported by J. S. DeMott, "Here Come the Intrapreneurs," *Time* (February 4, 1985), pp. 36–37.

22. E. C. Gottschalk, "Allied Unit, Free of Red Tape, Seeks To Develop Orphan Technologies," *Wall Street Journal* (September 13, 1984), p. 29.

23. M. Magnet, "Acquiring without Smothering," *Fortune* (November 12, 1984), p. 26.

24. C. Dolan, "Tektronix New-Venture Subsidiary Brings Benefits to Parent, Spinoffs," *Wall Street Journal* (September 18, 1984), p. 31.

25. Burgelman, pp. 162–164.

26. D. H. Thain, "Stages of Corporate Development," *The Business Quarterly* (Winter 1969), pp. 32–45.
    B. R. Scott, "Stages of Corporate Development" (Boston: Intercollegiate Case Clearing House, no. 9-371-294, 1971); and "The Industrial State: Old Myths and New Realities," *Harvard Business Review* (March–April 1973).
    R. V. Tuason, "Corporate Life Cycle and the Evaluation of Corporate Strategy," *Proceedings, The Academy of Management* (August 1973), pp. 35–40.

27. W. M. Bulkeley, "As Polaroid Matures, Some Lament a Decline in Creative Excitement," *Wall Street Journal* (May 10, 1983), p. 1.

28. M. J. Williams, "McDonald's Refuses to Plateau," *Fortune* (November 12, 1984), p. 40.

29. Thain, p. 39.

30. N. R. Smith and J. B. Miner, "Type of Entrepreneur, Type of Firm, and Managerial Motivation: Implications for Organizational Life Cycle Theory," *Strategic Management Journal* (October–December 1983), pp. 325–340.
    F. Hoy, B. C. Vaught, and W. W. Buchanan, "Managing Managers of Firms in Transition from Stage I to Stage II," *Proceedings, Southern Management Association* (November 1982), pp. 152–153.
    K. Smith and T. Mitchell, "An Investigation into the Effect of Changes in Stages of Organizational Maturation on a Decision Maker's Decision Priorities," *Proceedings, Southern Management Association* (November 1983), pp. 7–9.

31. Galbraith and Nathanson, p. 118.

32. D. A. Tansik, R. B. Chase, and N. J. Aquilano, *Management: A Life Cycle Approach* (Homewood, Ill.: Richard D. Irwin, Inc., 1980).
    J. R. Kimberly, R. H. Miles, and Associates, *The Organizational Life Cycle* (San Francisco: Jossey-Bass, 1980).

33. C. Waterloo, "Big Shakeout in Electronics Tests Concern," *Wall Street Journal* (November 9, 1983), p. 31.

34. C. W. Hofer, E. A. Murray, Jr., R. Charam, and R. A. Pitts, *Strategic Management: A Casebook in Business Policy and Planning* (St. Paul, Minn.: West Publishing Co., 1980), p. 19.
    M. Leontiades, "Choosing the Right Manager to Fit the Strategy," *Journal of Business Strategy* (Fall 1982), pp. 58–69.
    J. G. Wissema, H. W. Van Der Pol, and H. M. Messer, "Strategic Management Archetypes," *Strategic Management Journal* (January–March 1980), pp. 37–47.
    L. J. Stybel, "Linking Strategic Planning and Management Manpower Planning," *California Management Review* (Fall 1982), pp. 48–56.
    R. A. Bettis and W. K. Hall, "The Business Portfolio Approach—Where It Falls Down in Practice," *Long Range Planning* (April 1983), pp. 95–104.
    A. D. Szilagyi, Jr. and D. M. Schweiger, "Matching Managers to Strategies: A Review and Suggested Framework," *Academy of Management Review* (October 1984), pp. 626–637.

35. A. K. Gupta and V. Govindarajan, "Business Unit Strategy, Managerial Characteristics, and Business Unit Effectiveness at Strategy Implementation," *Academy of Management Journal* (March 1984), p. 36.

36. H. Deresky and T. T. Herbert, "The Strategic Contingency in the General Manager's Role," a paper presented to the Academy of Management, San Diego, California, August 1985, p. 11.

37. J. B. Miner and M. G. Miner, *Personnel and Industrial Relations,* 3rd ed. (New York: Macmillan, 1977), pp. 194–196.

38. Miner and Miner, p. 196.

39. M. A. Harris, "IBM: More Worlds to Conquer," *Business Week* (February 18, 1985), p. 85.

40. R. Pascale, "Fitting New Employees into the Company Culture," *Fortune* (May 28, 1984), pp. 28–42.

41. S. J. Carroll, Jr. and H. L. Tosi, Jr., *Management by Objectives* (New York: Macmillan, 1973), p. 3.

42. M. D. Richards, *Organizational Goal Structures* (St. Paul, Minn.: West Publishing Co., 1978), p. 128.

43. Carroll and Tosi, p. 16.

44. Galbraith and Nathanson, p. 99.

45. E. E. Lawler III, *Pay and Organizational Effectiveness* (New York: McGraw-Hill, 1971).
    E. A. Locke, "How to Motivate Employees" (Paper presented at the NATO conference on changes in the nature and quality of working life, Thessaloniki, Greece, August 19–24, 1979.) Cited in E. E. Lawler III, *Pay and Organizational Development* (Reading, Mass.: Addison-Wesley, 1981), p. 3.

Chapter 9

EVALUATION AND CONTROL

STRATEGIC MANAGEMENT MODEL

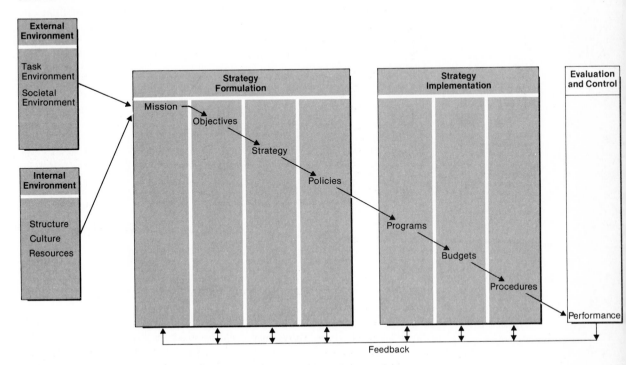

The last part of the strategic management model is the evaluation of performance and the control of work activities. Control follows planning. It ensures that the corporation is achieving what it set out to accomplish. Just as planning involves the setting of objectives along with the strategies and programs necessary to accomplish them, the control process compares performance with desired results and provides the feedback necessary to evaluate results and take corrective action, as needed.[1] This process may be viewed as a five-step feedback model as depicted in Fig. 9.1.

1. *Determine what to measure.* Top managers as well as operational managers need to specify what implementation processes and results will be monitored and evaluated. The processes and results must be capable of being measured in a reasonably objective and consistent manner. The focus should be on the most significant elements in a process—the ones that account for the highest proportion of expense or the greatest number of problems.

2. *Establish standards of performance.* Standards used to measure performance are detailed expressions of strategic objectives. They are *measures* of what are acceptable performance results. Each standard usually includes a *tolerance range* within which certain deviations will be accepted as satisfactory. Standards can be set not only for final output, but for intermediate stages of production output.

3. *Measure actual performance.* Measurements must be made at predetermined times.

4. *Compare actual performance with the standard.* If actual performance results are within the desired tolerance range, the measurement process stops here.

5. *Take corrective action.* If actual results fall outside the desired tolerance range, action must be taken to correct the deviation. The following must be determined:

    a) Is the deviation only a chance fluctuation?

    b) Are the processes being carried out incorrectly?

    c) Are the processes appropriate to the achievement of the desired standard?

    Action must be taken that will not only correct the deviation, but also prevent its happening again.

The strategic management model shows that evaluation and control information is fed back and assimilated into the entire management process.

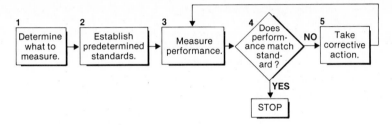

Figure 9.1   **Evaluation and control process.**

This information consists of performance data and activity reports (gathered in step 3 of Fig. 9.1). If undesired performance is the result of an inappropriate *use* of the strategic management processes, operational managers must know about it in order to correct employee activity. Top management need not be involved. If, however, undesired performance results from the processes themselves, top managers, as well as operational managers, must know about it in order to develop new implementation programs or procedures.

The measures used will depend on the organizational unit to be measured, as well as on the objectives to be achieved. Certain measures, such as return on investment, are very appropriate for evaluating the ability of a corporation or division to achieve a profitability objective. These measures, however, are inadequate for evaluating other objectives a corporation may want to achieve: social responsibility or employee development, for instance. Different measures are required for different objectives. Even though profitability is the major objective for a corporation, using return on investment alone may be insufficient as a control device. ROI, for example, can be computed only *after* profits are totaled for a period. It tells what happened—not what *is* happening or what *will* happen. A firm, therefore, needs to develop measures that predict likely profitability. These are referred to as "steering" or "feed-forward" controls because they measure variables that influence profitability.

The most commonly used measure of corporate performance (in terms of profits) is return on investment. As discussed in Chapter 2, it is simply the result of dividing net income before taxes by total assets. Although there are a number of advantages to using ROI, there are also a number of distinct limitations. Some of these are detailed in Table 9.1.

Other popular measures are earnings per share (EPS) and return on equity (ROE). Earnings per share also has several deficiencies when used to

9.1 MEASURING PERFORMANCE

Measures of Corporate Performance

Table 9.1 **Advantages and Limitations of ROI as a Measure of Corporate Performance**

Advantages

1. ROI is a single comprehensive figure influenced by everything that happens.
2. It measures how well the division manager uses the property of the company to generate profits. It is also a good way to check on the accuracy of capital investment proposals.
3. It is a common denominator that can be compared with many entities.
4. It provides an incentive to use existing assets efficiently.
5. It provides an incentive to acquire new assets only when doing so would increase the return.

Limitations

1. ROI is very sensitive to depreciation policy. Depreciation write-off variances between divisions affect ROI performance. Accelerated depreciation techniques reduce ROI, conflicting with capital budgeting discounted cash-flow analysis.
2. ROI is sensitive to book value. Older plants with more depreciated assets have relatively lower investment bases than newer plants (note also the effect of inflation), thus increasing ROI. Note that asset investment may be held down or assets disposed of in order to increase ROI performance.
3. In many firms that use ROI, one division sells to another. As a result, transfer pricing must occur. Expenses incurred affect profit. Since, in theory, the transfer price should be based on the total impact on firm profit, some investment center managers are bound to suffer. Equitable transfer prices are difficult to determine.
4. If one division operates in an industry that has favorable conditions and another division operates in an industry that has unfavorable conditions, the former division will automatically "look" better than the other.
5. The time span of concern here is short range. The performance of division managers should be measured in the long run. This is top management's time-span capacity.
6. The business cycle strongly affects ROI performance, often despite managerial performance.

SOURCE: James M. Higgins, *Organizational Policy and Strategic Management*, 2nd ed. Copyright © 1983 by CBS College Publishing. Reprinted by permission of The Dryden Press, CBS College Publishing.

evaluate past and future performance. For one thing, because alternative accounting principles are available, EPS may have several different but equally acceptable values, depending on the principle selected. Second, because EPS is based on accrual income, the conversion of income to cash can be near term or delayed. As a result, EPS does not consider the time value of money. Because of these and other limitations, earnings per share *by itself* is not an adequate measure of corporate performance.[2]

Stakeholder Measures As mentioned in Chapter 4, stakeholders in the corporation's task environment are often very concerned about corporate activities and performance. Each has its own set of criteria to determine how well the corporation is performing. These criteria typically deal with the direct and indirect impact of corporate activities on stakeholder interests. Freeman proposes that top management needs to "keep score" with these stakeholders by establishing one or more simple measures for each stakeholder category.[3] A few of these measures are listed in Table 9.2.

Assuming that any one measure is bound to have some shortcomings, Hofer recommends the use of three new measures to evaluate a corporation's performance results (see Table 9.3). These measures are based on *value added* and are attempts to measure directly the contribution a corporation makes to

Value Added Measures

Table 9.2   A Sample Score Card for "Keeping Score with Stakeholders"

Stakeholder Category	Possible Near-Term Measures	Possible Long-Term Measures
Customers	Sales ($ and volume) New customers Number of new customer needs met ("tries")	Growth in sales Turnover of customer base Ability to control price

Suppliers	Cost of raw material
	Delivery time
	Inventory
	Availability of raw material
		Growth rates of
		  Raw material costs
		  Delivery time
		  Inventory
		New ideas from suppliers

Financial Community	EPS Stock price Number of "buy" lists ROE	Ability to convince Wall Street of strategy Growth in ROE
Employees	Number of suggestions Productivity Number of grievances	Number of internal promotions Turnover
Congress	Number of new pieces of legislation that affect the firm Access to key members and staff	Number of new regulations that affect industry Ratio of "cooperative" vs. "competitive" encounters
Consumer Advocate	Number of meetings Number of "hostile" encounters Number of times coalitions formed Number of legal actions	Number of changes in policy due to C.A. Number of C.A. initiated "calls for help"
Environmentalists	Number of meetings Number of hostile encounters Number of times coalitions formed Number of EPA complaints Number of legal actions	Number of changes in policy due to environmentalists Number of environmentalist "calls for help"

SOURCE: R. E. Freeman, *Strategic Management: A Stakeholder Approach* (Cambridge, MA: Ballinger Publishing Co., 1984), p. 179. Copyright © 1984 by R. E. Freeman. Reprinted with permission from Ballinger Publishing Company.

Table 9.3   **Three New Measures of Corporate Performance**

Performance Characteristic	*Some Traditional Measures*	*Proposed New Measures*
Growth	Dollar sales, unit sales, dollar assets.	Value added*
Efficiency	Gross margin, net profits, net profits/dollar sales.	ROVA†
Asset utilization	ROI, return on equity, earnings per share.	ROVA/ROI

SOURCE: C. W. Hofer, "ROVA: A New Measure for Assessing Organizational Performance," in R. Lamb, ed., *Advances in Strategic Management*, vol. 2 (Greenwich, Conn.: JAI Press, 1983), p. 50. Copyright © 1983 by C. W. Hofer. Reprinted by permission.

* Value added = Dollar sales − Cost of raw materials and purchased parts.

† ROVA: Return on Value Added = $\dfrac{\text{Net profits before tax}}{\text{Value Added}} \times 100\%$.

society. Value added is the difference between dollar sales and the cost of raw materials and purchased parts. Return on value added (ROVA) is a second measure, one that divides net profits before tax by value added and converts the quotient to a percentage. Preliminary studies by Hofer suggest that ROVA tends to stabilize in the range of 12% to 18% for most industries in the maturity or saturation phases of market evolution. Hofer argues that ROVA may be a better measure of corporate performance across various industries than other measures currently in use.[4]

Shareholder Value   Because of the belief that accounting-based numbers such as return on investment and earnings per share are not reliable indicators of a corporation's economic value, many corporations are using shareholder value as a better measure of corporate performance and strategic management effectiveness.[5] *Shareholder value* (or shareholder wealth) is defined as the sum of dividends plus stock appreciation. It determines if a corporation is earning a rate of return greater than that demanded by investors in the security market. Rappaport, one of the principal advocates of this measure, explains its use.

> What I have termed the "shareholder value approach" estimates the economic value of any strategy as the expected cash flows discounted by the market discount rate. These cash flows in turn serve as the basis for expected shareholder returns from dividends and stock-price appreciation.[6]

A recent survey of the senior managers of Fortune 500 companies revealed that 30% select investment proposals on the basis of their expected contributions to shareholder wealth. The survey also noted that a number of corporations not now using this approach are starting to experiment with value-based techniques.[7]

Through its strategy, audit, and compensation committees, a board of directors closely evaluates the job performance of the CEO and the top management team. Of course, it is concerned primarily with overall profitability as measured by return on investment, return on equity, earnings per share, and shareholder wealth. The absence of short-run profitability is certainly a factor contributing to the firing of any CEO.[8] The board will also, however, be concerned with other factors. For example, McSweeney recommends the incorporation of a number of areas of concern on a scorecard for use by the board. Figure 9.2 is one example of such a scorecard.

As shown in Fig. 9.2, the board should evaluate top management not only on return, but also on factors relating to its strategic management practices. Has the top management team set reasonable long-run as well as short-run objectives? Has it formulated innovative strategies? Has it worked closely with operational managers to develop realistic implementation plans, schedules, and budgets? Has it developed and used appropriate measures

Evaluation of Top Management

General scoreboard	Good	Fair	Poor
Return on stockholders' equity			
Return on sales			
Management of stockholders' assets			
Development of sound organizational structure			
Development of successors			
Development of proprietary products			
Development of organization morale			
Development of corporate image			
Development of growth potential			
Percentage of industry by segments			
Divestments			
Acquisitions			
Application of research & development			
Application of engineering & technology			
International			

Figure 9.2   Scorecard to rate top management.
SOURCE: E. McSweeney, "A Scorecard for Rating Management," *Business Week* (June 18, 1974), p. 15. Reprinted from the June 18, 1974 issue of *Business Week* by special permission. Copyright © 1974 by McGraw-Hill, Inc.

of corporate and divisional performance for feedback and control? Has it provided the board with appropriate feedback on corporate performance in advance of key decision points? These and other questions should be raised by a board of directors as they evaluate the performance of top management.

The specific items that are used by a board to evaluate its top management should be derived from the objectives agreed to earlier by both the board and top management. If better relations with the local community and improved safety practices in work areas were selected as objectives for the year (or for five years), these items should be included in the evaluation. In addition, other factors should be included that tend to lead to profitability, such as market share, product quality, and investment intensity (from the PIMS research discussed in Chapter 6).[9]

Key Performance Areas

In order for top management to establish effective control systems for the entire corporation, it must identify "key performance areas." These areas must reflect important corporate objectives. According to Stoner, "Key performance or key result areas are those aspects of the unit or organization that *have* to function effectively in order for the entire unit or organization to succeed."[10] The broad controls that top management establishes for these key areas help to define the more detailed control systems and performance standards for lower-level managers. GE developed eight key performance areas and established standards for them. These areas are as follows:

1. *Profitability.* GE chose to use total dollar profits minus a charge for capital investment.

2. *Market position.* Market share, that is, the percent of available business for each product or service.

3. *Productivity.* Two measures were used—payroll dollar cost and the depreciation dollar costs of goods produced. These enabled GE to assess the efficiency with which labor and equipment were being used.

4. *Product leadership.* In each of GE's businesses, members of the engineering, manufacturing, marketing, and finance departments annually evaluated the costs, quality, and market position of each existing and each planned product.

5. *Personnel development.* Various reports were compiled to evaluate the manner in which GE was providing for present and future personnel needs.

6. *Employee attitudes.* Attitudes of employees toward the company were measured directly by regular attitude surveys, as well as indirectly by absenteeism and turnover.

7. *Public responsibility.* Indicators were developed to assess how well GE was carrying out its responsibilities to its employees, suppliers, and local communities.

8. *Balance between short-range and long-range goals.* An in-depth study of the interrelationships between key performance areas was carried out to ensure that immediate goals were not being attained at the expense of future profits and stability.[11]

Strategic Audits

Audits of corporate activities are used by various consulting firms as a way to measure performance and are increasingly suggested for use by boards of directors as well as by others in managerial positions. Management audits have been developed to evaluate activities such as corporate social responsibility, functional areas such as the marketing department, divisions such as the international division, as well as to evaluate the corporation itself in a strategic audit (see Chapter 2). The strategic audit approach is likely to be increasingly used by corporations that become concerned with closely monitoring those activities that affect overall corporate effectiveness and efficiency. To be effective, the strategic audit should be developed to parallel the corporation's strategic management process and/or model.

Measures of Divisional and Functional Unit Performance

Corporations use a variety of techniques to evaluate and control performance in divisions, SBUs, and functional units. If a corporation is composed of SBUs or divisions, it will use many of the same performance measures (ROI, for instance) that it uses to assess overall corporation performance. To the extent that it can isolate specific functional units, such as R&D, the corporation may develop responsibility centers.

   Budgets are certainly an important control device. During strategy formulation and implementation, top management approves a series of programs and supporting operating budgets from its business units.[12] During evaluation and control, actual expenses are contrasted with planned expenditures to assess the degree of variance. This is typically done on a monthly basis. In addition, top management will probably require *periodic statistical reports* summarizing data on key factors, such as the number of new customer contracts, volume of received orders, and productivity figures, among others.[13]

Evaluating a Division or SBU

At Norton Company, each SBU is evaluated in depth every two years. This evaluation is conducted by the Strategy Guidance Committee, composed of the CEO, the financial vice-president, eight vice-presidents in charge of operations, the controller, assistant controller, vice-president for corporate development, and an assistant vice-president. At the same time that the line manager in charge of an SBU comes before the committee with a detailed strategy for each major segment of the unit's operations, the committee is evaluating the unit's performance according to past objectives, and arriving at its strategic position within the corporation and, therefore, its potential.

The Strategy Guidance Committee looks at a strategic business unit from many viewpoints—return on net assets, return on sales, asset turnover, market share strategy. The committee might test sales growth rate against market growth rate against market share strategy. The committee also looks at competition, relative strengths and weaknesses, and cash generation plotted against market share strategy. It also places the unit on a balloon chart or growth/market share matrix for the entire company, to see how this unit fits in with all the others.[14]

The Strategy Guidance Committee looks at the SBU from all angles and asks a number of penetrating questions. Some of these questions are listed below.

Evaluation of a Strategic Business Unit at Norton Company

- How does this unit contribute to the overall scheme of things?
- Does it help to balance the total?
- Does it increase or decrease the cyclical nature of the company?
- How does it relate to other Norton technologies, processes, or distribution systems?
- How successfully does it compete?
- How is it regarded by its customers and by its competitors?
- Does it hurt or improve the company's image with the investment community?
- What are its mission and mode of operation in terms of build, maintain, or harvest?
- Is its current strategy appropriate?
- Can we win and, if so, how?
- If it has changed its strategy or performance since the last review, why has it changed?
- What does our analysis suggest about the unit's profitability in comparison with similar businesses?

SOURCE: D. R. Melville, "Top Management's Role in Strategic Planning," *The Journal of Business Strategy*, vol. 1, no. 4, (Spring 1981), p. 63. Reprinted by permission from the *Journal of Business Strategy*. Copyright © 1981 by Warren, Gorham & Lamont Inc., Boston. All rights reserved.

Responsibility Centers

Control systems can be established to monitor specific functions, projects, or divisions. Budgets typically are used to control the financial indicators of performance. Responsibility centers are used to isolate a unit so that it can be evaluated separately from the rest of the corporation. A responsibility center is headed by a manager responsible for the center's performance. It uses resources (measured in terms of costs) to produce a service or a product (measured in terms of volume or revenues). There are five major types of responsibility centers. They are determined by the way these resources and services or products are measured by the corporation's control system:[15]

1. *Standard cost centers.* Primarily used in manufacturing facilities, standard (or expected) costs are computed for each operation on the basis

of historical data. To evaluate the center's performance, its total standard costs are multiplied by the units produced to give the expected cost of production, which is then compared to the actual cost of production.

2. *Revenue centers.* Production, usually in terms of unit or dollar sales, is measured without consideration of resource costs (e.g., salaries). The center is thus judged in terms of effectiveness rather than efficiency. The effectiveness of a sales region, for example, is determined by its actual sales compared to its projected or previous year's sales. Profits are not considered because sales departments have very limited influence over the cost of the products they sell.

3. *Expense centers.* Resources are measured in dollars without consideration of service or product costs. Thus budgets will have been prepared for "engineered" expenses (those costs that can be calculated) and for "discretionary" expenses. Typical expense centers are administrative, service, and research departments. They cost an organization money, but they only indirectly contribute to revenues.

4. *Profit centers.* Performance is measured in terms of the difference between revenues (which measure production) and expenditures (which measure resources). A profit center is typically established whenever an organizational unit has control over both its resources and its products or services. By having such centers, a corporation can be organized into divisions of separate product lines. The manager of each division is given autonomy to the extent that she or he is able to keep profits at a satisfactory (or better) level. Some organizational units that are not usually thought of as potentially autonomous can, for the purpose of profit-center evaluations, be made so. A manufacturing department, for example, may be converted from a standard cost center (or expense center) into a profit center by allowing it to charge a *transfer price* for each product it "sells" to the sales department. The difference between the manufacturing cost per unit and the agreed-upon transfer price is the unit's "profit."

5. *Investment centers.* As with profit centers, investment center performance is measured in terms of the difference between its resources and its services or products. Since most divisions in large manufacturing corporations use huge assets, such as plants and equipment, to make their products, evaluating their performance on the basis of profits alone ignores the size of their assets. For example, two divisions in a corporation make identical profits, but one division owns a $3 million plant, whereas the other owns a $1 million plant. Both make the same profits,

but one is obviously more efficient: The smaller plant provides the stockholders with a better return on their investment.

The most widely used measure of investment center performance is ROI. Another measure, called residual income, is found by subtracting an interest charge from the net income. This interest charge could be based on the interest the corporation is actually paying to lenders for the assets being used. It could also be based on the amount of income that could have been earned if the assets had been invested somewhere else.

Sloan reports that the concept of rate of return on investments was crucial to General Motors' exercise of its permanent control of the whole corporation in a way consistent with its decentralized organization.[16] Donaldson Brown, who came to GM from DuPont in 1921, defined return on investment as a function of the profit margin and the rate of turnover of invested capital. Multiplying the profit margin by the investment turnover equals the percent of return on investment. Management can, therefore, increase the return on investment by increasing the rate of capital turnover in relation to sales (that is, increase volume) as well as by increasing profit margins (increase revenue and/or cut costs and expenses).[17]

Investment center performance can also be measured in terms of its contribution to *shareholder value*. One example is given by the CEO of a large corporation.

We value our businesses by computing the net present value of each unit's equity cash flow, using the appropriate cost of capital. Then we subtract out the market value of assigned debt and arrive at an estimate of the warranted market value of the unit. These techniques allow us to evaluate and rank our units based on their relative contribution to the creation of overall corporate equity value, which is our overall objective.[18]

9.2 STRATEGIC INFORMATION SYSTEMS

Before performance measures can have any impact on strategic management, they must be communicated to those people responsible for formulating and implementing strategic plans. Strategic information systems can perform this function. They may be computer-based or manual, formal or informal. They serve the information needs of top management.[19] As discussed in Chapter 5, an information system is meant to provide a basis for early warning signals that can originate both externally or internally. These warning signals grow out of the corporation's need to ensure that programs and procedures are being implemented to achieve corporate and divisional objectives.

As mentioned in Chapter 5, the information system should focus managers' attention on the critical success factors in their jobs. *Critical success factors* are those few things that must go well to ensure success in a corporation. They therefore represent those areas that must be given special and continuous attention to bring about high performance.[20] These critical success factors provide a focal point for directing the development of a computer-based information system. Taking this approach should result in an information system useful to strategic managers as it pinpoints key areas that require a manager's attention.

At the divisional or SBU level of a corporation, the information system should be used to support, reinforce, or enlarge its business-level strategy.[21] An SBU pursuing a strategy of overall cost leadership could use its information system to reduce costs either by improving labor productivity or the utilization of other resources such as inventory or machinery. Another SBU, in contrast, might wish to pursue a differentiation strategy. It could use its information system to add uniqueness to the product or service and contribute to quality, service, or image through the functional areas.[22] American Hospital Supply and both United and American Airlines took this approach to increase their market shares by offering unique information systems services to their customers. The choice of the business-level strategy will thus dictate the type of information system needed in the SBU to both implement and control strategic activities. Table 9.4 lists the differences between an information system needed to evaluate and control a low-cost strategy and an information system needed for product differentiation. The information systems will be constructed differently to monitor different activities because the two types of business-level strategies have different critical success factors.

9.3 PROBLEMS IN MEASURING PERFORMANCE

The measurement of performance is a crucial part of evaluation and control. The lack of quantifiable objectives or performance standards and the inability of the information system to provide timely, valid information are two obvious control problems.[23] Without objective and timely measurements, it would be extremely difficult to make operational, let alone strategic, decisions. Nevertheless, the use of timely, quantifiable standards does not guarantee good performance. The very act of monitoring and measuring performance can cause side-effects which interfere with overall corporate performance. Among the most frequent negative side-effects are a *short-term orientation* and *goal displacement*.

Short-Term Orientation

Hodgetts and Wortman state that in many situations top executives do not analyze *either* the long-term implications of present operations on the strategy they have adopted *or* the operational impact of a strategy on the corporate mission. They report that long-run evaluations are *not* conducted because executives (1) may not realize their importance, (2) may feel that

Table 9.4 Use of Information Systems to Monitor Implementation of Business Strategies

	Generic Strategies	
	Low Cost	Product Differentiation
Product Design & Development	Product engineering systems Project control systems	R&D data bases Professional work stations Electronic mail CAD Custom engineering systems Integrated systems for manufacturing
Operations	Process engineering systems Process control systems Labor control systems Inventory management systems Procurement systems Quality monitoring systems	CAM Quality assurance systems Systems for suppliers Quality monitoring systems
Marketing	Streamlined distribution systems Centralized control systems Econometric modeling systems	Sophisticated marketing systems Market data bases Graphic display systems Telemarketing systems Competition analysis systems Modeling systems Service-oriented distribution systems
Sales	Sales control systems Advertising monitoring systems Systems to consolidate sales function Strict incentive/monitoring systems	Differential pricing systems Office/field communications Customer/sales support systems Dealer support systems Customer order entry systems
Administration	Cost control systems Quantitative planning & budgeting systems Office automation for staff reduction	Office automation to integrate functions Environment scanning & nonquantitative planning systems Teleconferencing systems

short-run considerations are more important than long-run considerations, (3) may not be personally evaluated on a long-term basis, or (4) may not have the time to make a long-run analysis.[24] There is no real justification for the first and last "reasons." If executives realize the importance of long-run evaluations, they make the time needed to conduct them. The short-term nature of most incentive and promotion plans, however, provides a rationale for the second and third reasons.

A study of 112 large U.S. corporations revealed that only 44.4% had an explicit policy for rewarding the contribution of key line managers to strategic planning.[25] A similar study found that whereas 79% of the corporations sampled rewarded executives for short-term performance (typically an annual bonus linked to pretax profit), only 42% of the same firms offered longer-term incentive plans.[26]

Table 9.1 indicates that one of the limitations of ROI as a performance measure is its short-term nature. In theory, ROI is not limited to the short run, but in practice it is often difficult to use this measure to realize long-term benefits for the corporation. If the performance of corporate and division managers is evaluated primarily on the basis of an annual ROI, the managers tend to focus their effort on those factors that have positive short-term effects. As a result, division managers often undertake capital investments with early paybacks to establish a favorable division track record. Results are often inconsistent with corporate long-run objectives. Since managers can often manipulate both the numerator (earnings) as well as the denominator (investment), the resulting ROI figure becomes meaningless. Advertising, maintenance, and research efforts might be reduced. Mergers may be undertaken that will do more for this year's earnings than for the division's or corporation's future profits. Expensive retooling and plant modernization can be delayed as long as a manager can manipulate figures on production defects and absenteeism. Efforts to compensate for these distortions tend to create a burdensome accounting control system which stifles creativity and flexibility, leading to even more questionable "creative accounting" practices.[27] For example, the manager of Doughtie's Foods' wholesaling operation in Richmond, Virginia, admitted to SEC investigators that he routinely gave false inventory figures to his superiors in order to overstate his division's profits. He admitted that he did it "just to look good." His division had not been doing well and his bosses would regularly single him out for criticism at corporate planning meetings.[28]

A more insidious danger resulting from heavy emphasis on short-term performance measures is their effect on top-level strategic decisions. Hayes and Abernathy contend that such control measures have helped cause a decline in technological innovations: "Conditioned by a market-driven strategy and held closely to account by a 'results now' ROI-oriented control system, American managers have increasingly refused to take the chance on innovative product/market development."[29] Even the highly touted PIMS research (discussed in Chapter 6) has contributed to this short-run tendency by focusing on only those variables that affect ROI as a measure of corporate performance. For example, PIMS research has concluded that "increased investment almost invariably reduced ROI and cash flow in the short run. . . ."[30]

Goal Displacement

The very monitoring and measuring of performance (if not carefully done) can actually result in a decline in overall corporate performance. A dysfunctional side-effect known as *goal displacement* can occur. This is the confusion of means with ends. Goal displacement occurs when activities originally intended to help attain corporate objectives become ends in themselves—or are adapted to meet ends other than those for which they were intended.[31] Two types of goal displacement are *behavior substitution* and *suboptimization*.

Behavior Substitution   Not all activities or aspects of performance can be easily quantified and measured. It may be very difficult to set standards for such desired activities as cooperation or initiative. As a result, managers of divisions or functional units tend to focus more of their attention on those behaviors that are measurable than on those that are not.[32] They thus reward those people who do well on these types of measures. Since the managers tend to ignore behaviors that are either unmeasurable or difficult to measure, people receive little to no reward for engaging in these activities. The problem with this phenomenon is that the easy-to-measure activities may have little to no relationship to the desired good performance. Rational people, nevertheless, will tend to work for the rewards the system has to offer. As a result, employees will tend to substitute behaviors that are recognized and rewarded for those behaviors that are ignored without regard to their contribution to goal accomplishment. A U.S. Navy quip sums up this situation: "What you inspect is what you get." If the evaluation and control system of an auto plant rewards the meeting of quantitative goals while paying only lip-service to qualitative goals, consumers can expect to get a very large number of very poorly built cars!

The most frequently mentioned problem with Management By Objectives (MBO) is that the measurement process partially distorts the realities of the job. Objectives are made for areas where the measurement of accomplishments is relatively easy, such as with ROI, increased sales, or reduced cost. But these may not always be the most important areas. This problem becomes crucial in professional, service, or staff activities where quantitative measurements are difficult. If, for example, a manager is achieving all of the quantifiable objectives, but in so doing, alienates the work force, the result may be a long-term drop in performance. If promotions are strictly based on measurable short-term performance results, this manager may very likely be promoted or transferred before the negative employee attitudes result in complaints to the personnel office, strikes, or sabotage. The law governing the effect of measurement on behavior seems to be: *Quantifiable measures drive out nonquantifiable measures.*

Suboptimization   The emphasis in large corporations to develop separate responsibility centers can create some problems for the corporation as a whole. To the extent that a division or functional unit views itself as a separate entity, it may refuse to cooperate with other units or divisions in the same corporation if co-operation may in some way negatively affect its performance evaluation. The competition between divisions to achieve a high ROI can result in a refusal to share new technology or work process improvements. One division's attempt to optimize the accomplishment of its goals can cause other divisions to fall behind and thus negatively affect overall corporate performance. One common example of this type of suboptimization occurs when a marketing department approves an early shipment date to a customer as a means of getting an order and forces the manufacturing department into overtime production for this one order. Production costs are raised, which reduces the manufacturing department's overall efficiency. The end result may be that, although marketing achieves its sales goal, the corporation fails to achieve its expected profitability.

In designing a control system, top management should remember that controls should follow strategy. Unless controls are a means to ensure the use of the proper strategy to achieve objectives, there is a strong likelihood that dysfunctional side-effects will completely undermine the implementation of the objectives. The following guidelines are recommended:

9.4 GUIDELINES FOR PROPER CONTROL

1. Control should involve only the minimum amount of information needed to give a reliable picture of events. Too many controls create confusion.

2. Controls should monitor only meaningful activities and results, regardless of measurement difficulty. If cooperation between divisions is important to corporate performance, some form of qualitative or quantitative measure should be established in order to monitor cooperation.

3. Controls should be timely so that corrective action can be taken before it is too late. *Steering controls,* controls that monitor or measure the factors influencing performance, should be stressed in order to give advance notice of problems.

4. Long-term as well as short-term controls should be used. If only short-term measures are emphasized, a short-term managerial orientation is likely.

5. Controls should aim at pinpointing exceptions. Only those activities or results that fall outside a predetermined tolerance range should call for action.

6. Emphasize the reward of meeting or exceeding standards rather than punishment for failing to meet standards. Heavy punishment of failure

will typically result in goal displacement. Managers will "fudge" reports and lobby for lower standards.

Surprisingly, the best-managed companies may have only a few formal objective controls. They focus on measuring the critical success factors— those few things that must go well to ensure success. Other factors are controlled by the social system in the form of the corporate culture. To the extent that the culture complements and reinforces the strategic orientation of the firm, there is less need for an extensive formal control system. In their book, *In Search of Excellence,* Peters and Waterman state that "the stronger the culture and the more it was directed toward the marketplace, the less need was there for policy manuals, organization charts, or detailed procedures and rules. In these companies, people way down the line know what they are supposed to do in most situations because the handful of guiding values is crystal clear."[33]

9.5 STRATEGIC INCENTIVE MANAGEMENT

In an assessment of the strategic planning performance of large U.S. corporations, Steiner reports a significant weakness in rewarding managers for strategic thinking.[34] His view agrees with the data reported earlier that fewer than half of the large U.S. corporations have long-term incentive plans. Traditionally, the emphasis of executive compensation has been on equity and competitiveness.[35] This means that the level of compensation for chief executive officers has been a function of how much CEOs are paid at comparable firms. As a result, CEO compensation is related more to the size of the corporation than to the size of its profits.[36] This association between firm size and executive compensation, according to Rappaport, can only fuel top management's natural inclination to grow businesses as fast as possible.[37]

Boards of directors need to take the initiative in developing long-term controls and corresponding incentive plans. According to Andrews, "The best criterion for appraising the quality of management performance, in the absence of personal failures or unexpected breakdowns, is management's success over time in executing a demanding and approved strategy that is continually tested against opportunity and need."[38]

Executive compensation must be linked more clearly to strategic performance—to the management of the corporate portfolio, to the business unit's mission, to short-term financial as well as long-term strategic performance, and to the degree of risk involved in managing a portfolio effectively and efficiently.[39] The following three approaches are tailored to help match measurements and rewards with explicit strategic objectives and timeframes: (1) the *weighted-factor method,* (2) the *long-term evaluation method,* and

(3) the *strategic-funds method*. These approaches can also be combined to best suit a corporation's circumstances.[40]

1. *Weighted-factor method*. The *weighted-factor method* is particularly appropriate for measuring and rewarding the performance of top SBU managers and group-level executives when performance factors and their importance vary from one SBU to another. One corporation might contain the following variations: the performance of high-growth SBUs measured in terms of market share, sales growth, designated future payoff, and progress on several future-oriented strategic projects; the performance of low-growth SBUs, in contrast, measured in terms of ROI and cash generation; and the performance of medium-growth SBUs measured for a combination of these factors. Refer to Table 9.5 for an example of how the weighted-factor method could be applied to three different SBUs.

2. *Long-term evaluation method*. The *long-term evaluation method* compensates managers for achieving objectives set over a multiyear period. An executive is promised some company stock or "performance units" (convertible into dollars) on the basis of long-term performance. An executive committee, for example, might set a particular objective in

Table 9.5   A Weighted-Factor Approach to Strategic Incentive Management

Strategic Business Unit Category	Factor	Weight
High growth	Return on assets	10%
	Cash flow	0%
	Strategic-funds programs	45%
	Market-share increase	45%
		100%
Medium growth	Return on assets	25%
	Cash flow	25%
	Strategic-funds programs	25%
	Market-share increase	25%
		100%
Low growth	Return on assets	50%
	Cash flow	50%
	Strategic-funds programs	0%
	Market-share increase	0%
		100%

terms of growth in earnings per share during a five-year period. The giving of awards would be contingent on the corporation's meeting that objective within the designated time limit. Any executive leaving the corporation before the objective is met receives nothing.

As of 1984, approximately 15% of corporations with sales over $550 million had long-term income programs that compensated managers with some sort of deferred stock to achieve set goals over a multiyear period. The typical emphasis on stock price, however, makes this approach more applicable to top management than to business unit managers.[41]

3. *Strategic-funds method.* The *strategic-funds method* encourages executives to look at developmental expenses as different from expenses required to sustain current operations. The accounting statement for a corporate unit enters strategic funds as a separate entry below the current ROI. It is therefore possible to distinguish between those expense dollars consumed in the generation of current revenues and those invested in the future of the business. As a result, the manager can be evaluated on *both* a short- and a long-term basis and has an incentive to invest strategic funds in the future. Refer to Table 9.6 for an example of the strategic-funds method applied to a business unit.

According to Stonich, "An effective way to achieve the desired strategic results through a reward system is to combine the weighted-factor, long-term evaluation, and strategic funds approaches."[42] To do this, first segregate strategic funds from short-term funds, as in the strategic-funds method. Second, develop a weighted-factor chart for each SBU. Third, measure performance on three bases: the pre-tax profit in the strategic-funds approach; the

Table 9.6   **A Strategic-Funds Approach Applied to an SBU Profit and Loss Statement**

Sales	$ 12,300,000
Cost of sales	6,900,000
Gross margin	$ 5,400,000
Operating (general and administrative expense)	−3,700,000
Operating (return on sales)	$ 1,700,000 or 33%
Strategic funds	−1,000,000
Pre-tax profit	$ 700,000 or 13.6%

SOURCE: Paul J. Stonich, "The Performance Measurement and Reward System: Critical to Strategic Management," *Organizational Dynamics* (Winter 1984), p. 52. Copyright © 1984, Periodicals Division, American Management Associations, New York. All rights reserved. Reprinted by permission of the publisher.

weighted factors; and the long-term evaluation of the SBU's and the corporation's performance. These incentive plans will probably gain increasing acceptance with business corporations in the near future. General Electric and Westinghouse are two firms using a version of these measures.

9.6 SUMMARY AND CONCLUSION

The evaluation and control of performance is a five-step process: (1) determine what to measure, (2) establish standards for performance, (3) measure actual performance, (4) compare actual performance with the standard, and (5) take corrective action. Information coming from this process is fed back into the strategic management system so that both strategic and operational managers can correct performance deviations.

Although the most commonly used measures of corporate performance are the various return ratios, measures based on a value-added or shareholder value approach may be of some use. A number of corporations also monitor key factors related to ROI that may have predictive value. If a corporation has objectives other than profitability, it may wish to follow GE's example by establishing "key performance areas" for special attention. A stakeholder "scorecard" may also be of some value in assessing the corporation's impact on its environment. The strategic audit is recommended as a method to evaluate activities throughout the corporation.

Divisions, SBUs, and functional units are often broken down into responsibility centers to aid control. Such areas are often categorized as standard cost centers, revenue centers, expense centers, profit centers, and investment centers. Budgets and periodic statistical reports are important control devices to monitor the implementation of major programs in business units.

A strategic information system is an important part of the evaluation and control process. By focusing on critical success factors, it can provide early warning signals to strategic managers. The system can be tailored to the business-level strategy being implemented in the SBU in order to ensure the success of the strategy.

The monitoring and measurement of performance can result in dysfunctional side effects that negatively affect overall corporate performance. Among the likely side effects are a short-term orientation and goal displacement. These problems can be reduced if top management remembers that controls must focus on strategic goals. There should be as few controls as possible, and only meaningful activities and results should be monitored. Controls should be timely to both long-term as well as short-term orientations. They should pinpoint exceptions but should be used more to reward than to punish individuals.

Incentive plans should be based upon long-term as well as short-term considerations. Three suggested approaches are the weighted-factor method, the long-term evaluation method, and the strategic-funds method.

A proper evaluation and control system should act to complete the loop shown in the strategic management model. It should feed back information important not only to the implementation of strategy, but also to the initial formulation of strategy. In terms of the strategic decision-making process depicted in Fig. 6.1, the data coming from evaluation and control are the basis for step 1—evaluating current performance results. Because of this feedback effect, evaluation and control is the beginning as well as the end of the strategic management process.

DISCUSSION QUESTIONS

1. Is Fig. 9.1 a realistic model of the control process? Why or why not?

2. Why bother with value-added, shareholder value, or a stakeholder's scorecard? Isn't it simpler to evaluate a corporation and its SBUs just using standard measures like ROI or earnings per share?

3. What are the values to a corporation of establishing "key performance areas"?

4. How much faith can a division or SBU manager place in a *transfer price* as a surrogate for a market price in measuring a profit center's performance?

5. Why are goal displacement and short-run orientation likely side effects of the monitoring of performance? What can a corporation do to avoid them?

6. Why do less than half of the large U.S. corporations use long-term incentive plans?

7. Is the evaluation and control process appropriate for a corporation that emphasizes creativity? Are control and creativity compatible? Explain.

NOTES

1. L. G. Hrebiniak and W. F. Joyce, *Implementing Strategy* (New York: Macmillan, 1984), p. 195.

2. V. E. Millar, "The Evolution Toward Value-Based Financial Planning," *Information Strategy: The Executive's Journal* (Winter 1985), p. 28.

3. R. E. Freeman, *Strategic Management: A Stakeholder Approach* (Boston: Pitman Publishing Co., 1984), pp. 177–181.

4. C. W. Hofer, "ROVA: A New Measure for Assessing Organizational Performance," in R. Lamb (ed.), *Advances in Strategic Management*, Vol. 2 (Greenwich, Conn.: Jai Press, 1983), pp. 43–55.
C. W. Hofer and D. Schendel, *Strategy Formulation: Analytical Concepts* (St. Paul, Minn.: West Publishing Co., 1978), p. 130.

5. A. Rappaport, "Corporate Performance Standards and Shareholder Wealth," *Journal of Business Strategy* (Spring 1983), pp. 28–38.

6. A. Rappaport, "Have We Been Measuring Success with the Wrong Ruler?" *Wall Street Journal* (June 25, 1984), p. 22.

7. Millar, pp. 29–30.

8. L. R. Jauch, T. N. Martin and R. N. Osborn, "Top Management Under Fire," *Journal of Business Strategy* (Spring 1981), p. 39.

9. G. Badler, "Strategizing for a Spectrum of Possibilities," *Planning Review* (July 1984), pp. 28–31.

10. J. A. F. Stoner, *Management,* 2nd ed. (Englewood Cliffs, N.J.: Prentice-Hall, 1982), pp. 603–604.

11. J. A. F. Stoner, *Management,* 1st ed. (Englewood Cliffs, N.J.: Prentice-Hall, 1978), pp. 583–586.

12. C. H. Roush, Jr., "Strategic Resource Allocation and Control," in W. D. Guth (ed.), *Handbook of Business Strategy* (Boston: Warren, Gorham, and Lamont, 1985), pp. 20.1–20.25.

13. R. L. Daft and N. B. Macintosh, "The Nature and Use of Formal Control Systems for Management Control and Strategy Implementation," *Journal of Management* (Spring 1984), pp. 43–66.

14. D. R. Melville, "Top Management's Role in Strategic Planning," *Journal of Business Strategy* (Spring 1981), p. 63.

15. This discussion is based on R. N. Anthony, J. Dearden, and R. F. Vancil, *Management Control Systems* (Homewood, Ill.: Richard D. Irwin, Inc., 1972), pp. 200–203.

16. A. P. Sloan, Jr., *My Years with General Motors* (Garden City, N.Y.: Doubleday, Anchor Books, 1972), p. 159.

17. Sloan, p. 161.

18. Millar, p. 30.

19. J. A. Turner and H. C. Lucas, Jr., "Developing Strategic Information Systems," in W. D. Guth (ed.), *Handbook of Business Strategy* (Boston: Warren, Gorham and Lamont, 1985), p. 21.2.

20. A. C. Boynton and R. W. Zmud, "An Assessment of Critical Success Factors," *Sloan Management Review* (Summer 1984), p. 17.

21. G. L. Parsons, "Information Technology: A New Competitive Weapon," *Sloan Management Review* (Fall 1983), p. 11.

22. Parsons, p. 11.

23. Hrebiniak and Joyce, pp. 198–199.

24. R. M. Hodgetts and M. S. Wortman, *Administrative Policy,* 2nd ed. (New York: John Wiley & Sons, 1980), p. 128.

25. R. B. Higgins, "Human Resource Management Problems in Strategic Planning," in R. Lamb (ed.), *Advances in Strategic Management,* Vol. I (Greenwich, Conn.: Jai Press, 1983), p. 90.

26. J. B. Quinn, "Why Executives Think Short," *Newsweek* (July 13, 1981), p. 11c.

27. J. Dutton and A. Thomas, "Managing Organizational Productivity," *Journal of Business Strategy* (Summer 1982), p. 41.

28. R. L. Hudson, "SEC Charges Fudging of Corporate Figures Is a Growing Practice," *Wall Street Journal* (June 2, 1983), p. 1.

29. R. H. Hayes and W. J. Abernathy, "Managing Our Way to Economic Decline," *Harvard Business Review* (July–August 1980), p. 72.

30. C. P. Zeithaml, C. R. Anderson, and F. T. Paine, "An Empirical Re-examination of Selected PIMS Findings," *Proceedings, Academy of Management* (August 1981), p. 14.

31. H. R. Bobbitt, Jr., R. H. Breinholt, R. H. Doktor, and J. P. McNaul, *Organizational Behavior*, 2nd ed. (Englewood Cliffs, N.J.: Prentice-Hall, 1978), p. 99.

32. K. Cameron, "A Study of Organizational Effectiveness and Its Predictions," Working Paper, Center for Higher Education Management Systems, Boulder, Colorado, September 1983, p. 2.

33. T. J. Peters and R. H. Waterman, *In Search of Excellence* (New York: Harper & Row, 1982), pp. 75–76.

34. G. A. Steiner, "Formal Strategic Planning in the United States Today," *Long Range Planning* (June 1983), pp. 12–17.

35. M. R. Hurwich and R. A. Furniss, "Measuring and Rewarding Strategic Performance," in W. D. Guth (ed.), *Handbook of Business Strategy* (Boston: Warren, Gorham, and Lamont, 1985), p. 24.5.

36. G. R. Ungson and R. M. Steers, "Motivation and Politics in Executive Compensation," *Academy of Management Review* (April 1984), pp. 313–323.

37. A. Rappaport, "How To Design Value-Contributing Executive Incentives," *Journal of Business Strategy* (Fall 1983), p. 50.

38. K. R. Andrews, "Directors' Responsibility for Corporate Strategy," *Harvard Business Review* (November–December 1980), p. 32.

39. L. J. Brindisi, Jr., "Paying for Strategic Performance: A New Executive Compensation Imperative," in R. B. Lamb (ed.), *Competitive Strategic Management* (Englewood Cliffs, N.J.: Prentice-Hall, 1984), p. 334.

40. P. J. Stonich, "The Performance Measurement and Reward System: Critical to Strategic Management," *Organizational Dynamics* (Winter 1984), pp. 45–57.

41. Stonich, p. 52.

42. Stonich, p. 53.

PART FIVE

OTHER STRATEGIC CONCERNS

Chapter 10

STRATEGIC MANAGEMENT OF MULTINATIONAL CORPORATIONS

STRATEGIC MANAGEMENT MODEL

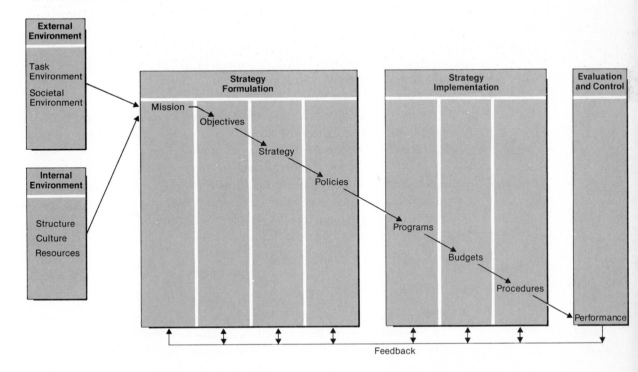

Throughout much of its history, the United States has been virtually self-sufficient. During the 1700s and 1800s, the distance between North America and Europe encouraged the United States to develop its own industries. As late as the 1960s, combined exports and imports of merchandise represented only 7% to 8% of the U.S. gross national product—the lowest of any major industrialized nation.[1] A large domestic market, plus a bountiful supply of natural resources and labor, enabled major corporations to grow and become successful with only a casual interest in "foreign" markets. High tariff laws served to keep the business interests of other countries out of the United States while the infant domestic companies matured.

Since World War II, however, international trade has increased dramatically. In the past quarter century, the volume of goods traded between nations has climbed from less than $100 billion to more than $1 trillion.[2] The United States became much more concerned about international trade. From 1973 to 1983, U.S. exports expanded 281% from $71.4 billion to $200.5 billion. At the same time, U.S. imports increased 368% from $70.1 billion to $258.1 billion.[3] Manufactured exports now equal approximately 20% of U.S. manufacturing output.[4] International considerations have become crucial to the strategic decisions of any large business corporation.

10.1 THE COMING GLOBAL VILLAGE

In 1965, Marshall McLuhan suggested that advances in communications and transportation technologies were drawing the people of the world closer together. As intercontinental travel times decreased, the world went toward becoming a "global village" of interdependent people.[5] People in all countries were finding themselves affected by huge multinational corporations (MNCs).

In 1984, for example, the Chicago Mercantile Exchange linked with a futures exchange in Singapore in a major step toward global 24-hour financial trading. The world's automobile manufacturers, as shown in Fig. 10.1, were heavily involved by 1984 in a series of joint ventures and complicated equity arrangements. Not only did General Motors and Chrysler have minority ownership in the Japanese firms of Suzuki, Isuzu, and Mitsubishi, French government-owned Renault had 15% equity in Swedish Volvo and almost majority ownership of American Motors.[6]

Going International

Three basic reasons can be listed for business corporations expanding their operations internationally:

1. Corporations can earn increased sales and profits by expanding market outlets and by exploiting growth opportunities. Foreign sales can thus absorb extra capacity and reduce unit costs. They can also spread economic risks over a wider number of markets. For example, while Ford's

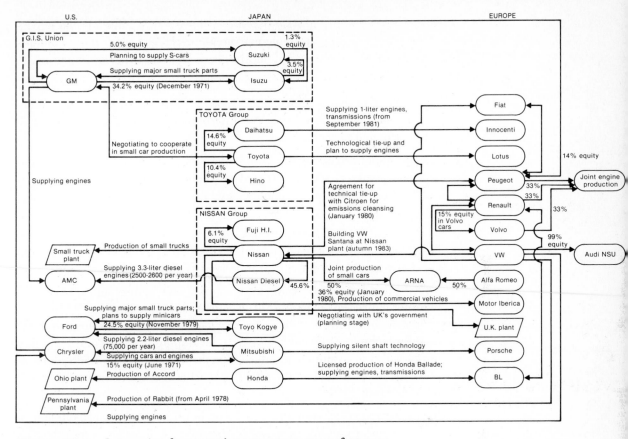

Figure 10.1 **International cooperation among auto manufacturers.**
SOURCE: J. McElroy, "Cheaper by the Dozen," *Road and Track* (June 1984), p. 122. Copyright © 1984 by CBS, Inc. All rights reserved. Courtesy Dodwell Associates. Reprinted with permission.

U.S. market share dropped below 25% in 1980, Ford of Britain's had risen to 32%, up six percentage points in four years.[7]

2. Corporations can gain competitive advantages by seeking low-cost production facilities in locations close to raw materials and/or cheap labor. They can achieve wider channels of distribution and access to new technology through joint ventures. Both General Electric and Société Nationale d' Étude et de Construction de Moteurs d'Aviation (SNECMA), the French engine maker, benefited from their joint venture in forming CFM International to produce and sell jet engines to airlines.[8]

3. In addition, companies can secure raw material resources by engaging in the worldwide exploration for, and the processing, transportation, and marketing of raw materials. For years, the major rubber companies have owned rubber plantations in Southeast Asia. Oil companies have, of course, gone international for the same reason.

There are a number of *disadvantages,* however, in international expansion. For one thing, the strategic management process is far more complex for a multinational than for a domestic firm. Dymsza lists six limitations to international expansion.[9]

First, the multinational company faces a multiplicity of political, economic, legal, social, and cultural environments as well as a differential rate of change in them.

Second, there are complex interactions between a multinational firm and the multiplicity of its national environments because of national sovereignties, widely disparate economic and social conditions, as well as other factors.

Third, geographical distance, cultural and national differences, variations in business practices, and other differences make communications difficult between the parent corporation and its subsidiaries.

Fourth, the degree of significant economic, marketing, and other information required for planning varies a great deal among countries in availability, depth, and reliability. Furthermore, in any given host country, modern techniques for analyzing and developing data may not be highly developed. For example, an international corporation may find it difficult and expensive to conduct the effective market research essential for business planning.

Fifth, analysis of present and future competition may be more difficult to undertake in a number of countries because of differences in industrial structure and business practices.

Sixth, the multinational company is confronted not only with different national environments but also with regional organizations such as the European Economic Community, the European Trade Area, and the Latin American Free Trade Area, all of which are achieving various degrees of economic integration. The United Nations and specialized international organizations such as the International Bank for Reconstruction and Development, the International Finance Corporation, and the General Agreement of Tariffs and Trade (GATT) may also affect its future opportunities.

Becoming International

Perhaps the best reason for U.S. corporations taking an international viewpoint in strategic management is the increasing rate of international investment and the marketing of imports in the United States. Investments by foreign interests in U.S. corporations and properties have increased from $416 billion in 1979 to $833 billion in 1984.[10] By year-end 1983, 13.5

million acres (1% of all privately owned U.S. agricultural land) was in non-U.S. hands.[11] During 1984, Nestlé S. A. of Switzerland paid $2.9 billion for Carnation Company. Saatchi and Saatchi PLC, Britain's largest advertising agency, bought the U.S. market research firm of Yankelovich, Skelly, and White. Over a one-year period, five of Japan's six largest steelmakers spent more than $500 million to buy U.S. assets and forge partnerships in metals-related industries. One example of this type of acquisition is Nippon Kokan K.K.'s purchase of 50% interest in Pittsburgh's National Steel Corporation.[12] A survey of 193 chief executives in 15 European countries in 1984 revealed that 45% preferred to invest in the United States than in any other country.[13]

The average U.S. consumer is becoming more involved and increasingly affected by international trade. Peoria-based Caterpillar Tractor Company laid off 22,000 U.S. workers in 1983 because of a worldwide sales slump aggravated by a debt crisis in Latin American countries.[14] Out of every dollar spent by Americans, 20 cents is now spent on imported items. During 1983, for example, K-Mart, J. C. Penney, and Sears Roebuck purchased a total of $5.2 billion worth of imported goods for resale to U.S. consumers.[15] The old slogan, "Buy American," no longer makes sense at a time when a large proportion of many U.S. products includes foreign-made parts. Chrysler Corporation, for example, is importing Plymouth Reliants and Dodge Aries from its Toluca, Mexico plant for sale in the United States. In an almost "Alice in Wonderland" manner, the reverse is also true. So-called foreign products are being made in the United States. Volkswagen produces (German-American?) cars in its New Stanton, Pennsylvania plant. Japan's Matsushita Electric Industrial Company purchases air conditioners from the U.S.'s General Electric Company for sale in the United States under the Panasonic brand name![16]

The Multinational Corporation

The multinational corporation is a very special type of international firm. Any U.S. company can call itself "international" if it has a small branch office in, say, Juarez or Toronto. An *international company* is one that engages in any combination of activities from exporting/importing to full-scale manufacturing in foreign countries. The *multinational corporation*, in contrast, is a highly developed international company with a deep worldwide involvement, plus a global perspective in its management and decision making.[17] A more specific definition of an MNC is suggested by Dymsza:[18]

1. Although a multinational corporation may not do business in every region of the world, its decision makers consider opportunities throughout the world.

2. A considerable portion of its assets are invested internationally. One authority suggests that a firm becomes global when 20% of its assets are in other countries. Another suggests that the point is reached when operations in other nations account for at least 35% of the corporation's total sales and profits.

3. The corporation engages in international production and operates plants in a number of countries. These plants may range from assembly to fully integrated facilities.

4. Managerial decision making is based on a worldwide perspective. The international business is no longer a sideline or segregated activity. International operations are integrated into the corporation's overall business.

Refer to Table 10.1 for a list of the world's largest multinational corporations in terms of total revenue. Note the strong presence of the Japanese trading companies and various oil firms.

Table 10.1   **World's Largest Multinational Corporations**

Rank	Company	Total Revenue (millions)	Corporate Headquarters	Industry
1.	Exxon	$88,651	U.S.A.	Energy
2.	Royal Dutch/Shell Group	80,610	Neth/U.K.	Energy
3.	General Motors	74,582	U.S.A.	Automobiles
4.	Mitsui & Co., Ltd.	63,149	Japan	Wholesaler
5.	Mitsubishi Corp.	62,831	Japan	Wholesaler
6.	Mobil	55,609	U.S.A.	Energy
7.	British Petroleum Co. Plc.	49,231	U.K.	Energy
8.	C. Itoh & Co. Ltd.	48,436	Japan	Wholesaler
9.	Marubeni Corp.	46,816	Japan	Wholesaler
10.	Sumitomo Corp.	45,806	Japan	Wholesaler
11.	Ford Motor	44,455	U.S.A.	Automobiles
12.	IBM	40,180	U.S.A.	Computers
13.	Texaco	40,068	U.S.A.	Energy
14.	Sears, Roebuck	35,883	U.S.A.	Wholesale/retail
15.	E.I. du Pont de Nemours	35,173	U.S.A.	Chemicals
16.	Nissho Iwai Corp.	34,039	Japan	Wholesaler
17.	Phibro–Salomon	29,757	U.S.A.	Minerals/metals
18.	Standard Oil, Indiana	27,937	U.S.A.	Energy
19.	General Electric	27,681	U.S.A.	Electrical equipment
20.	Standard Oil, California	27,342	U.S.A.	Energy

SOURCE: *Forbes* (July 2, 1984), pp. 129–132 and 134.

As described in Chapter 1, the strategic management process includes strategy formulation, implementation, and evaluation and control. In order to formulate strategy, the top management of a multinational corporation must scan both the external environment for opportunities and threats, and the internal environment for strengths and weaknesses.

The dominant issue in the strategic management process of a multinational corporation is the external environment. The type of relationship an MNC can have with each factor in its task environment varies from one country to another and from one region to another. International societal environments vary so widely that a corporation's internal environment and strategic management process must be very flexible. Cultural trends in West Germany, for example, have resulted in the inclusion of worker representatives in corporate strategic planning. Differences in the sociocultural, economic, political-legal, and technological aspects of societal environments among countries strongly affect how an MNC conducts its marketing, financial, manufacturing, and other functional activities.

Different sociocultural norms and values among nations will affect MNC activities importantly. For example, some cultures accept bribery and payoffs as a fact of life, whereas others punish them heavily. In Nigeria the accepted "dash" (money under the table) ranges from 15% of a multibillion dollar contract to a few naira to get a hotel operator to place a phone call. Most countries differentiate between "lubrication" or "grease" payments made to minor officials to expedite the execution of their duties and large-scale "whitemail" bribes intended to allow either a violation of the law or an illegal contribution designed to influence government policy. In some countries grease payments may be viewed by their citizens as an entitlement—necessary income to supplement low public salaries.[19] Since the dividing line between these two forms of extra payment is indistinct, an MNC must carefully monitor each country's norms to ensure its actions are in line with local practice. Ethics tend to become pragmatically bound to situations, and the top managers of MNCs may find themselves open to charges of being amoral.

In less developed countries (LDCs), most of the working population may be illiterate. As a result, there will likely be a shortage of skilled labor and supervisors. Manufacturing facilities that mesh with the technical sophistication of the work force must be designed. If U.S. managers are used in LDCs, they must be aware of the wide variance in working practices around the world and totally familiar with those in the country where they are stationed. For example, it is common in Europe for employees to get added compensation according to the number of their family members or because of unpleasant working conditions. Finnish paper mill workers get a "sauna

10.2 STRATEGY FORMULATION

Scanning the External Environment

Sociocultural Forces

premium" for missing baths when they are asked to work on Sunday. Fiji Island miners receive a daily half-hour "sex break" to fulfill marital obligations.[20] Other examples abound.

Differences in language and social norms will affect heavily the marketing mix for a particular country. Product presentation, packaging, distribution channels, pricing, and advertising must be attuned to each culture. For example, Western cosmetic firms such as Max Factor, Revlon, and Avon have had little success in selling their usual products in Japan. Certain cultural factors affect their sales: in Japan perfume is hardly used; suntans are considered ugly; and bath oil is impractical in communal baths.[21] In contrast, Mr. Donut franchise shops are very successful in Japan, even though there is no coffee and doughnut custom there. Doughnuts are presented as a snack rather than as a breakfast food and located near railroad stations and supermarkets. All the signs are in English in order to appeal to the Western interests of the Japanese.

Even if a product is desired by the public, literal translation of product names and slogans can ruin sales. For example, Pepsi Cola's "Come alive" jingle was translated into German as "Come alive out of the grave."[22] When General Motors introduced its Nova model into Latin America, it believed the name would translate well. Nova means constellation in Spanish. Nevertheless, people began to pronounce it "no vá," which in Spanish means "it does not go."[23] An advertisement for ink by the Parker Pen Company when translated into Spanish gave the false impression that the product helped prevent pregnancy.[24]

Religious beliefs may also make a significant impact on a country's business practices. For example, banks in Pakistan stopped paying interest to depositors in 1985 to conform with Islamic law. The alternative is a profit-sharing and loss-sharing system. Sudan and Iran are also moving toward a totally Islamic banking system.[25] In Japan, each time Mazda manufactures a new car model, a Shinto priest clad in traditional white robe, sandals, and black lacquered hat conducts "honorable purification" rites on the new product with top management in attendance.[26]

Economic Forces   The type of economic system in a country can affect strongly the kind of relationship an MNC can establish with a host country. The managers of an MNC based in a free-market capitalistic country may have difficulty understanding the regulations affecting trade with a centrally planned socialistic country. Licensing, acquisition, and joint ventures may be restricted severely by such a host country. In addition, in most countries inflation and currency exchange rates create further difficulties for an MNC. In Argentina, for example, the inflation rate during 1985 was around 1000%! An

MNC's financial policy in an economy subject to rapid inflation must be altered to protect the firm against inflationary losses. Cash balances must be minimized. Credit terms must be restricted. Prices must be constantly watched. In addition, balance of payments problems in a host country may lead to currency devaluation, as occurred in Mexico from 1980 through 1985 and in Italy during 1985. Such devaluation leads to an MNC's taking large losses in terms of the assets and profits of its subsidiary in the devaluating country. In addition, a socialistic country may control the prices of the products sold by the MNC in that country but may increase the price of the raw materials it sells to the MNC. This results in a severe profit squeeze as the host government attempts to pass the burden of inflation to "rich" multinational corporations.

As a result of these and other economic problems throughout the world, an MNC must be prepared to engage in countertrade and in hedging its foreign currency. *Countertrade* is a modern form of bartering which ranges from relatively simple barter transactions to intricate arrangements that can involve many nations and goods as well as complex financing and credits. Because less developed countries are often unable to pay cash for needed goods, exchanging goods and services is becoming increasingly attractive for them. From 1976 to 1984, countertrade grew from an estimated 2% to 33% of world commerce. For example, Sorimex, a Renault subsidiary, accepts coffee, phosphates, and other commodities in exchange for autos in agreements with such countries as Colombia, Tunisia, Turkey, Egypt, Rumania, and the People's Republic of China. Almost one-fifth of General Electric's $4 billion in exports in 1983 were under countertrade contracts. Banks now have countertrade divisions to turn commodities into cash for the bank's commercial customers.[27] Multinational corporations must also deal with fluctuating exchange rates by *hedging* their foreign-currency exposures in the forward foreign-exchange market where currencies are bought and sold for delivery at specific dates.[28] For example, if a U.S.-based multinational is scheduled to receive 100 million German marks in exchange for machine tools one year from today, it may lose money if the dollar rises in value in relation to that of the mark. One-hundred million marks may be worth 30 million U.S. dollars today, but only 25 million U.S. dollars next year. To avoid this risk, an MNC may choose to sell marks for dollars in the forward market for delivery in one year. This hedge "locks in" the MNC's dollar revenue at 30 million U.S. dollars regardless of currency fluctuations.

Political-Legal Forces

The system of laws and public policies governing business formation, acquisitions, and competitive activities constrains the strategic options open to a multinational company. It is likely that a particular country will specify guidelines for hiring, firing, and promoting people, as well as giving employment ratios of "foreigners" to its citizens and restricting management prerogatives regarding unions. In addition, there are likely to be government policies dealing with ownership, licensing, repatriation of profits (profits leaving the host country for the MNC's home country), royalties, importing, and purchasing. Beyond these, there are likely to be both some sentiment for keeping out foreign goods by erecting tariff barriers and some strong negative feeling about foreign control by an MNC of the host country's assets.

There are many examples of countries expropriating and nationalizing foreign as well as domestic holdings. In 1981, for example, France, under socialist leader François Mitterand, ordered a number of foreign-owned firms (among them, Honeywell-Bull Computers, ITT-France, and Rouseel-Uclaf Drugs) to sell a large percentage of their stock to the French government. Other countries have passed laws forbidding foreign nationals (including MNCs) from having majority control of firms in key industries. Mexico and India restricted foreign ownership during the 1970s. Canada passed legislation in 1981 requiring U.S. energy companies operating in Canada to sell a majority of their stock to Canadian owners by 1990. Responding to Malaysia's requirement that Malaysians have majority control of rubber plantations, Uniroyal sold its profitable rubber plants to a Malaysian company in 1984 and left the country.[29]

By the mid-1980s two international trends were evident. One was the desire by a number of countries to sell to private interests previously state-owned firms and to welcome the presence of foreign-owned MNCs. Similar to President Reagan's deregulation of government agencies, this *denationalization* or *privatization* of state-owned corporations was taking place in Canada, Japan, and most Western European nations. Great Britain, for example, sold the assets of Jaguar automobiles and 51% of British Telecom, the telecommunications monopoly. The second international trend was an increasing amount of trade barriers, local content regulations, and other *protectionist measures* designed to help domestic industry compete with foreign competition. Murray Weidenbaum, former Chairman of the U.S. Council of Economic Advisers, stated in 1984 that "Protectionist sentiment around the world is stronger now than it has been in decades."[30] As an example of local content laws, Mexico requires its six foreign-car manufacturers to use locally produced parts and material equal to half of each vehicle's value. Similar protectionist sentiment exists in the United States in the form of "voluntary" quotas on Japanese cars and foreign steelmakers and quotas on sugar and other imported goods.[31] There are examples like these for most nations in the world. Such protectionist and nationalistic tendencies serve to short-circuit the basic logic underlying the economic concept of *comparative advantage* (see Illustrative Example 10.1), resulting in higher prices for consumers and inefficient domestic industries.[32]

In order to introduce some stability into international trade, a number of countries have formed alliances and negotiated mutual cooperation agreements. One such agreement is the General Agreement on Tariffs and Trade (GATT) established in 1948 by twenty-three countries. This agreement was formed to create a relatively free system of trading, primarily through the reduction of tariffs. It provides a forum for negotiating mutual reduction of trade restrictions. Since 1948, most nations in the "free" world have become parties to GATT. According to Daniels, Ogram, and Radebaugh, "Through the most-favored-nation provision of GATT, countries have agreed to apply the same trade regulations to nearly all countries in the world. This greatly simplifies the negotiation process and allows exporters from almost any nation to have the same access, in terms of restrictions, to the market in any participating country."[33] An example of a political/trade alliance is the European Economic Community (Common Market), which agreed not only to reduce duties and other trade restrictions among member countries, but also to have a common tariff against nonmember countries. This provision was a major factor in encouraging firms from nonmember countries, such as the United States, to locate some manufacturing and marketing facilities inside the EEC to avoid tariffs.[34]

THE BASICS OF ABSOLUTE AND COMPARATIVE ADVANTAGE IN INTERNATIONAL TRADE

Illustrative Example 10.1

Suppose a country presently produces 1 million bushels of corn and 5 million bushels of beans each year. Its people desire more corn. Should it simply plant more corn and less beans? This seems like a reasonable solution until one notes that the soil and water are much better for growing beans than for corn. Each acre planted can produce twice as much bean crop as corn. It takes the same amount of work, and the seeds, fertilizer, and other costs are the same for the farmers regardless of the crop planted. Suppose that the neighboring country has different soil and on every acre planted is able to produce twice as much corn as beans.

The concept of *absolute advantage* in international trade suggests that when both countries are considered, the first country has advantage over the second country in producing beans, but the second has advantage over the first in producing corn. The logical conclusion is that the first country should specialize in producing beans (where it has absolute advantage) and the second should plant only corn (where it also has absolute advantage). The result would be that the first country would produce 7 million bushels of beans each year and *no* corn (with the 2 to 1 advantage of beans to corn,

(Continued)

the 1 million bushels of corn would be replaced by 2 million bushels of beans). The reverse would be true in the second country. If the countries are able to trade freely with each other, both countries would be able to have more corn and beans if they specialize in the crop with which there is advantage than if both countries tried to produce both crops.

Therefore, in answer to the question posed earlier, if a country wants more corn but has an absolute advantage in the production of beans, it should plant more beans. The excess beans can be exported to another country in exchange for more corn than the first country could ever produce with the same resources.

What happens, however, when the first country can produce more corn *and* beans per acre planted than can its neighboring country? Is there any benefit to trade? According to the concept of *comparative advantage*, it still makes sense to specialize as long as the first country is able to grow more of one crop than another crop per acre planted. As an analogy, suppose the best architect in town also happens to be the best carpenter. Would it make sense for him to build his own house? Certainly not, because he can earn more money per hour by devoting all his time to his job as an architect even though he has to employ a carpenter less skillful than himself to build the house. In the same manner, the first country will gain if it concentrates its resources on the production of that commodity it can produce most efficiently. It will earn enough money from the export of that commodity to still import what it needs from its less efficient neighbor country.

SOURCE: J. D. Daniels, E. W. Ogram, Jr., and L. H. Radebaugh, *International Business: Environments and Operations*, 3rd ed. (Reading, Mass.: Addison-Wesley, 1982), pp. 107–113.

There are also trade associations, such as the Organization of Petroleum Exporting Countries (OPEC), the International Tin Council, and the International Cocoa Organization, which attempt to stabilize commodity supplies and prices to the benefit of their member nations.

Technological Forces

As mentioned in Chapter 4, the question of technology "transfer" has become an important issue in international dealings. Most less developed countries welcome multinational corporations into their nation as conduits of advanced technology and management expertise. They realize that not only will local labor be hired to work for the firm, but that the MNC will have to educate the work force to deal with advanced methods and techniques. Reich, in his book *The Next American Frontier*, argues that production technologies are rapidly moving from the developed to the developing nations of the world.[35] Countries such as Korea, Hong Kong, Taiwan, Singapore, Brazil, and Spain, which specialized in the 1960s in simple products like clothing and toys, are now mass producing technologically complex products like automobiles, televisions, and ships. At the same time, the less developed countries of Malaysia, Thailand, the Philippines, Sri Lanka, and India have taken over the production of clothing, toys, and the like. With Korea and Taiwan on its heels technologically, Japan reduced its steelmaking capacity and began orienting itself in the 1980s beyond consumer electronics toward telecommunications.[36]

Political-legal considerations become important when aerospace firms, with their heavy dependence on government contracts, want to transfer technology developed for military purposes into profitable commercial products sold internationally. General Electric, for example, had a great deal of difficulty forming a joint venture with the French national engine firm SNECMA in the early 1970s. The venture involved the sharing of jet engines developed specifically for the prototype of the B-1 bomber. Although the U.S. federal government refused, for political reasons, to put the B-1 bomber into production, it did not like the idea of GE's selling such advanced technology to another country.[37] In the 1980s, the U.S. government has similar fears of semiconductor technology being sold to countries behind the "iron curtain." The Coordinating Committee for Multilateral Export Controls (Cocom), composed of the fifteen members of the North Atlantic Treaty Organization (NATO) minus Spain and Iceland plus Japan, compiles lists of items that cannot be sold to Communist countries without its approval. This has created a number of problems for MNCs wishing to sell high-technology products to China.[38]

Another technological issue raised in international trade is the determination of the appropriate technology to use in production plants located in host countries. For example, labor-saving devices (robots, for instance) that are economically justifiable in highly developed countries where wage rates are high, may be more costly than labor-intensive types of production in less developed countries with high unemployment and low wage rates. The knowledge of technology may be so low in a country that the MNC may be tempted to employ very few local people and automate the plant as much as possible to gain operating leverage. The host country's government, however, faced with massive unemployment, may strongly desire a labor intensive plant.[39] The basic question an MNC may face is whether the benefits to be gained by modifying technologies for the unique conditions of each country are worth the costs that must be incurred.

In searching for an advantageous market or manufacturing location, a multinational corporation must gather and evaluate data on strategic factors in a large number of countries and regions. Given the global perspective of MNCs, one company may use comparative advantage to its benefit by making machine parts in Brazil, assembling them as engines in Germany, install-

Assessing International Opportunities and Risks

ing the engines in auto bodies in Italy, and shipping completed cars to the United States for sale. This strategy serves to reduce the risk to the MNC of operating in only one country, but exposes it to a series of smaller risks in a greater number of countries. As a result, multinational corporations must be able to deal with political and economic risk in many diverse countries and regions.[40]

Some firms, such as American Can Company, develop an elaborate computerized system to rank investment risks. Smaller companies may hire outside consultants like Chicago's Associated Consultants International or Boston's Arthur D. Little, Inc. to provide political risk assessments. Among the many systems that exist to assess political and economic risks are the Political System Stability Index, the Business Environment Risk Index, Business International's Country Assessment Service, and Frost and Sullivan's World Political Risk Forecasts.[41] (For a summary of Frost and Sullivan's risk index, see the May 1985 issue of *Planning Review*.)[42] Regardless of the source of data, a firm must develop its own method of assessing risk. It must decide upon the most important factors from its point of view and assign weights to each. An example of such a rating method is depicted in Table 10.2.

Scanning the Internal Environment

Any corporation desiring to move into the international arena will need to assess its own strengths and weaknesses. Chang and Campo-Flores suggest that a corporation's chances for success are enhanced if it has or can develop the following capabilities:

1. *Technological lead.* An innovative approach or a new product or a new process gives one a short-term monopoly position.

2. *A strong trade name.* Snob appeal of a well-known product can permit a higher profit margin to cover initial entry costs.

3. *Advantage of scale.* A large corporation has the advantage of low unit costs and a financial base strong enough to weather setbacks.

4. *A scanning capability.* An ability to search successfully and efficiently for opportunities will take on greater importance in international dealings.

5. *An outstanding product or service.* A solid product or service is more likely to have staying power in international competition.

6. *An outstanding international executive.* The presence of an executive who understands international situations and is able to develop a core of local executives who can work well with the home office is likely to result in the building of a strong and long-lasting international organization.[43]

Table 10.2 Example of Weighted Rating of Investment Climate

Factors Listed in Order of Importance	Country A			Country B		
	(1) Assigned Weights Considering Importance of Adverse Developments	(2) Rating of Factor from 0 (Completely Unfavorable) to 100 (Completely Favorable)	(3) Weighted Rating (Column 1 × Column 2)	(1) Assigned Weights Considering Importance of Adverse Developments	(2) Rating of Factor from 0 (Completely Unfavorable) to 100 (Completely Favorable)	(3) Weighted Rating (Column 1 × Column 2)
1. Possibility of expropriation.	10	90	900	10	55	550
2. Possibility of damage to property from rebellion or war.	9	80	720	9	50	450
3. Remission of earnings.	8	70	560	8	50	400
4. Governmental restrictions of foreign business compared to domestic-owned enterprise.	8	70	560	8	60	480
5. Availability of local capital at reasonable cost.	7	50	350	7	90	630
6. Political stability.	7	80	560	7	50	350
7. Repatriation of capital.	7	80	560	7	60	420
8. Currency stability.	6	70	420	6	30	180
9. Price stability.	5	40	200	5	30	150
10. Taxes on business (including any discriminatory provisions).	4	80	320	4	90	360
11. Problems of dealing with labor unions.	3	70	210	3	80	240
12. Government investment incentives.	2	0	0	2	90	180
TOTAL WEIGHTED RATING OF INVESTMENT CLIMATE			5,360			4,390

Evaluating the Mission

Once a corporation has decided to become multinational in orientation, the first step is to restate the corporate mission. An example of such a mission statement is from General Electric Company:

> To carry on a diversified, growing, and profitable world-wide manufacturing business in electrical apparatus, appliances, and supplies, and in related materials, products, systems, and services for industry, commerce, agriculture, government, the community, and the home.[44]

Setting Objectives

Upon completing an assessment of its external and internal environments, a multinational corporation can determine specific objectives for foreign affiliates, corporate divisions, and the entire firm. Dymsza states that a multinational corporation usually starts with profitability goals in terms of amounts: return on investment, assets, or sales; rate of growth per year; or growth in earnings per share by major unit. It then sets specific marketing, production, logistics, technology, personnel, acquisition, and other goals for a given period. These goals provide the basis for determining strategies.[45]

Developing International Strategies

A multinational corporation can pick from a number of strategic options the ways to enter a foreign market or to establish manufacturing facilities in another country. An experienced firm with a global orientation will usually select a strategy based on specific product strengths and on host country attractiveness.

Exporting

Exporting is a good way to minimize risk and to experiment with a specific product; it can be conducted in a number of ways. An MNC could choose to handle all critical functions itself, or it could contract these functions to an export management company. To operate in a country such as Japan, which has a series of complex regulations, an MNC could use the services of an agent or distributor.

Licensing

Under a *licensing* agreement, the licensing firm grants rights to a firm in the host country to produce and/or sell a product. The licensee pays compensation to the licensing firm in return for technical expertise. This is an especially useful strategy if the trademark or brand name is well known, but the MNC does not have sufficient funds to enter the country directly. La Chemise Lacoste, the French sportswear concern, for example, sold the U.S. and Canadian licenses for the Lacoste trademark and its alligator emblem to General Mills to use in its Izod, Ltd. fashion unit. Anheuser-Busch is also using this strategy to produce and market Budweiser beer in Great Britain, Japan, Israel, Australia, Korea, and the Philippines. It also becomes an important strategy if the country makes entry via investment either difficult or impossible. Examples are Japan and Eastern European countries. There is always the danger, however, that the licensee may develop its competence to the point that it becomes a competitor to the licensing firm.

Joint ventures are very popular with MNCs. The corporation engages in international ownership at a much lower risk. A joint venture will typically be an association between an MNC and a firm in the host country or a government agency in that country. A quick method of obtaining local management, it also reduces the risks of expropriation and harassment by host country officials. Some of the joint ventures engaged in recently by U.S. firms with foreign partners are listed in Table 10.3.

    When more than two organizations participate in a joint venture, it is sometimes referred to as a *consortium*. For example, Airbus Industrie, the European producer of jet airplanes is a consortium owned by four partners from four countries: Aerospatiale of France (37.9%), Messerschmitt-Bokkow-Blohm of West Germany (37.9%), British Aerospace Corp. (20%), and Construcciones Aeronauticas S. A. of Spain (4.2%). Disadvantages of joint ventures include loss of control, lower profits, probability of conflicts with partners, and the likely transfer of technological advantage to the local partner. Joint ventures typically are meant to be temporary, especially by the Japanese who view them as a way to rectify a competitive weakness until they can achieve long-term dominance in the partnership.[46]

Joint Ventures

If an MNC wishes total control of its operations, it may want to start a business from scratch or acquire a firm already established in the host country.

Acquisitions

Table 10.3   **Some Recent Joint Ventures**

Joint Venture	U.S. Parent	Foreign Partner	Products
New United Motor Mfg.	General Motors	Toyota (Japan)	Subcompact cars
National Steel	National Inter-group	Nippon Kokan (Japan)	Steel
Siecor	Corning Glass Works	Siemens (Germany)	Optical cable
Honeywell/Ericsson Development	Honeywell	L. M. Ericsson (Sweden)	PBX systems
Himont	Hercules	Montedison (Italy)	Polypropylene resin
GMFanuc Robotics	General Motors	Fanuc (Japan)	Robots
International Aero Engines	United Technologies	Rolls-Royce (Britain)	Aircraft engines

SOURCE: "Are Foreign Partners Good for U.S. Companies?" *Business Week* (May 28, 1984), p. 59. Reprinted from the May 28, 1984 issue of *Business Week* by special permission. Copyright © 1984 by McGraw-Hill, Inc.

An *acquisition* has merits because assets can be bought in their entirety rather than on a piecemeal basis. Synergistic benefits may result if the MNC acquires a firm with strong complementary product lines and a good distribution network. Nestlé S. A. of Switzerland, for example, purchased Beech-Nut (baby foods), Libby, McNeill and Libby (fruit juices), Stouffer (hotels and frozen dinners), Ward-Johnson (candy), Hills Brothers (coffee), and Carnation (evaporated milk) to complement its successful Nescafé, Quik, Nestea, and L'Oreal consumer products. In some countries, however, acquisitions may be difficult to arrange due to a lack of available information about potential candidates. Government restrictions on ownership, such as Canada's requirement that all energy corporations in Canada be controlled by Canadians, also may discourage acquisitions. It may be possible, however, to have control of a foreign enterprise even though the MNC cannot attain more than 49% of the ownership. One way is to maintain control over some asset required by the foreign firm. Another device is to separate equity into voting and nonvoting stock so that the minority MNC investor has a majority of the voting stock.[47]

Green-Field Development

If a corporation does not wish to buy another firm's existing facilities via acquisition, it may choose a *green-field development,* or the building of a manufacturing facility from scratch. This is usually far more complicated and expensive than acquisition, but it allows the MNC more freedom in designing the plant, choosing suppliers, and hiring a work force. An Italian semiconductor manufacturer, SGS-Ates Componenti Elettronici S. p. A., selected this strategy. According to its vice-president of marketing, Richard Pieranunzi: "To find a company that exactly matched our needs would be difficult. And we didn't want to buy other people's problems."[48]

Production Sharing

Coined by Peter Drucker, the term *production sharing* combines the higher labor skills and technology available in the developed countries with lower-cost labor available in developing countries. Since 1970, U.S. imports under production-sharing arrangements have been increasing at a rate of more than 20% per year.[49] Among the multinational corporations using this strategy are Texas Instruments, RCA, Honeywell, General Electric, and GTE. By locating assembly plants in Ciudad Juarez, Mexico and packaging plants across the border in Texas, these firms are able to take advantage of Mexico's low labor costs. This was a result of the Mexican government's relaxation of its laws against foreign ownership of factories and its reduction of import taxes on raw materials.[50]

Management Contracts

A large multinational corporation is likely to have a large amount of management talent at its disposal. *Management contracts* offer a means through which an MNC may use part of its personnel to assist a firm in a host country for a specified fee and period of time. Such arrangements are common when a host government expropriates part or all of an MNC's holdings in its country. This allows the MNC to continue to earn some income from its investment and keep the operations going until local management is trained. Management contracts are also used by a number of less developed countries that have the capital but neither the labor nor the managerial skills required to utilize available technology.

Turnkey operations are typically contracts for the construction of operating facilities in exchange for a fee. The facilities are transferred to the host country or firm when they are complete. The customer is usually a government agency of, say, an Eastern European or Middle Eastern country that has decreed a given product must be produced locally and under its control. MNCs that perform turnkey operations are frequently industrial equipment manufacturers that supply some of their own equipment for the project and that commonly sell to the host country replacement parts and maintenance services. They thereby create customers as well as future competitors.

Turnkey Operations

MNCs may find that in times of national fervor in the less developed countries, facilities that mine and process raw materials are prime targets for expropriation. As a result, an MNC may *contract* with a foreign government or local firm to trade raw materials for certain resources belonging to the MNC. For example, several oil-producing countries have made arrangements with oil firms to let the firms take all exploration and development risks in exchange for a share of the sales of the oil produced.[51]

Subcontract Arrangements

Broadly viewed, strategic planning seeks to match markets with products and other corporate resources in order to strengthen a firm's competitive position. Since most multinational corporations manufacture and sell a wide range of products, it is necessary, when formulating strategy, to keep track of country attractiveness as well as product strength. Nevertheless, there is a strong tendency for top management in MNCs to plan around either products or markets, but not both.[52]

International Product Portfolio

To aid international strategic planning, Harrell and Kiefer have shown how portfolio analysis can be applied to international markets. As depicted in Fig. 10.2, each axis summarizes a host of data concerning the attractiveness of a particular country and the competitive strength of a particular product.

Country attractiveness is composed of market size, market rate of

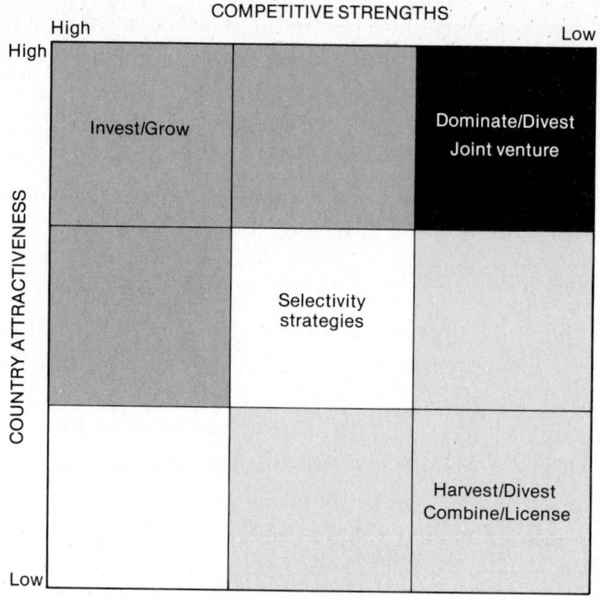

COMPETITIVE STRENGTHS

Figure 10.2   **Matrix for plotting products.**
SOURCE: G. D. Harrell and R. O. Kiefer, "Multinational Strategic Market Portfolios," *MSU Business Topics* (Winter 1981), p. 7. Reprinted by permission.

growth, government regulation, and economic and political factors. *Competitive strength* is composed of market share, product fit, contribution margin, and market support. The two scales form the axes of the matrix in Fig. 10.2. Those countries falling in the upper left generally should receive funding for growth, whereas countries in the lower right are prime for "harvesting," or divesting. Those countries falling on the lower left to upper right diagonal require selective funding strategies. Those falling in the upper right block require additional funding if the product is to contribute in the future to the firm's profits. Joint ventures or divestitures would be most appropriate if cash is limited. Those falling in the center and lower left blocks are probably good candidates for "milking." They can produce strong cash flows in the short run.[53]

10.3 STRATEGY IMPLEMENTATION

To be effective, international strategies must be implemented with national and cultural differences in mind. Among the many considerations an MNC must deal with, three of the most important are (1) selecting the local partner for a joint venture or licensing arrangement, (2) organizing the firm around the most appropriate structure, and (3) encouraging global rather than national management practices.

Joint ventures and licensing agreements between a multinational company **Partner Selection**
and a local partner in a host country are increasingly popular as a means of
entry into other countries, especially less developed countries.[54] National
policies as well as the complexity of the host country market often make
these the preferred strategies for balancing country attractiveness against financial risk. The key to the successful implementation of these strategies is
the selection of the local partner. In Fig. 10.3, Lasserre proposes a model
describing the many variables to be considered by both sides when assessing
a partnership. Each party needs to assess not only the strategic fit of each
company's project strategy, but also the fit of each company's respective re-

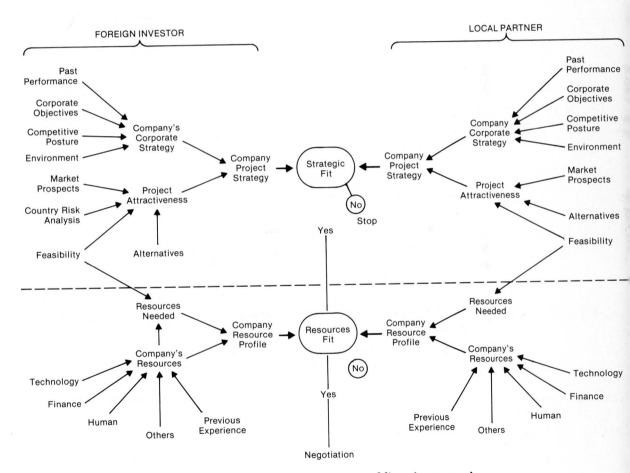

Figure 10.3   **Assessing partners to implement joint venture and licensing strategies.**
SOURCE: P. Lasserre, "Selecting a Foreign Partner for Technology Transfer," *Long Range Planning*
(December 1984), p. 45. Copyright © 1984 Pergamon Press, Ltd. Reprinted by permission.

sources. Lasserre contends that this process requires a minimum of one to two years of prior contacts between both parties.[55] The fact that joint ventures tend to have a high rate of costly failures suggests that few multinationals use such a careful selection process.[56]

Organization Structure

Rarely, if ever, do multinational corporations suddenly appear as full-blown worldwide organizations. They tend to go through three common evolutionary stages both in their relationships with widely dispersed geographic markets and in the manner in which they structure their operations and programs.

Stage 1: Initial Entry

The "parent" corporation is attracted to a particular market in another country and seeks to test the potential of its products in this market with minimal risk. The firm thus introduces a number of product lines into the market through home-based export programs, licensing agreements, joint ventures, and/or through local commercial offices. The product divisions at headquarters continue to be responsible for all functional activities.

Stage 2: Early Development

Success in Stage 1 leads the parent corporation to believe that a stronger presence and broader product lines are needed if it is to fully exploit its advantage in the host country. The parent company establishes a local operating division or company in the host country, such as Ford of Britain, to better serve the market. The product line is expanded. Local manufacturing capacity is established. Managerial functions (product development, finance, marketing, etc.) are organized locally. As time goes by, other related businesses are acquired by the parent company to broaden the base of the local operating division. As the subsidiary in the host country successfully develops a strong regional presence, it achieves greater autonomy and self-sufficiency.

Stage 3: Maturity

As the parent corporation becomes aware of the success of its subsidiaries in other countries and the skills of its local managers, it consolidates operations under a regional management organization. Greater attention is given to a wider range of investment opportunities, such as mergers and acquisitions. Although the regional or local company continues to maintain ties with the parent corporation and the product divisions in the home country, it tends to enjoy relative autonomy in terms of local policy-setting and managerial practices. As was the case with the North American Philips Corporation, originally an affiliate of N. V. Philips' Gloeilampenfabrieken, a subsidiary may become a totally separate company with local shareholders and publicly traded stock.[57] Table 10.4 summarizes some of the structural arrangements possible in each stage of MNC development.

Table 10.4 **International Activity and Structure**

Stage	Activities of Company	Organization Responsible for International Activities	Executive In Charge
1	Exports directly and indirectly, but trade is minor.	Export department.	Export manager, reporting to domestic marketing executive.
	Exports become more important.	Export division.	Division manager.
2	Company undertakes licensing and invests in production overseas.	International division.	Director of international operations, usually vice-president.
	International investments increase.	Sometimes international headquarters company as wholly owned subsidiary [of domestic parent company].	President, who is vice-president in parent company.
3	International investments substantial and widespread; diversified international business activities.	Global organizational structure by geographic areas, product lines, functions, or some combination. Also worldwide staff support.	No single executive in charge of international business.

SOURCE: Adapted from W. A. Dymsza, *Multinational Business Strategy* (New York: McGraw-Hill Book Company, 1972), p. 22. Copyright © 1972 by McGraw-Hill, Inc. Reprinted by permission.

Even though most international and multinational corporations move through these stages in their involvement with host countries, any one corporation may be at different stages with different products in different markets. An example of diversity in international operations is Hewlett-Packard. The company began international activity by exporting its products. It used its own staff for exports to Canada and export management companies (export intermediaries operating on a buy-and-sell basis and providing financing for export shipments) for exports to other countries. These exports were then sold in both cases to middlemen abroad. As sales expanded, Hewlett-Packard took over the exporting functions, opened its own sales office in Mexico, purchased a warehousing facility in Switzerland, organized a wholly owned manufacturing subsidiary in West Germany, and entered into a partly owned venture in Japan.[58]

A basic dilemma facing the globally oriented multinational corporation is how to organize authority centrally in order to operate as a vast interlocking system to achieve synergy and at the same time decentralize authority to allow local managers to make the decisions necessary to meet the demands of the local market or host government.[59] To deal with this problem, many mature MNCs structure themselves along the lines of a matrix organization combining *product* and *geography*.

Typically, multinational corporations do not organize themselves around business functions, such as marketing or manufacturing, unless they are in an extractive raw-materials industry. Basic functions are thus subsumed under either product or geographic units.[60] Two extremes of the usual matrix are Nestlé and American Cyanamid. Nestlé's structure is one in which significant power and authority have been decentralized to geographic entities. This structure is similar to that depicted in Fig. 10.4, with each geographic set of operating companies having a similar set of products. In contrast, American Cyanamid has a series of product groups with worldwide responsibilities. To depict this structure, the geographical entities in Fig. 10.4 would have to be replaced by product or strategic business unit names. There does appear to be a trend, however, toward the Nestlé version of the matrix structure in which the geographic unit dominates the product unit.[61] Each regional unit in this case is fairly self-sufficient and independent but will be loosely coordinated by headquarters to avoid duplication of effort, achieve economies of scale, or ensure uniformity of procedures.[62]

Management Practices

As is true of people from any highly developed society, U.S.-trained managers tend to believe that what works well in their society will work well anywhere. Thus, someone well-schooled in the virtues of MBO, participative decision making, theory Y practices, job enrichment, and management science will have a tendency to transplant these practices without alteration to foreign nations. Unfortunately, just as products often need to be altered to appeal to a new market, so too do most management practices.

In a study of forty different cultures, Hofstede found that he could ex-

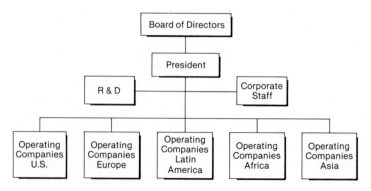

Figure 10.4   **Structure of a mature MNC.**

plain the success or failure of certain management practices on the basis of four cultural dimensions: power distance, uncertainty avoidance, individualism–collectivism, and masculinity–feminity.[63] He points out that management by objectives (MBO) has been the single most popular management technique "made in U.S.A." It has succeeded in Germany because the idea of replacing the arbitrary authority of the boss with the impersonal authority of mutually agreed-upon objectives fits the small power distance and strong uncertainty avoidance that are dimensions in the German culture. It has failed in France, however, because the French are used to large power distances—to accepting orders from a highly personalized authority. This cultural dimension goes counter to key aspects of MBO: small power distance between superior and subordinate and impersonal, objective goal setting. This same cultural dimension explains why the French, for whom vertical authority lines are very important, are significantly more reluctant than Americans to accept the multiple authority structures of project management or matrix organization.[64]

Because of these cultural differences managerial style and practices must be tailored to fit the situations in other countries. Most multinational corporations based in the United States, therefore, attempt to fill executive positions in their subsidiaries with well-qualified citizens of the host countries. IBM, for example, fills executive positions with the citizens of the many countries in which it operates.[65] This serves to placate nationalistic governments and to better attune IBM management practices to the host country's culture. Another approach to staffing the managerial positions of multinational corporations is to use people with an "international" orientation regardless of their country of origin or host country assignment. This approach allows for more promotion opportunities than does IBM's policy but it may result in a greater number of misunderstandings and conflicts with the local employees and with the host country government. In addition, it is estimated that anywhere from 25 to 40% of *expatriate* managers (people from a different country than the host country) fail to adjust to the host country's social and business environment. This is costly in terms of management performance, operations efficiency, and customer relations.[66]

In evaluating the activities of its international operations, the MNC should consider not only return on investment and other financial measures, but also the effect of its activities on the host country.

The three most widely used techniques for international performance evaluation are return on investment, budget analysis, and historical comparisons. In one study, 95% of the corporate officers interviewed stated that they use the same evaluation techniques for foreign and domestic operations. Rate of

10.4 EVALUATION AND CONTROL

Financial Measures

return was mentioned as the single most important measure.[67] The use of ROI, however, can cause problems when applied to international operations: "Because of foreign currencies, different rates of inflation, different tax laws, and the use of transfer pricing, both the net income figure and the investment base may be seriously distorted."[68] Consequently, Daniels, Ogram, and Radebaugh recommend that MNC top management emphasize budgets as a means of differentiating between the worth of the subsidiary and the performance of its management.

Since differences among countries magnify the usual problems of comparability, multiple performance indicators should be used. Dymsza suggests that MNCs use management audits for their operations in foreign countries.[69]

MNC/Host Country Relationships

As multinational corporations grow and spread across the world, nations find themselves in a dilemma. Most countries, especially the less-developed ones, want to have the many benefits an MNC can bring: technology transfer, employment opportunities, tax revenues, and the opportunity to build domestic business corporations in partnership with powerful and well-connected foreign-based companies. These countries also fear the problems an MNC can bring. After having welcomed an MNC with tax benefits and subsidies of various types, the host country may find itself in a double bind regarding the repatriation of profits. It can either allow the MNC to export its profits to corporate headquarters—thereby draining the nation of potential investment capital—or it can allow the MNC to send home only a small portion of its profits—thereby making the host country unattractive to other MNCs as a place to invest. For example, research reveals that between 1960 and 1968, profits sent to the United States from Latin America by MNCs exceeded new investment by $6.7 billion.[70] Host countries also note that less-developed countries seldom receive much benefit from MNC technology transfer in the form of increasing their exports. MNCs also have a tradition of placing business values above the cultural values of the host country.[71]

Given the pros and cons of the multinational corporation's presence in the world, Fayerweather proposes four basic relationships an MNC can assume vis-à-vis a host country. They range from positively *contributing* to the country's development to negatively *undermining* the basic culture of the country.[72]

Contributory Relationships

An MNC acts to directly augment or contribute to the goals or achievement of a host nation without any negative effect. In this relationship both the MNC and the local partner (if any) positively help each other as well as their respective countries. Renault's investment in American Motors Corporation has resulted in keeping AMC from going bankrupt, thus saving American jobs. Recent AMC profits have helped compensate for Renault's poorer performance in Europe, thus helping Renault's owner, the French government.

Reinforcing Relationships

The actions of an MNC reinforce the goals or achievement of a host nation but tend to have some negative side-effects. This is a somewhat less than ideal relationship. The MNC invests heavily in the country's development and may build the transportation and communication systems so necessary for economic development. Nevertheless, the MNC sends all its profits to its headquarters and its emphasis on its own cultural values sometimes conflicts with host country values. This is probably the type of relationship existing between the U.S.-based MNCs that are production sharing in Mexico.

Frustrating Relationships

Actions of an MNC challenge the goals of the nation or impede its immediate functioning in ways to which the nation cannot respond effectively so that its government is frustrated. Nestlé's aggressive marketing of baby formula to mothers in less-developed countries is an example of this type of relationship. In countries where breast-feeding is more nutritious and healthier for babies than bottle-feeding (due to the poor quality of water and sanitary conditions) the use of Nestlé's baby formula contributed to malnutrition and other sickness in the babies. Because many LDC governments were unable to deal with the situation, church groups from the developed countries plus the United Nations put enough pressure on Nestlé to cause it to stop its aggressive marketing practices in the LDCs.[73]

Undermining Relationships

The effect of an MNC is to reduce the basic logic (in terms of norms, values, and philosophy) of a nation so that its functioning is weakened or undermined. MNCs' development of oil resources in the Middle Eastern countries caused a clash between traditional Moslem values and Western values; this probably contributed to the Iranian revolution and disruptions in other Moslem countries. The resulting antagonism from such a relationship is reflected in the following comment by a Third World representative:

> Poor countries have often been swindled out of a decent return for their produce in the name of market mechanism, deprived of their economic independence, seduced by imported life styles, foreign value systems, irrelevant research designs—all in the name of freedom of choice.[74]

To the extent that an MNC fails to contribute to or reinforce the functioning of a host country, it may find its assets expropriated and its home-country management team asked to leave. For those corporations that go to less-developed countries to locate and extract needed raw materials but see the host countries only as something to manipulate and use, a certain cycle results:

First, they are welcomed by the host country as a source of foreign currency, a major employer, a means of upgrading the country's skills, a stimulant to the economy, and a catalyst to attract other investors. *Second,* after a few years, pressure increases on the firm to process in addition to only extracting the material. This often leads to a second phase of investment by the company and more benefits to the country. *Third,* the company is now sufficiently dependent to be vulnerable to a request to have local participation in ownership, either through private parties or directly by the host government. *Fourth,* nationalization advances to a takeout stage after more years of evolving relationships, usually involving compensation for assets and some arrangement of management. *Fifth,* recalling that the primary reason for the original investment was a source of materials, and recognizing that government owned operations are almost always inefficient, the company is forced to pay increasing prices and turns to alternative sources if they exist.[75]

10.5 SUMMARY AND CONCLUSION

A knowledge of international considerations is becoming extremely important for the proper understanding of the strategic management process in large corporations. Just as U.S. firms are becoming more involved every year with operations and markets in other countries, imports and subsidiaries from other countries are becoming more a part of the American landscape. International corporations have been transforming themselves slowly into multinational corporations (MNCs) with a global orientation and flexible management styles.

The dominant issue in the strategic management process of a multinational corporation is the effect of widely different external environments on internal activities. A firm's top management must therefore be well schooled in the differences among nations in terms of their sociocultural, economic, political-legal, and technological environment variables. Data search procedures and analytical techniques must be used to assess the many possible investment opportunities and their risks in world business. Assuming that top management feels that the corporation has the requisite internal qualifications to become multinational, it must determine the appropriate set of strategies for entering and investing in potential host countries. These may vary from simple exportation to the formation with other companies of very complex consortiums. The corporation's product portfolio must be constantly monitored for strengths and weaknesses.

Attention must also be paid to selecting the most appropriate local partner, organization structure and management system for a worldwide enterprise. An overall system of control and coordination must be balanced against a host country's need for local flexibility and autonomy. An MNC should use a series of performance indicators so that return on investment, budget analysis, and historical comparisons can be viewed in the context of a strategic audit of operations in the host country. Above all, the top management of a multinational corporation has the responsibility to ensure that the MNC contributes to and reinforces the functioning of the host nation rather than frustrating or undermining its government and culture.

1. What differentiates a multinational corporation from an international corporation?

2. If the basic concepts of absolute and comparative advantage suggest free trade as the best route to prosperity for all nations, why do so many countries use protectionist measures to keep out imports?

3. Should MNCs be allowed to own more than half the stock of a subsidiary based in a host country? Why or why not?

4. Should the United States allow unrestricted trade between corporations in the United States and communist countries? Why or why not?

5. In developing an international product portfolio matrix, what specific factors should be included to assess a country's attractiveness?

6. Given the many disadvantages of joint ventures (loss of control, lower profits, probability of conflicts with partners, and the likely transfer of technological advantage to a partner), plus its typical temporary nature, why is it such a popular strategy?

7. What is the overall impact of multinational corporations on world peace? How do they help? How do they hinder?

1. B. D. Henderson, *New Strategies for the New Global Competition* (Boston: Boston Consulting Group, 1981), p. 1.

2. A. L. Malabre, Jr., "World Trade Suffers as Economies Slow," *Wall Street Journal* (August 3, 1981), p. 1.

3. *International Financial Statistics Yearbook*, Volume XXXVII (Washington, D.C.: International Monetary Fund, 1984), p. 595.

4. B. R. Scott, "National Strategy for Stronger U.S. Competitiveness," *Harvard Business Review* (March–April 1984), p. 77.

5. M. McLuhan, *Understanding Media: The Extensions of Man* (New York: McGraw-Hill Paperbacks, 1965).

6. J. McElroy, "Cheaper by the Dozen," *Road and Track* (June 1984), pp. 122–128.

7. L. Birger, "Once Threatened by Henry Ford II, European Fords Carrying Detroit," *The Tribune*, Albuquerque, N. Mex. (June 2, 1980), p. C-10.

8. "USAir Orders Engines for Its Boeing Jets," *Wall Street Journal* (August 3, 1981), p. 22.

9. Adapted from W. A. Dymsza, *Multinational Business Strategy* (New York: McGraw-Hill, 1972), pp. 50–51.

10. United States Commerce Department, Washington, D.C. Reported by B. Boyd in "Moneylist," *Ames Tribune,* Ames, Iowa (February 11, 1985), p. 1.

11. *Wall Street Journal* (May 24, 1983), p. 35.

12. G. Anders, "European Executives Consider U.S. Prime Area for Expansion Abroad, Journal Poll Shows," *Wall Street Journal* (December 5, 1984), p. 34.
    "Saatchi and Saatchi PLC To Buy Yankelovich; Price Is $13.5 Million," *Wall Street Journal* (October 31, 1984), p. 37.
    T. F. O'Boyle, "Some Japanese Steelmakers Are Weighing Making Investments in U.S. Steel Industry," *Wall Street Journal* (October 12, 1984), p. 2.

13. Anders.

14. O. Ullmann, "Third World Debt Plays Poorly for Caterpillar, Peoria," *Des Moines Register* (September 25, 1983), p. 5F.

15. "Drastic New Strategies To Keep U.S. Multinationals Competitive," *Business Week* (October 8, 1984), p. 172.

16. A. Nag, "Chrysler Tests Consumer Reaction to Mexican-Made Cars Sold in U.S.," *Wall Street Journal* (July 23, 1984), p. 13.
    "Matsushita Selling G. E. Products in U.S.," *Des Moines Register* (July 8, 1984), p. 3F.

17. Dymsza, p. 5.

18. Dymsza, pp. 5–6.

19. S. J. Kobrin, "Morality, Political Power and Illegal Payments by Multinational Corporations," *Columbia Journal of World Business* (Winter 1976), p. 106.

20. J. D. Daniels, E. W. Ogram, Jr., and L. H. Radebaugh, *International Business: Environments and Operations,* 3rd ed. (Reading, Mass.: Addison-Wesley, 1982), p. 640.

21. Daniels, Ogram, and Radebaugh, 3rd ed. (1982), p. 513.

22. D. Ricks, M. Y. C. Fu, and J. S. Arpan, *International Business Blunders* (Columbus, Ohio: Grid, Inc., 1974).

23. Daniels, Ogram, and Radebaugh, 3rd ed. (1982), pp. 522–523.

24. D. A. Ricks and V. Mahajan, "Blunders in International Marketing: Fact or Fiction," *Long Range Planning* (February 1984), pp. 78–82.

25. "Banks in Pakistan To Stop Paying Interest in 1985," *Wall Street Journal* (June 18, 1984), p. 23.

26. S. Chang, "The Gods and the U.A.W. Are Smiling: Mazda's New Boss Plans To Make Cars, and Jobs, for Yanks," *People* (February 18, 1985), pp. 90–91.

27. R. T. Grieves, "Modern Barter," *Time* (June 11, 1984) p. 48.
    D. B. Yoffie, "Profiting from Countertrade," *Harvard Business Review* (May–June 1984), pp. 8–12, 16.

28. P. F. Drucker, "Insulating the Firm from Currency Exposure," *Wall Street Journal* (April 30, 1985), p. 28.

29. "Uniroyal Sells a Unit for Over $71 Million to Malaysian Concern," *Wall Street Journal* (December 24, 1984), p. 12.

30. M. L. Weidenbaum, "Facing the Problems of the World Economy," *Journal of Business Strategy* (Winter 1984), p. 68.

31. H. DeNero and A. Mahini, "Local-Content Laws Abroad Needn't Cut Profitability," *Wall Street Journal* (July 23, 1984), p. 10.
    W. R. Cline, "Protectionism: An Ill Trade Wind Rises," *Wall Street Journal* (November 6, 1984), p. 30.

32. A. Pine, "Study Says Curb on Japan's Cars Lifts U.S. Prices," *Wall Street Journal* (February 14, 1985), p. 3.

33. Daniels, Ogram, and Radebaugh, 3rd ed. (1982), p. 28.

34. Y. N. Chang and F. Campo-Flores, *Business Policy and Strategy* (Santa Monica, Calif.: Goodyear Publishing, 1980), p. 601.

35. R. B. Reich, *The Next American Frontier* (New York: Times Books, 1983).

36. R. A. Shaffer, "Japanese Now Target Communications Gear as a Growth Industry," *Wall Street Journal* (January 13, 1982), p. 1.

37. G. W. Weiss, Jr., "The General Electric-SNECMA Jet Engine Development Program" (Boston: *Intercollegiate Case Clearing House*, no. 9-380-739, 1980).

38. J. Mark, "High-Tech Exports to China Still Being Delayed, Despite Eased Rules, U.S. Firms Finding," *Wall Street Journal* (January 3, 1985), p. 16.

39. R. Stobaugh and R. T. Wells, Jr., *Technology Crossing Borders* (Boston: Harvard Business School Press, 1984), p. 4.

40. P. Banker, "You're the Best Judge of Foreign Risks," *Harvard Business Review* (March–April 1983), pp. 157–165.

41. T. N. Gladwin, "Assessing the Multinational Environment for Corporate Opportunity," in W. D. Guth (ed.), *Handbook of Business Strategy* (Boston: Warren, Gorham and Lamont, 1985), pp. 7.28–7.41.

42. W. D. Coplin and M. K. O'Leary, "The 1985 Political Climate for International Business: A Forecast of Risk in 82 Countries," *Planning Review* (May 1985), pp. 36–43.

43. Chang and Campo-Flores, pp. 602–604.

44. Dymsza, p. 1.

45. Dymsza, pp. 96–102.

46. V. Pucik and N. Hatvany, "Management Practices in Japan and Their Impact on Business Strategy," in R. Lamb (ed.), *Advances in Strategic Management,* Vol. I (Greenwich, Conn.: Jai Press, 1983), p. 124.

47. Daniels, Ogram, and Radebaugh, 3rd ed. (1982), p. 490.

48. S. P. Galante, "Foreign Semiconductor Firms Try New Strategy in U.S.," *Wall Street Journal* (August 23, 1984), p. 20.

49. K. P. Power, "Now We Can Move Office Work Offshore To Enhance Output," *Wall Street Journal* (June 9, 1983), p. 30.

50. S. Koepp, "Hands across the Border," *Time* (September 10, 1984), p. 36.

51. For further discussion of these strategies, refer to a text on international business such as that by Daniels, Ogram, and Radebaugh.

52. G. D. Harrell and R. O. Kiefer, "Multinational Strategic Market Portfolios," *MSU Business Topics* (Winter 1981), p. 5.

53. Harrell and Kiefer, p. 8.

54. P. Lasserre, "Selecting a Foreign Partner for Technology Transfer," *Long Range Planning* (December 1984), pp. 43–49.

55. Lasserre, pp. 48–49.

56. J. P. Killing, "How To Make a Global Joint Venture Work," *Harvard Business Review* (May–June 1982), p. 120–127.

57. R. L. Drake and L. M. Caudill, "Management of the Large Multinational: Trends and Future Challenges," *Business Horizons* (May–June 1981), pp. 84–85.

58. Daniels, Ogram, and Radebaugh, 2nd ed. (1979), p. 359.

59. Stobaugh and Wells, pp. 16–17.

60. S. M. Davis, *Managing and Organizing Multinational Corporations* (New York: Pergamon Press, 1979), p. 241.

61. Drake and Caudill, p. 87.

62. T. T. Herbert, "Strategy and Multinational Organization Structure: An Interorganizational Relationship Perspective," *Academy of Management Review* (April 1984), p. 264.

63. G. Hofstede, "Motivation, Leadership, and Organization: Do American Theories Apply Abroad?" *Organizational Dynamics* (Summer 1980), pp. 42–63.
G. Hofstede, "National Cultures in Four Dimensions: A Research-Based Theory of Cultural Differences among Nations," *International Journal of Management and Organization* (Spring–Summer 1983), pp. 46–74.
G. Hofstede, "The Cultural Relativity of the Quality of Life Concept," *Academy of Management Review* (July 1984), pp. 389–398.

64. G. Inzerilli and A. Laurent, "Managerial Views of Organization Structure in France and the USA," *International Studies of Management and Organization* (Spring–Summer 1983), p. 113.

65. W. H. Newman, J. P. Logan, and W. H. Hegarty, *Strategy, Policy, and Central Management,* 9th ed. (Cincinnati, Ohio: South-Western Publishing Company, 1985), p. 611.

66. M. Mendenhall and G. Oddou, "The Dimensions of Expatriate Acculturation: A Review," *Academy of Management Review* (January 1985), pp. 39–47.

67. Daniels, Ogram, and Radebaugh, 3rd ed. (1982), p. 552.

68. Daniels, Ogram, and Radebaugh, 3rd ed. (1982), p. 552.

69. Dymsza, pp. 74–78.

70. K. Paul and R. Barbato, "The Multinational Corporation in the Less Devel-

oped Country: The Economic Development Model versus the North–South Model," *Academy of Management Review* (January 1985), p. 9.

71. P. Wright, "MNC-Third World Business Unit Performance: Application of Strategic Elements," *Strategic Management Journal* (July–September 1984), pp. 231–240.

72. Adapted from J. Fayerweather, *International Business Strategy and Administration* (Cambridge, Mass.: Ballinger Publishing, 1978), p. 124.

73. J. E. Post, "Assessing the Nestlé Boycott," *California Management Review* (Winter 1985), pp. 113–131.

74. M. Ul Haq, *The Poverty Curtain: Choices for the Third World* (New York: Columbia University Press, 1976) as quoted by Wright, p. 232.

75. F. T. Haner, *Business Policy, Planning and Strategy* (Cambridge, Mass.: Winthrop Publishers, 1976), p. 441.

Chapter 11

STRATEGIC MANAGEMENT OF NOT-FOR-PROFIT ORGANIZATIONS

STRATEGIC MANAGEMENT MODEL

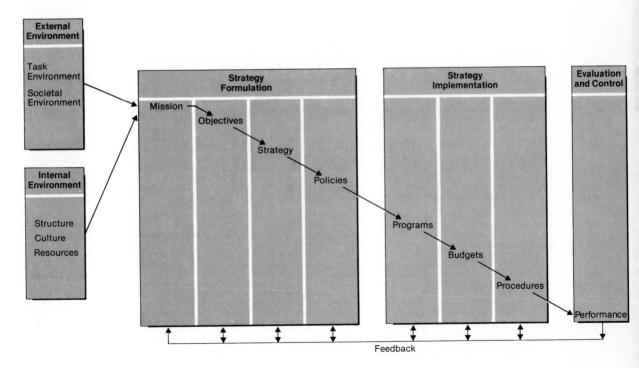

Traditionally, studies in strategic management have dealt with profit-making firms to the exclusion of nonprofit or governmental organizations. The little existing empirical research suggests that not-for-profit organizations are in the initial stage of using strategic management.[1] From their study of 103 not-for-profit organizations, Unterman and Davis conclude: "Not only have not-for-profit organizations failed to reach the strategic management stage of development, but many of them have failed to reach even the strategic planning stages that for-profit enterprises initiated 15 to 20 years ago."[2] Nevertheless, an increasing number of not-for-profits, especially hospitals, are concerned with strategic issues and strategic planning, even though it may be only an informal process.[3] A knowledge of not-for-profit organizations is important if for no other reason than the fact that they employ over 20 million people in the United States (compared to approximately 70 million in the profit-making sector).[4] Private nonprofit organizations, in particular, represent 5.2% of all corporations, partnerships, and proprietorships in the United States, receive 3.5% of all revenue, and hold about 4.3% of the total assets of business firms. During the 1970s, nonprofit firms increased both in total number and revenues *faster* than did profit-making firms.[5] It is estimated that over one-third of the world's gross product is generated by "non-market" corporations (which include state-owned corporations and regulated utilities).[6] In the United States alone, in addition to various federal, state, and local government agencies, there are about 3,500 not-for-profit hospitals; 3,000 colleges and universities; and approximately 300 national church and synagogue bodies, plus hundreds of thousands of local churches, synagogues, and charities.[7]

The first ten chapters of this book dealt primarily with the strategic management of profit-making corporations. The purpose of this chapter, however, is to highlight briefly the major differences between the profit-making and the not-for-profit organization to indicate how their differences might affect the strategic management process.

11.1 CATEGORIES OF ORGANIZATIONS

All profit-making and not-for-profit organizations can be grouped into four basic categories. In some instances, it is difficult to clearly state where one category leaves off and another begins: "The wide and growing involvement of government in all aspects of life has caused a convergence or blurring of the various sectors."[8] Four categories are as follows:

1. *Private for-profit* businesses dependent on the market economy for generating the means of survival (ranging from small businesses to major corporations).

2. *Private quasi-public* organizations created by legislative authority and

given a limited monopoly to provide particular goods or services to a
population subgroup (primarily public utilities).

3. *Private nonprofit* organizations operating on public goodwill (donations, contributions, and endowments or government stipends), but
constituted outside the authority of governmental agencies or legislative bodies.

4. *Public* agencies of government (federal, state, and local) constituted by
law and authorized to collect taxes and provide services.[9]

Typically, the term *not-for-profit* includes private nonprofit corporations
such as hospitals, institutes, private colleges, and organized charities, as well
as public governmental units or agencies such as welfare departments, prisons, and state universities. Regulated public utilities are in a grey area somewhere between profit and not-for-profit. They are profit making and have
stockholders, but take on many of the characteristics of the not-for-profit organization, such as a greater dependence on rate-setting government com-
missions than on customers.

The not-for-profit sector of the American economy is becoming increasingly
important for a number of reasons. *First,* society desires certain goods and
services that profit-making firms cannot or will not provide. These are referred to as "public" or "collective" goods because people who may not
have paid for the goods also receive benefits from them. Paved roads, police
protection, museums, and schools are examples of public goods. A person
cannot use a private good unless she or he pays for it. Generally once a public good is provided, however, anyone can partake of it.

    Second, a private nonprofit firm tends to receive benefits from society
that a private profit-making firm cannot obtain. Preferred tax status to non-
stock corporations is given in section $501(c)(3)$ of the Internal Revenue
Code in the form of exemptions from corporate income taxes. Private nonprofit firms also enjoy exemptions from various other state, local, and federal
taxes. Under certain conditions they also benefit from the tax deductibility of
donor contributions and membership dues. In addition, they qualify for special third-class mailing privileges.[10] These benefits are allowed because private nonprofit organizations are typically service organizations which are
expected to use any excess of revenue over costs and expenses to either improve service or reduce the price of their service. This service orientation is
reflected in the fact that not-for-profit organizations do not use the term *customer* to refer to the consumer or recipient of the service. The recipient is
typically referred to as a patient, student, client, case, or simply "the public."

11.2 WHY NOT-FOR-PROFIT?

**11.3
IMPORTANCE
OF REVENUE
SOURCE**

The feature that best differentiates not-for-profit organizations from each other as well as from profit-making corporations is their source of income.[11] The profit-making firm depends upon revenues obtained from the sale of its goods and services to customers. Its source of income is the customer who buys and uses the product, and who typically pays for the product when it is received. Profits result when revenues are greater than the costs of making and distributing the product, and are thus a measure of the corporation's *effectiveness* (a product is valued because customers purchase it for use) and *efficiency* (costs are kept below selling price).

The not-for-profit organization, in contrast, depends heavily on dues, assessments, or donations from its membership or on funding from a sponsoring agency such as the United Way or the federal government. Revenue, therefore, comes from a variety of sources—*not* just from sales to customers/clients. It may come from people who do not even receive the services they are subsidizing. Such charitable organizations as the American Cancer Society and CARE are examples. In another type of not-for-profit organization—such as unions and voluntary medical plans—revenue comes mostly from the people, the members, who receive the service. Nevertheless, the members typically pay dues *in advance* and must accept later whatever service is provided whether they want it or not, whether it is what they expected or not. The service is often received long after the dues are paid. As a result, some members who have paid into a fund for many years may leave the organization or die without receiving services, whereas newcomers may receive many services even though they have paid only a small amount into it.

Therefore, in profit-making corporations, there is typically a simple and direct connection between the customer or client and the organization. The organization tends to be totally dependent on sales of its products or services to the customer for revenue and is therefore extremely interested in pleasing the customer. As shown in Fig. 11.1, the profit-making organization (organization A) tries to influence the customer to continue to buy and use its services. The customer, in turn, directly influences the organization's decision-making process by either buying or not buying the item offered.

In the case of the typical not-for-profit organization, however, there is likely to be a very different sort of relationship between the organization providing and the person receiving the service. Since the recipient of the service typically does not pay the entire cost of the service, outside sponsors are required. In most instances, the sponsors receive none of the service but may provide from partial to total funding of needed revenues. As indicated earlier, these sponsors may be the U.S. Congress (using taxpayers' money) or charitable organizations, such as the United Way (using voluntary donations). As shown in Fig. 11.1, the not-for-profit (NFP) organization may be

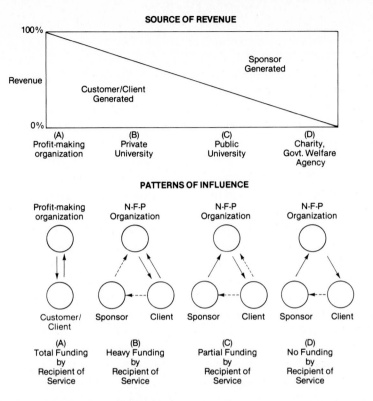

Figure 11.1   **The effect of sources of revenue on patterns of client-organization influence.**
SOURCE: Thomas L. Wheelen and J. David Hunger, "The Effect of Revenue upon Patterns of Client-Organization Influence." Copyright © 1982 by Wheelen and Hunger Associates. Reprinted by permission.

partially dependent on sponsors for funding (organizations B and C) or totally dependent on the sponsors (organization D).

The pattern of influence on the organization's strategic decision making derives from its sources of revenue. As shown in Fig. 11.1, a private university (organization B) is heavily dependent on student tuition and other client-generated funds for around 71% of its revenue.[12] As a result, student desires are likely to have more influence (as shown by an unbroken line) on the university's decision making than are the desires of the various sponsors, such as alumni and private foundations. The relatively marginal influence on the organization by the sponsors is reflected by a broken line. In contrast, a public university (depicted in Fig. 11.1 as organization C) is more heavily dependent on outside sponsors, such as a state legislature, for revenue funding. Student tuition and other client-generated funds form a smaller percentage (typically only 37%) of total revenue. As a result, decision making is heavily influenced by the sponsors (unbroken line) and only marginally influenced directly by the students (broken line). In the case of organization D in Fig. 11.1, however, the client has no direct influence on the organization because the client pays nothing for the services received. In this type of situation, the organization tends to measure its effectiveness in terms of sponsor satisfaction. It has no real measure of its efficiency other than its ability to carry out its mission and achieve its objectives within the dollar contribution it has received from its sponsors. In contrast to other organizations where the client contributes a significant proportion of the needed revenue, this type of not-for-profit organization (D) actually may be able to increase the amount of its revenue by heavily lobbying its sponsors while reducing the level of its service to its clients!

Regardless of the percentage of total funding generated by the client, the client may attempt to influence indirectly the not-for-profit organization through the sponsors. This is depicted by the broken lines connecting the client and the sponsor in organizations B, C, and D in the figure. Welfare clients or prison inmates, for example, may be able to improve indirectly the services they receive by pressuring government officials by writing letters to legislators or, even, by rioting. And students at public universities may lobby state officials for student representation on governing boards.

The key to understanding the management of a not-for-profit organization is thus to learn who pays for the delivered services. To the extent that the recipients of the service pay only a small proportion of the total cost of the service, it is likely that top management will be more concerned with satisfying the needs and desires of the funding sponsors or agency than those of the people receiving the service. As previous studies indicate, acquisition of resources may become an end in itself.[13]

11.4 CONSTRAINTS ON STRATEGIC MANAGEMENT

Because not-for-profit organizations are truly different from profit-making organizations, there are a number of characteristics peculiar to the former that constrain its behavior and affect its strategic management. Newman and Wallender list the following five constraining characteristics:

1. Service is often intangible and hard to measure. This difficulty is typically compounded by the existence of multiple service objectives developed in order to satisfy multiple sponsors.

2. Client influence may be weak. Often the organization has a local monopoly, and payments by clients may be a very small source of funds.

3. Strong employee commitment to professions or to a cause may undermine their allegiance to the organization employing them.

4. Resource contributors—notably fund contributors and government—
    may intrude upon the organization's internal management.

5. Restraints on the use of rewards and punishments may result from char-
    acteristics 1, 3, and 4.[14]

It is true that a number of these characteristics may be found in profit-making as well as in not-for-profit organizations. Nevertheless, as Newman and
Wallendar state, the "... frequency of strong impact is much higher in not-
for-profit enterprises. ..."[15] As a result, the strategic management process
for any given situation will be different in a not-for-profit organization than in
the typical profit-making corporations discussed in earlier chapters.

Long-range planning and decision making are affected by the listed constraining characteristics and serve to add at least four *complications* to strategy formulation.

Impact on Strategy Formulation

1. *Goal conflicts interfere with rational planning.* Since the not-for-profit
    organization typically lacks a single clear-cut performance criterion
    (such as profits), divergent goals and objectives are likely.[16] This is
    especially true if there are multiple sponsors. Differences in the concern
    of various important sponsors may prevent top management from stat-
    ing the organization's mission in anything but very broad terms, fearing
    a sponsor may disagree with a particular narrow definition of mission
    and cancel funding. In such organizations it is the reduced influence of
    the clients that *permits* this diversity of values and goals to occur with-
    out a clear market check.

2. *An integrated planning focus tends to shift from results to resources.*
    Since not-for-profit organizations tend to provide services that are hard
    to measure, there is rarely a net "bottom line." Planning, therefore,
    becomes more concerned with resource inputs, which can easily be
    measured, than with service, which cannot. Goal displacement, there-
    fore, becomes even more likely than in business organizations.

3. *Ambiguous operating objectives create opportunities for internal poli-
    tics and goal displacement.* The combination of vague objectives and a
    heavy concern with resources allows managers considerable leeway in
    their activities. Such leeway makes possible political maneuvering for
    personal ends. In addition, since the effectiveness of the not-for-profit
    organization hinges on the satisfaction of the sponsoring group, there is
    a tendency to ignore the needs of the client while focusing on the de-
    sires of the powerful sponsor. This problem is compounded by the fact

that boards of trustees are often selected not on the basis of their managerial experience, but on the basis of their ability to contribute money, raise funds, and work with politicians. Board members therefore tend to ignore the task of determining strategies and policies—leaving this to the paid executive director.[17]

4. *Professionalization simplifies detailed planning but adds rigidity.* In those not-for-profit organizations where professionals hold important roles (as in hospitals or colleges), professional values and traditions may prevent the organization from changing conventional behavior patterns to fit new service missions to changing social needs. This, of course, can occur in any organization that hires professionals. The strong service orientation of most not-for-profit organizations, however, tends to encourage the development of static professional norms and attitudes.

Impact on Strategy Implementation

The five constraining characteristics affect how a not-for-profit organization is organized in both its structure and job design. Three *complications,* in particular, can be highlighted.

1. *Decentralization is complicated.* The difficulty of setting objectives for an intangible, hard-to-measure service mission complicates the delegation of decision-making authority. Important matters are therefore centralized and lower-level managers are forced to wait until top management makes a decision. With the heavy dependence on sponsors for revenue support, the top management of a not-for-profit organization always must be alert to how the sponsors may view an organizational activity. This leads to "defensive centralization" in which top management retains all decision-making authority to avoid any actions to which the sponsors may object.

2. *Linking pins for external-internal integration become important.* Given the heavy dependence on outside sponsors, a special need arises for people in "buffer" roles who can relate to both inside and outside groups. This is especially necessary when the sponsors are diverse (revenue comes from donations, membership fees, and federal funds) and the service is intangible (for instance, a "good" education) with a broad mission and multiple shifting objectives. The job of a "Dean for External Affairs," for example, consists primarily of working with school alumni and fund raising.

3. *Job enlargement and executive development may be restrained by professionalism.* In organizations that employ a large number of professionals, managers must design jobs that appeal to prevailing professional norms. Professionals have rather clear ideas about which

activities are, and which are not, within their province. Enriching a nurse's job by expanding his or her decision-making authority regarding drug dosage, for example, may cause conflict with medical doctors who feel such authority is theirs alone. In addition, promoting a professional into a managerial job may be viewed as a punishment rather than as a reward.

Special *complications* arising from the constraining characteristics also affect how behavior is motivated and performance is controlled. Two problems, in particular, are often noticed.

Impact on Evaluation and Control

1. *Rewards and penalties have little or no relation to performance.* When desired results are vague and the judgment of success is subjective, predictable and impersonal feedback cannot be established. Performance is judged either intuitively ("You don't seem to be taking your job seriously") or on the basis of those small aspects of a job that can be measured ("You were late to work twice last month").

2. *Inputs rather than outputs are heavily controlled.* Since inputs can be measured much more easily than outputs, the not-for-profit organization tends to focus more on the resources going into performance than on the performance itself. The emphasis is thus on setting maximum limits for costs and expenses. Because there is little to no reward for meeting these standards, people usually respond negatively to controls.

Not-for-profit organizations tend to deal with the complications resulting from constraining characteristics in a number of ways. Although these responses may occur in profit-making organizations as well, they are more typical of not-for-profit organizations.

11.5 TYPICAL RESPONSES TO CONSTRAINTS

One approach, which is also used in profit-making firms at times, is to appoint a strong leader to the top management position: "The leader has personal convictions about the values to be used in decision-making and either has enough power to make important choices, or is so influential that her or his values are accepted by others who make decisions."[18] This manager thus can force a change in the planning of the organizational mission and objectives without antagonizing the sponsors, as well as in the organizing and controlling of activities. The danger with this approach, however, is that change can occur only from the top down. Rather than accepting the normal risks inherent in making an important decision, lower-level managers "play it safe" and either wait for guidance from above to see which way "the wind is blowing" or pass the decision upward in the hierarchy.

Select a Dynamic and Forceful Leader

Develop a Mystique

The organization can be integrated toward successful goal accomplishment by developing a "mystique" that dominates the enterprise and attracts likely sponsors. A strong conviction shared by all employees, as well as the sponsors, about the importance of a particular mission or service objective can also serve to motivate unusually high performance and client satisfaction. This sense of mission typically focuses on providing a unique service to a highly visible client group, such as mentally retarded children. Once established, the mystique sets the character and values decision makers and others are expected to follow.[19] Thus it is similar to the corporate culture discussed earlier. One danger in using mystique to focus activities and to motivate performance is that the mission can move far afield from that desired by the sponsoring groups.

Generate Rules and Regulations

Since the constraints may force people in not-for-profit organizations to be concerned more with pleasing the sponsors than with achieving a mission of satisfying the client, top management may respond by generating rules and regulations regarding activities with the client. Minimum standards may be developed regarding the number of contact hours spent with each client, the number of reports completed, and/or the "proper" method of working. The danger inherent in this approach is that it tends to emphasize form over substance and to confuse looking good and keeping busy with actual performance. More goal displacement develops and feeds upon itself. "Burnout" develops among dedicated employees who may feel they are being forced to spend too much energy fighting the system rather than helping the client.

Appoint a Strong Board

A board of directors or trustees can help ensure vigilance in setting and monitoring the objectives of the organization. To the extent that the board actively represents the sponsors and special interest groups that determine the organization's revenues, it has a great deal of power: "The potential for control by some not-for-profit boards far exceeds that of the boards of a corporation which represents only the owners."[20] The board can perform a watchdog role over the organization by demanding clear-cut, measurable objectives and a mission of client satisfaction. The danger with this approach, however, is that the board may get too involved in operational activities. In organizations with a large number of professional employees, the senior administrator may be viewed as a "hybrid" professional—part professional and part manager (for instance, a physician serving as a hospital administrator). The board thus tends to involve itself not only with strategic matters, but also with operational matters such as hiring, directing, and developing the budget.[21] Nevertheless, like the boards discussed in Chapter 3, not-for-profit boards can range in their degree of involvement in strategic management from the passive phantom or figurehead boards to the active catalyst type.

A fifth approach to dealing with complications in a not-for-profit organization is to institute an information system that ties measurable objectives to budgeted line items. One such system is the *planning, programming, budgeting system* (PPBS) developed by the U.S. Department of Defense. It assists not-for-profit administrators in choosing among alternative programs in terms of resource use. It includes five steps:

Establish Performance-Based Budgets

1. Specify objectives as clearly as possible in quantitative, measurable terms.

2. Analyze the actual output of the not-for-profit organization in terms of the stated objectives.

3. Measure the cost of the particular program.

4. Analyze alternatives and search for those that have the greatest effectiveness in achieving the objectives.

5. Establish the process in a systematic way so that it continues to occur over time.[22]

Another system is *zero base budgeting* (ZBB). It is a planning process that requires each manager to justify budget requests in detail each year a budget is constructed. This procedure serves to avoid developing annual budgets based upon the previous year's budget plus a certain percentage increase. ZBB forces a manager to justify the use of money for old established programs as well as for new ones. The system requires three steps:

1. Identify each activity with a program in order to relate input to output.

2. Evaluate each activity by systematic analysis.

3. Rank all programs in order of performance.[23]

Zero base budgeting has been used by the U.S. Department of Agriculture since 1971 and has been employed in nearly a dozen state and local governments as well as in other federal agencies and in over one hundred business firms.[24] Its main value is to tie inputs with outputs and to force managers to set priorities on service programs. It is also a very useful adjunct to MBO, which is being increasingly adopted by many not-for-profit organizations.

The danger with emphasizing performance-based budgets is that members of an organization become so concerned with justifying the existence of pet programs that they tend to forget about the effect of these programs on achieving the mission. The process may become very political. It gives the appearance of rational decision making, but it can be just another variant of trying to please the sponsors and looking good on paper.[25]

11.6 POPULAR NOT-FOR-PROFIT STRATEGIES

Because the mission of the not-for-profit organization is typically to satisfy an unmet need of a segment of the general public, its objective becomes one of satisfying that need as much as is possible. To the extent that revenues exceed costs and expenses, the not-for-profit therefore is likely to use the surplus (otherwise known as "profit") to expand or improve its services. If, however, revenues are less than costs and expenses, strong pressures from both within and without the organization often prevent it from reducing its services. To the extent that management is able to find new sponsors, all may be well. For many not-for-profits, however, there is an eventual limit to contributions with no strings attached. The organization is thus painfully forced to reject contributions from sponsors who wish to alter a portion of the organization's basic mission as a requirement of the contribution.

As a result of various pressures to provide more services than the sponsors and clients can pay for, not-for-profit organizations are developing strategies to meet their desired service objectives. Two popular strategies are *strategic piggybacking* and *interorganizational linking.*

Strategic Piggybacking

Coined by Nielsen, the term *strategic piggybacking* refers to the development of a new activity for the not-for-profit organization for the purpose of generating funds needed to make up the difference between revenues and expenses.[26] The new activity is related typically in some manner to the not-for-profit's mission, but its purpose is to help subsidize the primary service programs. In an inverted use of portfolio analysis, top management invests in new, safe *cash cows* to fund its current cash-hungry stars, question marks, and dogs.

Although this strategy is not a new one, it is becoming increasingly popular in the 1980s. As early as 1874, for example, the Metropolitan Museum of Art retained a professional to photograph its collections and to sell copies of the prints. Profits were used to defray the museum's operating costs. Surpluses generated from the sale of food, wine, liquor, and tickets to the Boston Pops performances help support the primary mission of the Boston Symphony Orchestra—the performance of classical music. More recently, various income generation ventures have appeared under various auspices, from the Girl Scouts to UNICEF, and in numerous forms, from small gift shops to vast real estate developments.[27] The Small Business Administration, however, views this activity as "unfair competition."[28] The Internal

Revenue Service advises that a not-for-profit that engages in a business "not substantially related" to the organization's exempt purposes may jeopardize its tax-exempt status, particularly if the income from the business exceeds approximately 20% of total organizational revenues.[29]

Edward Skloot, president of the New York consulting firm New Ventures, suggests that a not-for-profit organization have five resources before beginning a revenue-earning activity.[30]

1. *Something to sell.* The organization should assess its resources to see if people might be willing to pay for a good or service closely related to the organization's primary activity.

2. *Critical mass of management talent.* There must be enough people available to nurture and sustain an income venture over the long haul.

3. *Trustee support.* If the trustees have strong feelings against earned-income ventures, they may actively or passively resist commercial involvement.

4. *Entrepreneurial attitude.* Management must be able to combine an interest in innovative ideas with businesslike practicality.

5. *Venture capital.* Given that it often takes money to make money, engaging in a joint venture with a business corporation can provide necessary start-up funds as well as marketing and management support. For example, Massachusetts General Hospital receives $50 million from Hoechst, the West German chemical company for biological research, in exchange for exclusive licenses to develop commercial products from certain research discoveries. The Children's Television Workshop, in partnership with Anheuser-Busch, developed a theme park for young children in Langhorne, Pennsylvania.[31]

Inter-organizational Linking

A major strategy often used by not-for-profit organizations to enhance their capacity to serve clients or to acquire resources is developing cooperative ties with other organizations.[32] Not-for-profit hospitals increasingly are using this strategy as a way to cope with increasing costs and declining revenues. Through cooperation with other hospitals, services can be purchased and provided more efficiently than if done alone. Currently, close to one-third of all nongovernmental not-for-profit hospitals in the United States are part of a *multihospital system,* defined as "two or more acute care hospitals owned, leased, or contract-managed by a corporate office."[33] By belonging to a system, a formerly independent hospital can hope to benefit in terms of staff utilization and management efficiency.[34]

11.7 SUMMARY AND CONCLUSION

Strategic management in not-for-profit organizations is in its initial stages. Approaches and techniques, such as MBO, which work reasonably well in profit-making corporations, are being tried in a number of not-for-profit organizations. Nevertheless, private nonprofit and public organizations differ in terms of their sources of revenue and thus must be treated differently. The relationship between the organization and the client also is more complicated. Moreover, not-for-profit organizations have certain constraining characteristics that affect their strategic management process. These characteristics cause variations in the way managers in not-for-profit organizations formulate and implement strategic decisions. Not-for-profit organizations therefore are more likely than profit-making corporations to look for dynamic and forceful leaders who can pull together various constituencies, develop a mystique about their activities, generate many rules and regulations regarding the client, appoint a strong board of directors/trustees to represent sponsoring agencies and special interest groups, and develop performance-based budgets. As increasing numbers of not-for-profit organizations find it difficult to generate the necessary funds from sponsors to achieve key service objectives, they are turning to *strategic piggybacking* and *interorganizational linking* strategies.

Not-for-profit organizations form an important part of society. It is therefore important to understand their reason for existence and what makes them different from profit-making corporations. The lack of a profit motive often results in vague statements of mission and unmeasurable objectives. This, coupled with a concern for funding from sponsors, may cause a lack of consideration for the very client the organization was designed to serve. Programs may develop that have little or no connection with the organization's mission. Nevertheless, it is important to remember that not-for-profit organizations usually are established to provide goods and services judged valuable by society that profit-making firms cannot or will not provide. It is dangerous to judge their performance on the basis of simple economic considerations because they are designed to deal with conditions under which profit-making corporations could not easily survive.

DISCUSSION QUESTIONS

1. Are not-for-profit organizations less efficient than profit-making organizations? Why or why not?

2. Do you agree that the source of revenue is the best way to differentiate between not-for-profit and profit-making organizations as well as among the many kinds of not-for-profit organizations? Why or why not?

3. Is client influence always weak in the not-for-profit organization? Why or why not?

4. Why does the employment of a large number of people who consider themselves to be professionals complicate the strategic management process? How may this also occur in profit-making firms?

5. How does the lack of a clear-cut performance measure, such as profits, affect the strategic management of a not-for-profit organization?

6. What are the pros and cons of *strategic piggybacking?*

7. In the past, a number of profit-making businesses such as city bus lines and railroad passenger services have changed their status to not-for-profit as governmental agencies took them over. Recently, however, a number of not-for-profit organizations have been converting to profit-making. For example, more than 20 of the 115 nonprofit Health Maintenance Organizations (HMOs) formed with federal money have converted to for-profit status.[35] Why would a not-for-profit organization want to change its status to profit-making?

NOTES

1. M. S. Wortman, Jr., "Strategic Management: Not-for-Profit Organizations," *Strategic Management,* eds. D. E. Schendel and C. W. Hofer (Boston: Little, Brown, 1979), pp. 353–381.
M. S. Wortman, Jr., "Strategic Management in Voluntary and Nonprofit Organizations: Reality, Prescriptive Behavior and Future Research," in M. Moyer (ed.), *Managing Voluntary Organizations* (Toronto, Ontario: York University, 1983), pp. 146–167.

2. I. Unterman and R. H. Davis, "The Strategy Gap in Not-For-Profits," *Harvard Business Review* (May–June 1982), p. 30.

3. W. F. Crittenden and D. D. White, "An Examination of Strategic Planning Characteristics in Voluntary Organizations," *Proceedings, Southern Management Association* (November 1982), pp. 140–142.
S. M. Vonderhaar, J. Strauss, and H. LeVan, "Impact of Selected Environmental Variables on the Long-Range Planning Process in U.S. Hospitals," *Proceedings, Southern Management Association* (November 1982), pp. 212–214.

4. B. P. Keating and M. O. Keating, *Not-For-Profit* (Glen Ridge, N.J.: Thomas Horton & Daughters, 1980), p. 18.

5. D. R. Young, *If Not For Profit, For What?* (Lexington, Mass.: D. C. Heath, Lexington Books, 1983), p. 9.

6. J. Ruffat, "Strategic Management of Public and Non-Market Corporations," *Long Range Planning* (April 1983), p. 74.

7. W. F. Glueck, *Business Policy and Strategic Management,* 3rd ed. (New York: McGraw-Hill, 1980), pp. 22–24.

8. M. D. Fottler, "Is Management Really Generic?" *Academy of Management Review* (January 1981), p. 2.

9. Fottler, p. 2.

10. Keating and Keating, pp. 23–24.

11. Keating and Keating, p. 21.

12. "Revenues and Expenditures of Colleges and Universities, 1981–82," *The Chronicle of Higher Education* (April 4, 1984), p. 14.

13. D. Mott, *Characteristics of Effective Organizations* (San Francisco: Harper & Row, 1972) as reported by H. L. Tosi, Jr. and J. W. Slocum, Jr., "Contingency Theory: Some Suggested Directions," *Journal of Management* (Spring 1984), p. 11.

14. W. H. Newman and H. W. Wallender, III, "Managing Not-For-Profit Enterprises," *Academy of Management Review* (January 1978), p. 26.

15. Newman and Wallender, p. 27. The following discussion of the effects of these constraining characteristics is taken from Newman and Wallender, pp. 27–31.

16. P. C. Nutt, "A Strategic Planning Network for Non-Profit Organizations," *Strategic Management Journal* (January-March 1984), p. 57.

17. Unterman and Davis, pp. 30–32.

18. Newman and Wallender, p. 27.

19. Newman and Wallender, p. 28.

20. Keating and Keating, p. 130.

21. E. H. Fram, "Changing Expectations for Third Sector Executives," *Human Resource Management* (Fall 1980), p. 9.

22. Keating and Keating, pp. 140–141.

23. Keating and Keating, pp. 143–144.

24. S. M. Lee and J. P. Shim, "Zero-Base Budgeting—Dealing with Conflicting Objectives," *Long Range Planning* (October 1984), p. 103.

25. M. W. Dirsmith, S. F. Jablonsky, and A. D. Luzi, "Planning and Control in the U.S. Federal Government: A Critical Analysis of PPB, MBO, and ZBB," *Strategic Management Journal* (October–December 1980), pp. 303–329.
E. E. Chaffee, "The Link between Planning and Budgeting," Working Paper, National Center for Higher Education Management Systems, Boulder, Colorado, October 1981, p. 12–13.

26. R. P. Nielsen, "SMR Forum: Strategic Piggybacking—A Self-Subsidizing Strategy for Nonprofit Institutions," *Sloan Management Review* (Summer 1982), pp. 65–69.
R. P. Nielsen, "Piggybacking for Business and Nonprofits: A Strategy for Hard Times," *Long Range Planning* (April 1984), pp. 96–102.

27. E. Skloot, "Should Not-For-Profits Go into Business?" *Harvard Business Review* (January–February 1983), pp. 20–26.

28. "When Should the Profits of Nonprofits Be Taxed?" *Business Week* (December 5, 1983), p. 191.

29. Skloot, p. 21.

30. Skloot, pp. 20–24.

31. Skloot, p. 24.

32. K. G. Provan, "Interorganizational Cooperation and Decision Making Autonomy in a Consortium Multihospital System," *Academy of Management Review* (July 1984), pp. 494–504.

33. *Directory of Multihospital Systems* (Chicago: American Hospital Association, 1980).

34. Provan, p. 496.

35. D. Wellel, "As HMOs Increasingly Become Big Businesses, Many of Them Convert to Profit-Making Status," *Wall Street Journal* (March 26, 1985), p. 4.

NAME INDEX

SUBJECT INDEX